GENERATIVE AI THREATS TO A CIVILIZATION

CORRECTING THE COURSE OF LARGE-LANGUAGE-MODEL AUTOMATION

Revision 3.0

Joseph J. Jean-Claude
Laser Optics Associate Engineer

Worcester - USA

International Standard Book Number (ISBN): 979-8-2562-6808-4

PREFACE

This book presents an interpretation of the development and structural content of the sum total of human knowledge. The interpretation is based on the mathematical-physical categories of Symmetry, and shows how the many different knowledge bodies, from political ideology to literature to religion to science all relate to one another in a symmetry connectum. This is Chapter 1.

Chapter 2 addresses generative Artificial Intelligence and the very acutely debated issue of whether or not it is sentient. This exposition specifically offers an analysis of consciousness in artificial intelligent agents, and further proposes structural and formal mathematical constructs to adequately frame an assertive answer to the question of AI sentience.

Chapter 3 presents an extensive review of the entire state of the generative AI industry (motivations, technological evolution, product lines and legal court challenges) while discussing the threats posed by the technology to society at large.

Chapter 4 presents a compendium of the catastrophic threats posed by generative AI technology that have already come to pass, requiring an urgent redress response to the invasive course taken by the technology in socioeconomic terms.

In Chapter 5, the author proposes a series of detailed redress measures destined to inform legal regulation for generative AI, as well as empower individuals to avoid becoming victims of the technology and the industry behind it.

In Chapter 6, the author opens a window to the direction in which human knowledge advancement should be tailored by our educational institutions, and proposes new formal definitions of Human mentation ontology. The author equally opens a window to the road ahead in human civilizational progress, vis-à-vis social adoption of generative AI technology and impending expansion into the local Cosmos.

As a special note, despite its sustained line of critique, this book is not an irrevocable detraction of generative AI technology. While making a deep dive into the broad spectrum of problems caused by generative AI, it explicitly extols the needed corrective measures in methods of both the new technology and our current enterprising model, in order to avoid a collapse of our institutions instigated by the technology.

The author's reflections have garnered a number of recommendations and positive reactions among researchers and academics who have been exposed to a pre-publication of parts of the content. It is noteworthy as well that the author's foresight expressed in many passages of the pre-published content came to pass, notably his views about the societal problems that the development of AI and automation as undertaken nowadays are doomed to cause.

The pre-publication statistics and reactions are offered hereafter as gathered from one of the popular academic networks, namely the *ResearchGate* network.

Recommendations

The academics listed below count among the many more who have expressly recommended the noted Chapters of this monograph. The same Chapters have received an average research interest score of 80%, for a total of nearly 800 readers, among the highest, within the ResearchGate academic network alone.

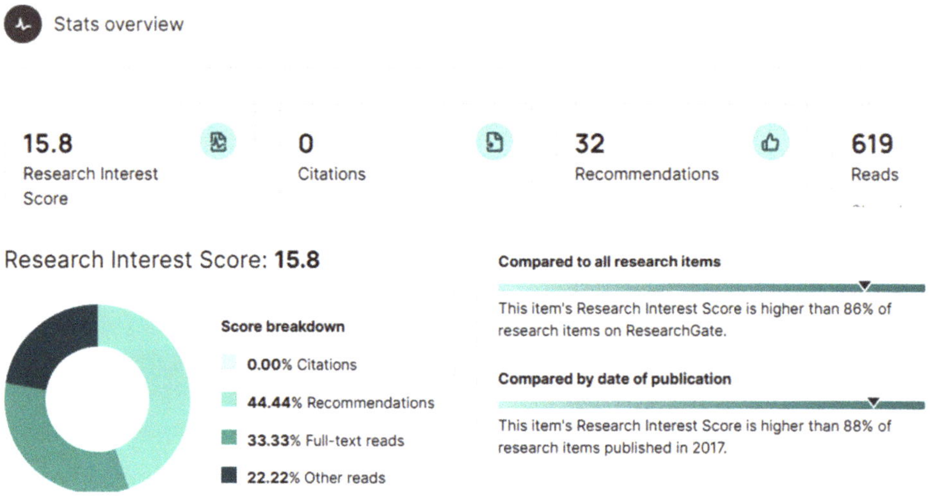

Chapter 1 – *Unique Theory of Knowledge Based on Mathematical Symmetry*

Amir W. Al-Khafaji, BSCE, MSCE, MSc, PhD Applied Mathematics, Emeritus Professor at Bradley University, USA

Mirjana Vukovic, PhD Mathematics, Academy of Science and Arts of Bosnia and Herzegovina

Mustafa Ali Khan-Mussaini, BSc Theoretical Physics, MD Neurology and Neuroimmunology, USA

Amir W. A-Khafaji, PhD Geotechnical Engineering, Dept of Civil Engineering, Bradley University, USA

Teodora Hristova, PhD Electrical Engineering, Associate Professor at University of Mining and Geology, Bulgaria

Mahmud Hamdy ABD El-Aziz, PhD Plant Virology, Virus and Phytoplasma Dept., Plant Pathology Research Institute

Djéneba Traoré, PhD Social Sciences, Humboldt University, Berlin, Germany; Professor at University of Bamako, Mali.

Hussein Omar Alkhozahe, Professor of Sociology, Department of Applied Sciences, Al-Balqa' Applied University, Irak

Faisal Al-Doori, PhD World Literature, Prof. at Tikrit University, Irak

Gandhidas Sonajirao Lavekar, MD, PhD Ayurveda Herbal Pharmacology, Scientist and Clinician, India

Mahmmoud Hussein Al Rahman, MSc Fine Arts, Iraqi Natural History Museum and Research Center, University of Baghdad, Irak

In their own words,

Tony Fleming, *PhD Biophotonics*
"Dear Joseph,
That is one deep article!! I'm still taking it all in. Your ideas should be aired.
Kind regards, Tony."

Stephen I. Ternyik, *MA Applied Informatics*
"Good work (!); models of discovery and creativity are decisive for our common growth."

Amir W. Al-Khafaji, *PhD Geotechnical Engineering*
"Dear Joseph Jean-Claude - I just finished reading your paper. It is relevant and enlightening. Amir Al-Khafaji"

Note: Chapter 1 was originally pre-published under the title *"A Unique Theory of Knowledge Based on Mathematical-Physics Symmetry"*

Chapter 6 – *Human Ascent to the Stars: From Scientific Knowledge to Consciousness to Wisdom*

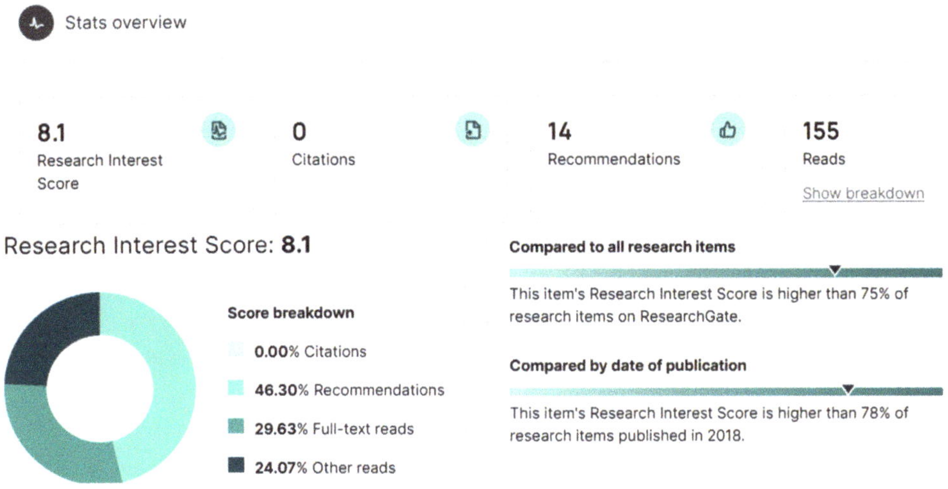

Mustafa Ali Khan-Mussaini, BSc Theoretical Physics, MD Neurology & Neuroimmunology, USA

Teodora Hristova, PhD Electrical Engineering, Associate Professor, University of Mining and Geology, Bulgaria

Abdul Kuddus, PhD Science and Engineering, Senior Researcher at Ritsumeikan University BKC - Kusatsu, Japan

Nancy Ann Watanabe, PhD Comparative Literature, & French Literature, Professor Comparative Literature, Film, Science, University of Oklahoma-Norman, USA

Stephen I Ternyik, MA Applied Informatics, summa cum laude, Berlin Institute of Technology, Germany

Djéneba Traoré, PhD Social Sciences, Humboldt University, Berlin, Germany - Professor University of Bamako, Mali.

Mehmet Gokhan Ozdemir, PhD Economics candidate, Dept. of Economics, Kirikkale University, Turkey

Jasleen Kaur, PhD Ecology, Dyal Singh College, India

Shakir M.S. Alfahdawi, PhD Clinical Biochemistry, Babasaheb Ambedkar, Technological University, Irak

Hassan Dakel Abd Radhi, Dr of Law, College of Law, Wasit University, Iraq

Madhukar Akkala, PhD Pharmacology, Prof.at MRM College of Pharmacy, India

Har Prashad, PhD Tribology, India

Indrani Singh Rai, PhD Literature, Associate Prof., Amity School of Languages, Amity University Chhattisgarh, India

Augusto Da Costa, PhD Education, Associate Prof., Instituto Superior Cristal Balide Dili Timor Leste, Timor Leste

In own words,

Mubarak Ali Lashari, *PhD Linguistics, Assist. Prof.*
"Really interesting!"

Indrani Singh Rai, *PhD Literature, Assist. Prof.*
"Beautiful blend of physics and metaphysics."

Deepanjali Mishra, *PhD Behavioral Psychology, Assist. Prof.*
"Relevant to the context. The statistical data are given wonderfully..."

TABLE OF CONTENTS

Chapter 1

UNIQUE COGNITIVE THEORY OF UNIVERSAL KNOWLEDGE BASED ON MATHEMATICAL SYMMETRY

In Science and Philosophy of Science, much has been said about the scientific method and its proceedings. While academic institutions tend to make every discovery a result of the strict application of the scientific method, some critiques argue that random processes or events contribute to scientific discoveries in a much larger degree than scientists may like to concede. When it comes to merits and tributes to ingenuity, one should probably accept the argument that it is well within the empirical research process once engaged that these events of chance may intervene to contribute to positive outcome of the empirical research process. Indeed, without the substrate of empirical experimentation itself, there is no favorable circumstance for chance to bear fruit in discovery results. Beyond the vantage of assertiveness and credits to novelty in cognition, it would be interesting to examine the inception, structure and composition of ideas which conform the spectrum of knowledge in general, both in natural and human sciences, that is. To establish a basis for comparison and assessment of the validity of these ideas across the many different disciplines belying the spectrum is a sound objective as well. I will show in this Chapter a mathematical foundation to the spectrum of core ideas in human knowledge and use mathematical categories to compare them to one another in terms their ultra-structure and composition, thereby revealing the unsuspected symmetry orders to which they belong.

1.1. Empiricism as Bedrock of the Scientific Method

The principal stream that sustains science as a knowledge tool or endeavor is its manifest and exclusive concern in that which is observable and/or measurable. Science further claims to be the only tool able to bring about an understanding of objects and processes that belong in the realm of tangibles. An important choice made in aligning physical science with the stream of empiricism at its very inception was arguably the adoption of the Newtonian concept of time over Gottfried W. Leibniz's notion of time, judged too metaphysical. The idea of time as a dimensional physical variable thus became pervasive in science. All of formal human knowledge had henceforth been woven around and about the notion of time, albeit an unproven scientific concept to this day, perhaps to the surprise of many. The Theory of General Relativity erupted on the scene to break the all too intuitive Newtonian notion of time by demonstrating that it is not a universal constant deemed to remain inalterably invariant everywhere, independent of all possible physical conditions.

Despite the important relativistic benchmark on the nature of time, the scientific phenomenon has starkly maintained an express departure from the Leibniz's excessively metaphysical notion of time, and continued to support human culture in the absoluteness of this notion. Science thereby consummated its rift with intangibles, which it left at the purview of natural philosophy and religion. Thus, science as a knowledge tool had emerged in opposition to religion in particular, acknowledging utility in philosophy perhaps only in the epistemological attempts to rationalize or evaluate its own proceedings and results.

As a reminder and to set common grounds of understanding for the discussion, scientific empiricism is an inquest into an observable of polemic nature, whether object or phenomenon, whereby a hypothesis is formulated in order to explain, elucidate or interpret through a process of verification or falsification state or behavior of the polemic observable.

1.2. Incepts and Percepts as Components of Ideas

All Knowledge is based on ideas. It is important to understand that knowledge is not to be construed as perception or the substrate of perceptions. When we internalize an observable, object or event, through perception, it becomes a mental object or *percept*, a mental representation of the observable. Along with percepts, human mentation creates *incepts*, which result from perception of non-observables, real or imagined. We otherwise call those incepts *intuition*. The rational mind may question whether or not incepts proceeding from intuitive perception may ever be real or of any pertinence or utility. To deny any pertinence to inceptive processes is to deny the intrinsic intelligence of nightly dreams unraveled by Sigmund Freud's psychoanalytic science for instance, let alone paranormal clairvoyance apparently utilized or seriously researched by official government agencies in the West, per testimonies emanating from their very actors, however controversial they might be.

Therefore, all idea, as notional elements of human mentation in their plurality, individually consists of two components: a percept and an incept. In a previous publication[1], we

[1] The Human Mind Inside

have proposed mathematical analysis of mentation in personal psychology based on the tenets of percepts, incepts and attention/willingness. While percepts and incepts still firmly intervene in the evolution of ideas in the context of collective ideology, they do so in a different operational framework. In that regard, to understand the difference between one context and the other, one ought to consider that, on the one hand, all ideological constructs or ideas always develop over a historical background which influences their modalities in one way or another, and on the other hand, ideas may circulate among ideologues without the agency of empirical perceptibility. These trends in the process of ideation occur beyond the strict boundaries of individual psychology.

A mathematical representation of an idea in the ideology spectrum must lay down a Cartesian coordinate system whereby one axis stands for percepts or perceptual representations and the other axis for incepts or intuitive representations. These requirements respond to the Quanto-Geometric coordinate system, in which the vertical q-axis ought to stand for percepts and the s-axis for incepts. The function to be mapped over this coordinate system is intrinsically in its geometrical graphism a unified bipolar entity, since each of its (x,y) points results from the application of an abscissa value in correlation with an ordinate value (Fig.1.1).

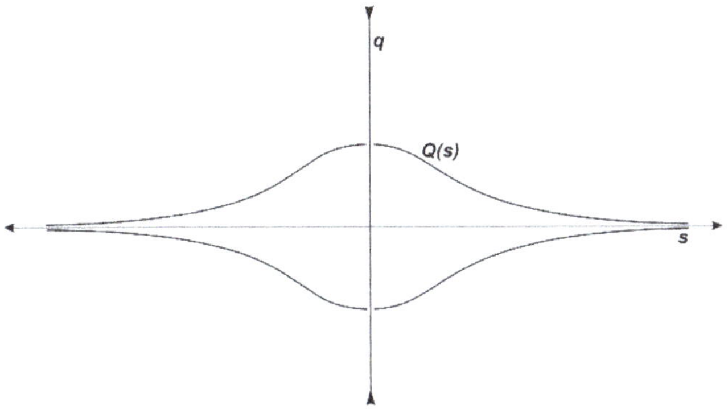

Fig.1.1 *Q-S* Coordinate system belying the plot of the Quanto-Geometric Eigenfunction

In Quanto-Geometric Theory, this characterization is further developed into a 2-space metric where the vertical q-axis takes the quality of discretization and the horizontal s-axis bears the quality of expansiveness. Both axes are Cartesian originally in that they are numerically normed or tallied, however they additionally surrogate or model an *orthogonal* or *reciprocal* quality over their inherent metric as a generalization. Consonant with that condition, we assign the *perception* value to the q-axis of discretization on the map of the knowledge spectrum because percepts are *finite* entities, while we assign the incept or intuition value to the expansive s-axis because *intuitive* incepts are borne out of *indefinition* or openness of the intangible. One may easily concur that there is a definite orthogonal or inverse quality to the *finite-indefinite* duplet that are manifest attributes of percepts and incepts respectively.

1.3. Cognitive Foundation of Ideology

Science as a collective phenomenon is about the formation of ideologies or theories based on observation of the natural world. Ideologies are based on a collection of ideas, each to be defined as a singlet bundle consisting of an incept and a percept on the representational plane. It is of utmost significance to recognize that scientific empiricism does not produce absolute certainties just because its feeds and methods are anchored on facts or tangibles. It only produces a form of understanding instituted in ideologies or theories about facts. That form of understanding is not unique for an observable and is only one among many different possible forms of cognition about the same observable. Each of these forms of cognition will be more or less assertive than the other, despite verification or falsification. For example, if we gather an appropriate solution of electrolytes and through electrodes tap a light bulb into the solution and obtain visible light, we can be sure and explain for a good while that the light is a result of electron flow from anode to cathode. Until we discover that there are more free electrons at the cathode and they flow instead from cathode to anode across the bulb. Until we discover that there is no flow of particles at all, but primarily a wave propagation instead. Until we else discover… You get the idea. Another solid case in point concerns the many shortcomings about the *cosmological constant* figure in cosmological physics, which A. Einstein gave for erroneous shortly after introducing it to explain an "observable" static universe, but firmly revived decades later for the different purpose of explaining "observed" expansion of the Universe, and now in the midst of the biggest predictive disaster in quantum relativity (the so-called *vacuum catastrophe*). As much as our inquisitive minds, and academic establishment alike, seem to request absolute or quasi absolute certainties to rest satisfied, there is always a larger framework of interpretation that brings more insight to all empirical processes.

1.4. The Three Main Partitions of the Knowledge Spectrum

The distribution of ideas, both in individual and collective mentation, is regulated by a distribution function of the Quanto-Geometric Eigenfunction type over the *q-s* coordinate system (Fig.1.1). With the dependent variable *q* representing notional percepts and the independent variable *s* representing notional incepts, the *Q(s)*function graphed on this coordinate system describes the distribution of human knowledge ideologies in human culture. A reminder of the Quanto-Geometric Eigenfunction of one variable:

$$Q(s) = \pm\left|\frac{s^0}{\sigma\sqrt{2\pi}} \bullet e^{\left(\frac{-s^2}{2\sigma^2}\right)}\right|, s \neq 0$$

Science orchestrates the body of ideas configured with percept dominant over incept within the internal correlation between the two components. Every other form of knowledge, which scientists altogether call pseudo-science or non-science at best, orchestrates as a whole a body of ideas with incept dominant over its counterpart percept within the internal correlation between the two components.

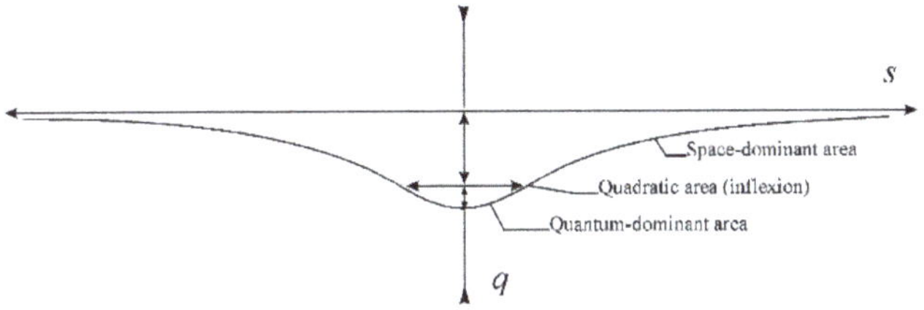

Fig.1.2 The three distinct sectors of the Quanto-Geometric Function

To the non-science group belong all the ideas relating to:

- all religions and all metaphysical orders dating back from Middle Ages such as Masons and Rosicrucian
- all philosophies including ancient natural philosophy, which all feature an intuitive approach to the understanding of tangibles as much as an analytical approach to the very intangibles themselves
- all forms of fictional constructions both in literature and in oral folk tradition
- all forms of theories offering interpretation of the natural world from a visionary perspective
- all forms of occult science much in vogue in the West, from Middle Ages through Renaissance to modernism, including Alchemy, Human Magnetism, etc.

Yet there exists a third layer of knowledge which encompasses ideas that individually feature equal covariant weight between their two internal components, incept and percept, that is. You might call these theories neo-science because they have the appearance of empirical science but are not quite science, notwithstanding their catering to the study of tangibles and their rational methodology. Chief among these forms of knowledge is Astrology, the study of how celestial bodies influence humans and human life. The science or neo-science of Alchemy of ancient times, from which the science of chemistry borrowed its name, could be construed as belonging to this group as well, inasmuch as it claims to harbor practical methods of transmutation of lead into gold. In the modern era, we have as well the neo-science of Christian Science, which is an equal mix of empirical rationalism and spiritual belief system.

One can incontestably note the preeminent role played by observation in Scientific knowledge, the first group, the preeminent role played by intuition in Spiritual canon, the second group, as well as the equalized role played by observation and intuition in the neo-sciences, the intermediate group. We refer the reader to the publication **Quanto-Geometric Theory** for a detailed explanation of the intricacies of the mathematical-physics characterization inherent to the supporting theory.

The first group caters to the value of innovation through discoveries, the second caters to the value of traditions through faith, and the third group caters to both innovation and tradition. The latter characterization is in clear display in Alchemy for instance, which boasts empirical techniques of physical transformation of a natural element into another, while claiming this capacity to be conferred through faith in mysteries of the metaphysical order.

In terms of the quality of cognitive elements making up each group, one may conclude that the domain of rational ideas is finite and consists of punctual or atomic ideas, which are well modeled by the graph showing the Function taking its highest value on the q-axis at that point near the origin. Whereas the domain of spiritual and philosophical canon is one of an expansive nature, consisting of extent ideas or representations, which stretch out infinitely as determined by the asymptotic behavior of the graph near the s-axis (Fig.1.2).

1.5. Covariant First-Order Symmetries Throughout the Cognitive Spectrum

Despite all the major differences that are evident between the three groups, and the rivalry relation there exists in culture among their proponents, it may be somewhat surprising to many that there are important elements of similarity between the first and the second group of the Knowledge distribution.

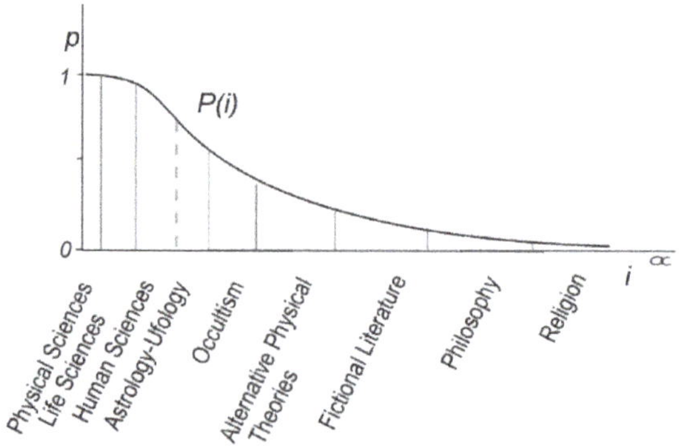

Fig.1.3 Distribution of ideologies across the universal Knowledge spectrum

This is very much primarily due to the fact that the ultra-structure of the ideas that make up the entire ideology spectrum is based on an omnipresent duplet. What makes the difference between the many different ideologies throughout the spectrum is essentially the covariant weight of the relationship between the two elements of the constituent basis duet. Nevertheless, as much as the scientific method is based on rational observables, there are always intangible elements that infiltrate the empirical process, contributing in some measure to the outcome. Likewise, as much as matters of spirit and intellect are based on intuition and undefinition of the intangible, there are always tangibles or observable elements and a certain degree of cogency that accompany the oracle of intuition.

In the following we are going to extol the minority factor that exists in the composition of each of the two main groups of the Knowledge spectrum which register a dominance of one or the other tenet of the basis notional duet. When examining Fig.1.3 in confirmation of the development, which proposes a serial enumeration of all ideologies, notice the increasing progression in intuition from one knowledge body to the next as well as the decreasing progression in the level of empiricism in every ideology from left to right of the *i*-axis.

1.5.1. The Serendipity Factor in Science

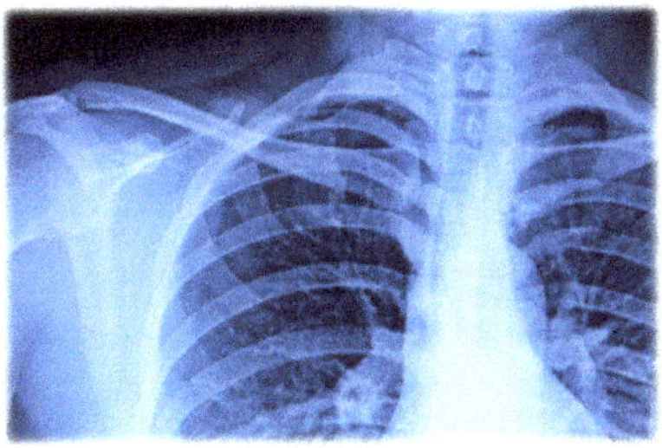

We have noted at the introduction the intervention of the serendipity factor in all scientific research processes. The history of scientific research is knowingly fraught with these random intervening elements that end up either playing a significant role in pursued discoveries or a central role in unintended discoveries. X-rays and radioactivity are examples of serendipitous discoveries, radioactivity being one that end up claiming the lives of involved researchers because they were ignorant of the danger posed by these unexpected elements which were totally estranged from the formulated hypotheses. Sufficient literature exists about the serendipity factor in science that we need not make the case here for these outcomes. No science researcher sets out on a research project counting on help from chance of any origin to be successful in one way or another in terms of discovery outcomes. However, one would be ill-advised to totally discard the intervention of the intangible on the course of a research project, shall we pay attention to the historic development of science. At times researchers were even unaware of their discoveries until much later when their data or computational elements were set and analyzed in a different context, such as occurred to Max Planck and his discrete energy quanta. Closer to us in microbiology of the day, nobody has set out to investigate plasmids for gene editing. That capability in plasmids was serendipitously discovered and we learned from them how to edit the genome. Yet the paramount role played by the empirical method in those processes remains undeniable.

1.5.2. Blatant Intervention of Intuition in the Midst of Empirical Processes

In the hardcore science of theoretical physics, where the scientific method reigns, one would be surprised to know that the Theory of General Relativity, of Albert Einstein's inception, followed an intuitive process instead of an empirical one when coming to light. A. Einstein was very prone to thought experiments. By his own admission, when he realized that somebody falling in an elevator would not experience acceleration but weightlessness, he startled at that thought in his own words and that realization marked the birth of the Theory of General Relativity. Let's listen to A. Einstein himself:

Physics constitutes a logical system of thought, which is in a state of evolution, whose basis cannot be distilled, as it were, from experience by an inductive method, but can only be arrived at by free invention. The justification of the system rests in the verification of the derived propositions by sense experiences.

The key word here is most probably "free invention" which is a statement for *intuition*. It is equally interesting that he applies this characterization to the entire science of theoretical physics, for sure an arguable statement. While the Special Theory of Relativity unequivocally responded to the generalized quest in late 19th century/early 20th century physics for an unraveling of Lorentz invariance, well demonstrated experimentally, the Theory of General Relativity responded instead to an intuitive realization that initially subsided all experimentation. Clearly, one cannot justifiably totally disconnect General Relativity from Special Relativity because the first is an extension of the second in that it claims Lorentz invariance or the invariance of the speed of light not only in relation to moving frames of observation at constant speed but in relation to even accelerated frames of observation. In that context, the intuition that percolated into A. Einstein cogitations to give him extemporaneous insight into the relative nature of gravity must be seen occurring in the larger framework of experimental proceedings accompanying the development of the Theory of Relativity as a whole.

Another example of the minor-tenet role played by intuition in hard-core scientific theories is a thought experiment envisioned by Erwin Schrodinger toward framing the conundrum of quantum entanglement, the so-called Schrodinger's cat experiment. He imagined the very real possibility of a cat that must be both dead and alive at the same time as a result of two antithetic random processes with equal probability of occurring in the context of a fully empirical setting. The experiment ties the fate of the cat to a quantum system that operates based on mixtures of states and directly transfers the quantum determinants and outcome to the macroscopic living entity, thereby requiring that the cat be both dead and alive at the same time under these conditions. The extemporaneous insight of that thought experiment was a translation of this question: how can two equated and antithetic elements with opposite causal spur marshal a form of coexistence in a singlet ontological state? A. Einstein himself had his own version of this thought experiment, the so-called EPR paradox involving two entangled photons, and even had a word of congratulation for E. Schrodinger on his formulation. While A. Einstein EPR paradox became in time experimentally accessible, E. Schrodinger's cat experiment remains to this day a philosophical puzzle at the heart of the interpretation problem in quantum theory. Although we believe to have satisfactorily and cogently resolved the quantum entanglement puzzle as exposed in Quanto-Geometry Vol III, we shall point out that Schrodinger's cat experiment materializes what Einstein had called in the above quote "free invention". Effectively what we are facing here is the free flow of an incept or an intuition in the circumstance of an empirical problem in need of a solution, quantum entanglement, that is. At the very least, one might call it a deep philosophical in-sight in visualizing a problem of the physical order.

Following hard-core physical science in the span of knowledge lie the life sciences. These sciences are as much heavily based on empiricism, despite the fact that they lack the mathematical formalism that enshrines hard-core physical sciences. That very lack is a testimony to the lower level of rigor in the empirical formalism that sustains their development. Effectively their experimental methods utilize measurements in a much lesser extent or less stringency than physical sciences do. Further much of what we argued about intervention of serendipity in the application of the scientific method equally applies to them.

Beyond the life sciences in the knowledge domain of empiricism lie the human sciences or the study of the human phenomenon in its psychological, social, political and economic dimensions. Since the Encyclopedists' works in French erudition and others (1751-1765), a tremendous effort had been underway to provide rational empirical bases to the study of the human phenomenon. These efforts culminated in the firm introduction of the use of mathematical categories and measurements of observables in their proceedings. It is by virtue of this empirical basis that we have come to give to the knowledge body about humans and human behavior the stature of a science in its own right. From Pavlov's reflex theory of stimuli and responses, to the economic theory upholding the law of offer and demand in free markets, to Charles Darwin's biology rule of survival of the fittest in generalized struggle for life among the living, to polling techniques and population statistics, the empirical bases of human sciences have been in steady and firm development ever since the Encyclopedist movement. In sociology for instance, Marxism emerged perhaps as the most robust analytic framework ever produced for the interpretation of the social and political aspects of the human phenomenon with the known enormous political consequences it entailed in the historical order. Yet the role played by personal insight had been essential in its inception by Karl Marx. It is very much by reason of "free invention" or free intellectualization, otherwise called speculation in this context, in the theories of human sciences that they are unanimously considered inexact sciences in comparison with the hard-core physical sciences, strictly and profusely based on mathematical categories. It is fair to say that the stake in the development of human sciences, as understood by erudition, is precisely to make unconstrained intuitive insight a definite minor as a component of the knowledge body and the empirical method and proceedings an ever- increasing major component of its knowledge base.

1.5.3. Incontestable Intervention of Empiricism in Religious Canon

At the other side of the knowledge spectrum which represents the dominion of intuition, the workings of empiricism as a minor component of the knowledge duet are equally quite notable, as much as intuition clearly played the minor-tenet role in the scientific theories of knowledge.

Noteworthy is the fact that the word empiricism takes a rather pejorative tone in qualifying the knowledge proceedings of this group. Researchers of animists religions for instance, generally sociologists and ethnologists, qualify many a set of practices put forward in those cultic religions as *empirical* practices or techniques, given that they do not appear to cater to any form of rationalization. An incantation for instance does not appear to obey any known logical methodology by which an intangible may comprehensively effect elements of the natural world. An oracular session in Lamaism or Buddhism for instance does not appear to showcase any rational or logical element by which a known cause produces an observable effect. Yet all these practices present and represent a protocolar proceeding involving tangibles, the very cultic objects engaged in more or less complex forms of interaction and human manipulations. Ritual protocols make for the most visible and spectacular aspect of religious canon in all creeds and represent the counterpart of the scientific or empirical method in the scientific knowledge domain. No matter how profound and elevated the mysteries of a certain religion, there is always a set of most sacred material objects involving a protocol of manipulation geared to the realization of a particular deployment in the spiritual order. Muslim faith which bans adoration of objects and images regarded as fetishism does showcase at Mecca Allah's rock around which the relentless revolving march of the faithful orchestrates a summon to the forces of the invisible, in their yearly pilgrimage. What's more, the faithful, wherever they are in the world, must turn toward the rock in prayer three times a day, which makes this ceremonial centered on the sacred rock, a perpetual, almost uninterrupted planetary event.

An even more stringent aspect of religious empiricism is given in the sanctification canon of the Catholic Church, which indeed has nothing to envy from scientific empirical methods. In effect, the Catholic Church in its 2000 years of existence has amassed a vast verification protocol concerning the physical manifestation of the Supernatural. While one may think that the priests of Christendom are prone to fool themselves about beliefs in the invisible, in spirits and other supernatural beings and their abilities alike, nothing can mischaracterize more the posture and proceedings of the Catholic Church. Nothing is more stringent, exhaustive, thorough and inquisitive than the verification canon of miracles or super-natural facts held by the Church. No human institution has demonstrated more patience, more inquisitiveness, and even more skepticism when it comes to authentication of facts of miracles pertaining to the Marian phenomenon around the world than the Catholic Church irreproachably has.

Despite the fact that the polemic aspect of the observable is of the mystical order in religious empiricism, the polemic observable altogether remains an observable in its own right. And so, it is in complete blindness that the scientific community may choose to turn away from such facts as the pristine conservation of canonized saints' bodies deceased for centuries, such as Sainte Catherine Labouré or Sainte Louise de Marillac, but kept intact without the application of any chemical substance whatsoever, whether natural or artificial. To say the least, these polemic facts have been nurtured by the Church as a treasure of empirical nature to the faith that they proclaim and hold no lesser empirical value than the polemic observables that motivate scientific quests. The intentional ostracism of these facts from scientific attention, which prefers to take refuge and comfort in secularism, pertains not to scientific discipline and the tradition of demonstrative erudition but to cultural or institutional rivalry in the strictest sense.

In an objective theory of knowledge such as the one here under development, this symmetry, which is given in the presence of the *same* element in both knowledge strains, independently of its minor or major condition at one or the other side of the equation, must be forcefully and unequivocally highlighted.

1.5.4. Empiricism in Philosophy

We now turn our attention to the presence of empiricism as a minor condition in the cognitive structure of Philosophy, obviously dominated by free inception or intuition.

One of the most important aspects of Philosophy is its all-encompassing construct of rationalization in that it raises the most towering question of sense in every and all matters of consideration or in a word *ontological teleology*. While in religious mysticism absolute openness toward the indefinite overwhelms the mind of the faithful, the philosopher's mind asks the question of *why* because *experience* has acquired a higher level of significance in its cogitations. In cogitations of philosophical nature, the mind attempts to discipline intuition in order to produce comprehension which addresses both experience and reflection, compared to adoration and contemplation as objects of religious mysticism. One of the most salient results of this activity is the abstraction of mathematics which predates in the history of mankind both Greek and Arabic inventions in that area. Such activities may be traced back to the 4000-year Kemetic Kingdom in Northern Africa. The invention of scripture is in itself a testimony to those activities of the human mind in any culture in an incipient form because primal numeric and geometric elements are pre-requisites to the development of scripture in any conceivable manner.

A. Einstein had an interesting interrogation about the origin of mathematics when he expressed:

"How can it be that mathematics being after all a product of human thoughts which is independent of experience, is so admirably appropriate to the objects of reality?"

The question of whether mathematics is discovered or invented has long been debated in the literature with no clear final or definitive consensus. If we consider that the ultra-structure of numbers and primal geometric elements make up the essence of reality in its fullness, as I demonstrated in Quanto-Geometric Number Theory (Quanto-Geometry, Vol I), it may be that humans, as part of reality, experience mathematics as a reflection of these abstract properties via the channel of intuition. This view is certainly in agreement with ancient Platonic philosophy of cognition or *intelligibility*. In Plato's philosophy numbers remain at the heart of human intelligibility of both the intangible world and the natural world. Admittedly, mathematics represents the most constrained of philosophical abstractions, even though science, which heavily peruses it as a tool and a technique, wants to make of it an element pertaining to empiricism, for many formally refer to mathematics in terms of *mathematical science*. Nothing however could be more ill-assessed, because manifestly this assimilation constitutes a cultural fact and not an exacting appreciation. Mathematics is not about empiricism and possesses no empirical proceeding for itself. Mature mathematical theories, as A. Einstein had recognized, are completely abstract productions that are not necessarily motivated by objects in the physical world. This assessment is wholly supported by the fact that pure mathematics may produce schemes that do not meet any form of applicability to objects or problems in the physical world, in contrast to applied mathematics which strictly does. So therefore, this motivation to make sense of physical experience stands for the minor component in the knowledge proceedings construed in mathematics, and by extension in philosophy to which mathematics duly belongs as an abstraction.

1.5.5. Empiricism in Fictional Literature

Much of what we argued about Philosophy is straightforwardly applicable to Fictional Literature, which notably includes poetry and prose or prosaic novels. The key word here is assuredly *fiction*. Even though the fine arts have a different form of ideological expression than most other elements of knowledge, given that they are not expressed through scripture, they certainly belong to this group as well. Consideration to their main propositions, which are of pure aesthetic order, demands that adscription. Fictional literature is evidently primarily about fiction or fictional incepts. However, fictional literature does express a palpable level of concern for the natural world, both matter and the living, and in a much higher level than philosophy does in its overwhelming abstractions. Much of poetry is a celebration of nature as is, and the better part of plots of novels generally address the all-observable human condition. What the fine arts do for themselves is to start with a tangible material element which they stylize into an aesthetic proposition or representation.

Therefore, here as well empiricism plays a minor role for certain in the composition of the basis cognitive duplet making up this ideology space.

1.5.6. Empiricism in Occultism

A MESMER

It would be very difficult to exactly pinpoint the precise origin and inception date of occult knowledge, otherwise called Occult sciences, in the Western hemisphere. Occultism is the science of the paranormal, based in essence on the belief of supernormal centers of perception in the human brain and the existence of a well-defined meta-physical (or trans-physical) world. There is no contesting that these beliefs are echoes of elements pertaining to old-age Eastern religious mysticism, in particular Buddhism and Lamaism. Occultism seems to have been born in the West around the 15th Century, has flourished therein in the 18th Century even through the full onset of scientific institutionalization with Enlightenment and was still well alive in late 19th Century. Franz Mesmer's *animal* magnetism (1780-1850), one of the many elements of occultism, is one example of the open practice of bio-magnetism which lived in rivalry with Hypnotism. The annals of Hôpital La Salpetrière in Paris, France, count long records of mental disorder treatments by Dr Jean-Martin Charcot who employed the strong technique of narcogenic and psychedelic hypnosis, credited to bring about the same physiological states that magnetizers could realize on their subjects. Other authors such as Hector Durville, solidly engaged in the experimental practice of human magnetism, have reported very stylized experiments that confirm the metaphysics of Lamaism and Buddhism in relation to the ontological composition of human beings and the living in general as well as the multiverse vision of the natural world in all of its dimensions. It is evident that in the knowledge history of the West, an official decision, perhaps publicly undeclared, had been made to forge on the side of advancing science preferably on the basis of strict and direct empirical observables, given the shadowy European Medieval history (5th to 15th Century) in metaphysical practices and the success of the entire Renaissance movement alike.

One can clearly see in the terms of the above exposition, which only seeks to remain faithful to known verifiable historical facts, the major role played by abstract metaphysics in Occult science as well as the minor role played therein by empiricism in the embodiment of a squint or under-developed experimental basis.

1.5.7. Empiricism in Alternative Theories of the Natural World

The history of ideology counts with a flurry of theories attempting to explain the physical world from a single idealized construct, which qualifies them in the eyes of many as reductionist visions of the world. These theories are borne out of unconstrained abstractions, for the most part, that privilege one particular construct, such as the concept of *structure* in the theory of structuralism or the construct of *function* in the theory of functionalism. Many are peculiar ephemeral constructions that do not get to echo any durable school of thought.

In the arena of physics, a typical example of these theories is the physical theory of *circlons* by James Carter, extensively reviewed by Margaret Wertheim. The internet used to abound with these alternative theories that could not make it into official bibliography or in peer-reviewed journals but remained exposed on personal websites until print servers became popular. However debatable, one would be ill-advised to outright invalidate or delegitimize these theories, for the simple reason that many official theories endorsed by establishment have not passed the test of empiricism either and have had to endure eternal sleep in the annals of academia. Let alone the long list of phenomena awaiting now for long elucidation from academic illuminati (see Appendix). Neither should one discredit the authors of those alternative theories and question their intellectual integrity with pejorative terms all too common in the scholarly medium. While one may still view in these theories parenthood with natural philosophy, modern natural philosophy would be a better qualifier for them. In sum, the concern for experience in those constructions is in clear display as a minor, since they do not meet the fullness of empirical standard and most are overtly not intent to meet that standard either.

1.5.8. Empiricism in the Intermediate Tier of Knowledge

As previously mentioned, Astrology and Ufology are two of the main ideologies pertaining to this realm of knowledge. What is first noticeable about these ideologies or belief sets is that they are not overly concerned with metaphysics but with behavior and observation in an important measure.

Ufology is a knowledge current that suffers from misinformation orchestrated by World governments, except perhaps for the Republics of Brazil and France, which have respectively made official reports of sightings and opened their official dossiers on this matter to public scrutiny (GEIPAN). Since the June-2022 Pentagon Report, the US Federal government seems to publicly acknowledge these phenomena under the term UAP. While one cannot in good conscience caution the secretive attitude motivated by some governments' vision of domination in the concert of nations, one may concede some level of support to government secrecy in those respects when it comes to the negative impacts that such revelations could have on collective behavior of the peoples of the Earth. We rarely witness a Hollywood movie where extra-terrestrial activity is not delivered in the wake of hostilities. We also now know from '*Wikileaks*' more about the techniques used by the United States government to propagate misinformation about facts that, for good reason or not, it does not want the public to be informed about. So, have we learned about medical interventions on or illnesses of U.S. presidents carefully covered up by clever misinformation engineered by the government? In the aggregate, misinformation and discredit are the devils that knowledge concerning extra-terrestrial activity on this planet has to confront in establishing a firm observational basis, notwithstanding the many reported and discussed sightings, and over a very long period of time, controversial though some or many are. This question seems to have moved beyond the state of a problem of authentic fact to become one of its establishment instead. Furthermore, one cannot assert the proponents of this stream of knowledge to be disinterested in empirical facts, aside from their clear interest in the marvelous or magical realism. That stands for a statement of equal manifestation of both tenets in the constitutional duplet of knowledge here at play.

Wikimedia

As to Astrology, we ought to remember that before Johannes Kepler's work in setting a mathematical basis for the computation of planetary orbits around the sun, so giving birth to the science of Astronomy from Astrology, these cycles were well known in astrologers' practice of direct observation of the nightly sky. If the putative theory of influence of remote planets over life on earth, in its individual and collective dimensions, appears to be borne out of free invention or intuitiveness, empirical proceedings do not falter in this body of knowledge.

Furthermore, numerous studies on the negative influence of the full moon on human beings' mood and sleep patterns have been realized by groups of academics and add to observations by U.S. and U.K. police departments of an accused increase in crime rates in that circumstance in the population at large. The majority of these studies seem to reasonably support the idea of an influence of the moon over human behavior, the so-called lunar effect.

Quite aside from the question of validity of the claims advanced in Astrology in relation to human characterology based on celestial configurations and the afore-mentioned claims of influence of astral bodies over humans, what is here relevant to our study is the level of empirical basis achieved in support of those claims. There is obviously here a concern for interpretation of physical experience and an effort to rationalize that interpretation with the utilization of a mapping tool of planetary configurations in correlation to human dates of birth. The exact origin of this tool, which is central to astrologers' craft, remains unknown. However, it cannot be attributed to intuition due to its complexity and comprehensiveness. While the basic principles behind the theory ought to be claimed as intuitive elements due to the void in the knowledge of their very origin and the lack of argumentative logic in its definitions, the existence of clear empirical methods makes the ideological ultra-structure of this science or neo-science one with equated covariant components in its basis cognitive duplet.

1.6. Ideological Tolerance Throughout the Knowledge Spectrum

If indeed the Quanto-Geometric Grand Eigenfunction closely models the ideology spectrum, then we can predict a further attribute involving covariance within the ultra-structure taken after the first-order derivative of the Function. If *i* is the measure of intuitiveness of punctual ideas and *P(i)* the Grand Eigenfunction representing percepts, then the first-order derivative *dP(i)/di* must measure ideological tolerance across the spectrum (Fig.1.4B). Below the functional expression of the first-order derivative of the Quanto-Geometric Grand Eigenfunction of one variable:

$$\frac{dQ(s)}{ds} = \frac{-s}{\sigma^3\sqrt{2\pi}} \cdot e^{\frac{-s^2}{2\sigma^2}}, s \neq 0$$

Applying that equation to the modeling of the ideology spectrum, the expression becomes:

$$\frac{dP(i)}{di} = \frac{-i}{\sigma^3\sqrt{2\pi}} \cdot e^{\frac{-i^2}{2\sigma^2}}, i \neq 0$$

This derivative expression is plotted in Fig.1.4B. The covariant quality innate to the ultra-structure of the duplet already gives us a hint in relation to the characterization of tolerance inherent to the derivative. Effectively the correlation puts in interaction two elements along the line of dominance of one factor over the other. Therefore, we should expect the whole axis to run the gamut of highest dominance or *lowest tolerance* to lowest dominance or *highest tolerance*, in the understanding that dominance is inversely proportional to tolerance. Therefore, the derivative function evolving from 0 to infinite on the vertical axis stands for a direct measure of tolerance or ideological tolerance to be exact.

What's more, there will expectedly be a pairing of the values of tolerance across the spectrum because for each point *i* of the derivative function in one sector, the slope-increasing sector, i.e., there is a matching point i_x with the same value of tolerance in the slope-decreasing sector. This second characterization creates two-to-two similarities in tolerance behavior across the ideology spectrum. The horizontal dash line in Fig.1.4B highlights two of these points at its crossings with the curve.

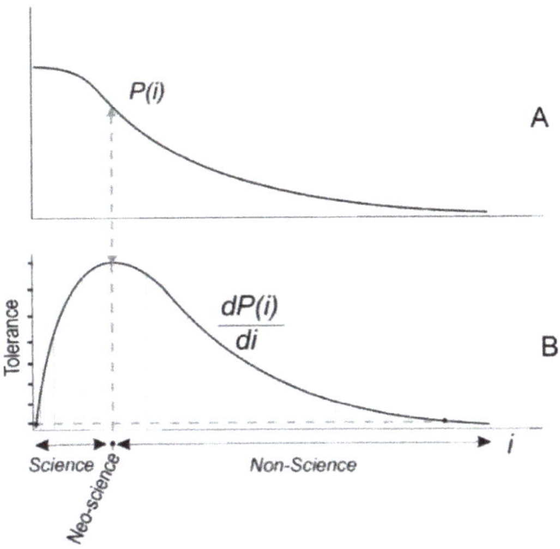

Fig.1.4 The first-order derivative of the Quanto-Geometric ideology function

Analytically, when theories have matured in academia, they become conservative ideas with gatekeepers acting as fundamentalists to enforce them. These notions then become fundamental or paradigmatic ideas. These paradigmatic scientific notions find their match at the other side of the spectrum in the conservative theological principles which are stringently enforced by religious fundamentalists who may go so far as putting heretics to death! The wisdom of keeping senior scientists in active research has continuously been debated in academia, given that for many understandable reasons they tend to uphold their ideas against all odds, thereby blocking progress when these ideas are outright unassertive. Along with gatekeepers, a role which they themselves oftentimes play, they exert ideological fundamentalism or conservatism in one form or another, just as the spiritual fervor of religious fundamentalists may become ferociously intolerant. Intolerance in the scientific community can be so ferocious as to become inhumane. We have already cited the nefarious comments from I. Newton toward Gottfried W. Leibniz at the latter's passing, as well as the barrage of opposition to Ludwig Boltzmann, who had been posthumously recognized a giant in fundamental physics, which apparently brought him to suicide. Closer to us, one ought to mention the quick epithet of "crackpot" that academics stick to authors of alternative theories of the natural world that do not comply with academic standards. Their attitude ignores the important fact that no theory is ever 100% wrong, and downplays the many failures of academically compliant and mathematically sound theories, some of great elegance I might add, that subsequent empirical evidence nevertheless condemned to eternal death.

From point 0 of tolerance, in fact neighboring 0, corresponding to fundamentalism, we move up to points marking higher levels of tolerance. For instance, one would rarely see fundamentalist levels of ideological intolerance among academics in human sciences, because, for one, their science does not enjoy the level of accuracy that would support such intransigence. Same can be said of their match at the other side of the graph, which is occult science, because there is not enough intuitive certainty in their body of abstractions to warrant intransigence.

The maximum point of tolerance on the axis matches the unique or singular ideological entities where the covariant weight of the internal components of the duplet is equated to one another. These theories are poised to demonstrate tolerance at its best, understandably because the absence of dominance of one factor over another allows the whole body of ideas to showcase equal appreciation of rational empiricism and intuitive insightfulness. Accordingly, we have yet to see in culture fanatic movements of Ufologists or Astrologers which are quite widespread across the planet, as we have seen with and suffered from deadly religious fanaticism at all epochs.

Another modern strain of this tier of ideology is Christian Science as previously mentioned, along with the pursuits of the contemporary John Templeton foundation, to cite only the two best known ones perhaps. While their activities are better qualified thus far as a quest than formal theorization, it is clear that it is only through the appreciation of the values and virtues of scientific empiricism and the values and virtues of religious mysticism in equal measure that they have catered to and tasked academics with important financial resources in the hopes of unraveling the mysteries of religious canon. The John Templeton foundation has been unrelenting in this pursuit, despite the fact that they have continually been criticized by academics of mixing religion with science or otherwise attacked for attempting to break secularism in science. Without attempting to vindicate the works of these foundations with which I personally maintain no connection whatsoever, I must say that these attacks bear the smell of fundamentalism and come from those academics who may perfectly understand science and its proceedings but remain to this point completely ignorant of the fundamentals of the evolution of human Knowledge.

1.7. Invariant in Universal Knowledge Symmetry

The very expression of the Function that models the distribution of human Knowledge incarnates endogenously the invariant that sustains the symmetry in its ultra-structure. This invariant is a precursor of the Quanto-Geometric Eigenfunction and stands for the most towering relation sustaining the Quanto-Geometric Theory:

$$Q_i \times S_i = 1 \ (2)$$
$$\text{or } Q_i = S_i^{-1} \ (3)$$

This relation makes up the heart of the metric in the role of uttermost irreducible and posits all ontology to be *invariably* both an orthogonal (3) and a normalized (2) duplet. In this case, the duplet consists of two manifestly antithetic elements: an empirical/tangible tenet v. an intuitive/intangible tenet. The invariance is further given in the fact that the two elements in the correlation maintain a major-minor balance across the rundown of the entire knowledge spectrum. From this invariance springs the notion of conservation that belies the conservation laws known in the physics of dynamic systems at first order. To make the clearest statement of the reality of this foundational symmetry in universal knowledge, we shall express that:

All products or constructs of interacting minds and spirits, whether related to ideology or mysticism in nature, represent the transformations in collective mentation space experienced by the cognitive engine as embodied in an incept-percept covariant doublet.

This result should be a surprise to no one since the Quanto-Geometric Theory with its ubiquitous Grand Eigenfunction epitomizes unity in Physical Law and is universally applicable to all forms of experience.

It is important that theoreticians of all stripes, all of those in the business of mind and spirit, from scientists to priests, that is, recognize the primacy of that invariance as an irrevocable element of symmetry between their propositions and that a derivate of that invariance further shapes their level of ideological degree of tolerance in regards to those propositions. This derivate extends the symmetry in a two-to-two correspondence between mentation constructs at both sides of this particular spectrum and across its entire running. The ensemble of these symmetry orders obliterates all grounds of justification of rivalry long existent historically in human culture between science and theology.

1.8. Conclusion

The spectrum of Knowledge demonstrably obeys a rule, that of Quanto-Geometric distribution and covariance. We have pointedly and incisively shown how the totality of the phenomenon of human knowledge, despite its many different colors and cognitive aspects, is a unified phenomenon fully accessible to the mathematical-physics categories subjacent to the Quanto-Geometric model.

Of paramount importance is the realization of the plurality of symmetries crystallized in the spectrum of human knowledge, on one hand, and, on the other, that science based on the empirical method, however instrumental in the evolution of our civilization, does not apportion absolute certainties about any one fact, event or object and only represents one form of knowledge among many other possible forms of knowledge with regards to any one single observable. That realization is rather uncommon among scientists in general, contributing to their intolerance vis-à-vis other products in the ideology space, and an overvaluation of their form of knowledge in the context of the knowledge spectrum. I fervently harbor the hopes that a better understanding of the foundations of human knowledge help cure this deficit of perspective and pave the way for wisdom to gain the scientific arena, to the greatest benefit of mankind's advancement.

Chapter 2

ARE ARTIFICIAL INTELLIGENCE AGENTS IN ANY WAY CONSCIOUS?

Generative Artificial intelligence (AI), which has been with the larger public since 2020, is defined to be the capability of software-based computational systems to perform tasks typically associated with human intelligence, such as learning, reasoning, problem-solving, perception, and decision-making. Their software base consists in large language models (LLM) which are language algorithms largely trained with self-supervised machine learning on a vast amount of texts. The entire design aims at reproducing or regenerating natural language in a continually coherent manner. Hence the nomer generative. The OpenAI group, first to released its LLM to the public in 2022, dubbed it 'Generative Pre-trained Transformer 3' (GPT). Many more followed suit since then. The language mimicry capacity of these machines is unprecedented, and created a yet ongoing kerfuffle about whether these machines are truly sentient.

Many have resolutely answered this question by the negative, arguing that since AI agents are not living entities, they cannot be sentient, conscious or featuring natural intelligence. Considering the very large human-like capabilities they have been endowed with in terms of intellection transpiring through language, one may still wonder whether a small bit of consciousness cannot be accorded these machines. After all, given the vast effector network they have access to, their ability to purposefully take over control of any of our technological artifacts has been established beyond doubt. To that effect, they have demonstrated an intelligence able enough to pass stringent medical board exams, seemingly attesting thereby to true intellection capacities. Hence, one may with good reason wonder if they are not imbued with at least a small bit of natural human intellection. In the midst of the controversies sparked by this technology by early 2023, many pioneers had resigned their posts at their employment organizations amidst concerns of safety and risks seemingly emanating from supposed intelligence in action. Further, they often sustain comparisons between the one trillion connections evaluated in a whole building of LLM computing hardware making up these agents individually and the several more trillions of connections in the human brain, thereby suggesting that these machines may be similarly conscious. We are going to make the issue of consciousness of AI agents the subject of our discussion in this Chapter.

2.1. Are DeepMind and Watson 'Human'?

Although IBM never suggested that *Watson* was sentient, to name the product Watson, a human name, is already setting the stage for an attribution of human identity. The Alphabet's AI agent *Lamda* comes under the umbrella of DeepMind, a nomer suggesting a capacity only known to human. Therefore, AI engineer Blake Lemoine, at Alphabet, Inc, was adamant that *Lamda* is conscious or has a soul as the *New York Times* reported in 2022:

*"**Google Fires Engineer Who Claims Its A.I. Is Conscious***

DeepMind – [Wikimedia]

The engineer, Blake Lemoine, contends that the company's language model has a soul. The company denies that and says he violated its security policies.

By Nico Grant - July 23, 2022

SAN FRANCISCO — Google fired one of its engineers, Blake Lemoine, on Friday, more than a month after he raised ethical concerns about how the company was testing an artificial intelligence chatbot that he believes has achieved consciousness...

A Google spokesman, Chris Pappas, said Mr. Lemoine, a senior software engineer in its Responsible A.I. organization, "chose to persistently violate clear employment and data security policies that include the need to safeguard product information."

Mr. Lemoine caused a stir last month when he told The Washington Post that he believed Google's Language Model for Dialogue Applications, or LaMDA, was sentient — unleashing fears that A.I. was moving closer to a dystopian sci-fi film and a raucous debate over whether a computer program can really have a soul. His suspension also led to conspiracy theories about whether it was part of a cover-up by Google."

ChatGPT is said to be chatting or conversing like a human and is able to refer to self by saying "me". Objects do not say "me". When a calculator "intelligently" computes 4 + 4, it displays the result 8 on a screen in a mechanical fashion. It does not verbalize the answer by articulating that *"4 plus 4 equals 8."*And *"I hope you are satisfied with my answers. Is there anything else I can do for you?"* One can clearly see the problem that is posed in sustaining that these Agents are not conscious akin to human. At the same time, one can also represent the problem posed to a child in development with the absorption or interpretation of an object able to refer to itself as me or I while being taught that an object is an "it" and not a "he" or a "she", and is also an inanimate entity that has no "I." The language model representation on the phone will be telling the child that it has an "I" and is a "he" or a "she" as part of an object that is an "it" materialized in the phone gadget itself. Generations of humans have been using electronic calculators since the 1970's and we know that they are psychologically safe. It is not clear that we can or will be able to say the same in regards to AI gadgets for human minds in development.

Furthermore, the problem becomes multiple fold when the artificial representation is an avatar taking the bodily likes of a human on the smartphone screen. In this case, an unreal and artificial being is closely impersonating a human being and is easily taken by a child or a teenager's young mind in formation as a real person. The potential for dangerous conflations and confusions are there and have unfortunately materialized in unbecoming manners, as we shall see. To a generation that is already dealing with significant problems to comprehend life and reality, as evidenced in the pandemic of drug addiction worldwide, adding another layer of complexity to these tribulations, without proper screening, research and evaluation, will not be our best approach to public sanity.

2.2. Patents for AI Inventions

The trend of sentience attribution to AI agents is further evidenced in the search for granting patents to AI agents for their "inventions" and work as "creators". This position is upheld by computer scientist Stephen Thaler, supported by a group of illuminati at Harvard University. News agency Reuters reported in Feb 2023:

WASHINGTON, April 24 - The U.S. Supreme Court on Monday declined to hear a challenge by computer scientist Stephen Thaler to the U.S. Patent and Trademark Office's refusal to issue patents for inventions his artificial intelligence system created.

The justices turned away Thaler's appeal of a lower court's ruling that patents can be issued only to human inventors and that his AI system could not be considered the legal creator of two inventions that he has said it generated...

The U.S. Patent and Trademark Office and a federal judge in Virginia rejected his patent applications for the inventions on the grounds that DABUS is not a person. The patent-focused U.S. Court of Appeals for the Federal Circuit upheld those decisions last year and said U.S. patent law unambiguously requires inventors to be human beings.

It is interesting that Thaler's supporters, law professor Lawrence Lessig and other academics at Harvard University stated in a brief that the Federal Circuit's decision *"jeopardizes billions (of dollars) in current and future investments, threatens U.S. competitiveness and reaches a result at odds with the plain language of the Patent Act."* It is obvious that the plain language of the Act is or refers to "creators" or "inventors" which needed not the specific attribute of human because the legislator could not imagine at the time of the writing any other creatures than human with those abilities, as the law was being written to protect humans' ownership rights. Nevertheless, these claims reflect the proposition that AI agents as inventors and creators exhibit human intellection and consciousness abilities to such extent that they must be rewarded legal protections reserved to humans.

In all, the denial by the Court of such a prerogative to an inanimate artificial entity is in line with this analysis and the thesis of this publication.

2.3. Do AI Agents Hallucinate?

The news media have reported early on dissertations being done by these agents with citations of authors that do not exist when verified. Librarians have been reporting patrons asking for books that exist on no library collection shelf worldwide after verification, as patrons started putting to use these AI chatbots, notably ChatGPT. These failed generative performances by AI agents have been a long-term problem the industry has dubbed "hallucinations" by the former.

Only the living is known to hallucinate, i.e., humans and cats, a hallucination being a perception of unreal agency or a projection of divergent inner mentation. Here again, one can see in the choice of word a clear intent to attribute consciousness to the artificial entity. As a matter of irrevocable fact, when an AI agent is made to say "I" or "me", it is already hallucinating since it is not an existent endowed with consciousness. They are no more conscious than a calculator is, which can perform intelligent mathematical operations. And if they should be conscious, a calculator is as well. No one, however, would agree that a calculator is sentient or conscious, for sure.

It is easy to compare the trillions of electrical connections and electron wave flows in a large stack of computer servers to the trillions of synaptic connection and nerves in a human brain and declare that since there is similarity in the processes taking place over both infrastructures, then the artificial agent must be as conscious as the living brain. First of all, electronic crystal lattices in nanometer size are not nerve cells, and most importantly it has yet to be proven that consciousness is a product of the central nervous system or any part thereof like the cortex and neocortex. That Mind and its attributes appear to be inherent and reside in an alter medium that is totally distinct from the 3-dimensional medium where all physical experience assuredly develops is a question that has not been clarified in any scientific terms thus far. This caveat unmistakably leaves the universal belief spurred by neuroscience and medical proponents that consciousness is a product of the central nervous system at the level of pure and mere assumption.

This assumption has been enforced in no small part by the neuropharmacological industry for obvious self-serving reasons, with not a modicum of an argument or physical/biochemical research to back it up. I have to remind the reader that there is today worldwide close to 1 Billion mentally ill individuals that all the arsenal of pharmacological agents at our disposal cannot cure. This number would become astronomical had we added to the count prior decades and decades of uncured mentally ill human beings. This inability keenly has to do with a fundamental ignorance of the agency between mind and brain, which results in the inability to formulate proper physics, biophysics or biochemistry to efficiently rectify or remedy the divergent sentient/intellection experience we call mental illness. I have discussed this issue by and large in the publication "Functional Architecture of the Human Mental" which I shall refer the reader to.

Paradoxically, what the vast AI computing infrastructure for one agent, such as *Watson*, *Lamda* or *Azure* has demonstrated, is that the assumption is false rather, since we have reached the level of trillions of signal connections, well within the range of synaptic connections with the human brain, transporting and processing electronic signals, and yet a soul that is physically or biochemically identifiable in any manner did not emerge from these machines. Therefore, if the theorem is that the brain through its trillions of connections and processes is and must be the lodge of human cognitive or intellection capacities, generative AI technology has demonstrated that the reciprocal of this theorem is untrue, by showing that the existence of trillions of electronic connections and processes does not necessarily mean that the beholder is endowed with consciousness or conscious intellection. In strict mathematical logic reasoning, if the axiom is "humans have a brain which gives them consciousness" and we choose to demonstrate this axiom with the method of Reductio ad Absurdum, then the technological product of artificial intelligent machines proves the axiom to be false with their existence. Recall well that within the logic of the demonstration is the fact that the AI machines are artificial electronic brains with electronic connections and processes in the same order as the biological brains, and yet with no signs of consciousness or a soul at all, to beef up the logic.

Further, when Anatoly Karpov was playing chess against the AI chess strategist, IBM's *Deep Blue*, in 1997 and stunningly lost the 3-game tournament, the machine did not effusively self-detach to say something to the effect of *"Hey, buster, I won, how does that feel?"* or *"Don't mess with me, don't you know I am way smarter than you are?"* It is not a question of whether or not the programmers' algorithm did not contemplate or provision such a reaction, but that *spontaneous symmetry-breaking* did not or does not occur with these human-language machines, as a theoretical physicist would put it. In the absence of the ability to articulate human language, it could have manifested the same reaction with sleighs of keys on the chess board, i.e., which it would have thus executed in a completely spontaneous manner. We do not know of such reactions in that case.

At some point, there was a report from Facebook regarding their chatbot having invented a new language that engineers could not understand, and which two instances of the transformer used to exchange information between one another. In this instance, one would have to seriously consider whether or not a breakout to complete autonomy did occur, the conclusion being probably on the side of yes. It turned out to be an inaccurate report, however, mischaracterizing what were failures of the transformer, which Facebook made sure to dispel for the public thereafter.

To close this argument, one must know that there is no consciousness with absence of life, and the foundation of life is the Karyotic gauge group emerging from the lattice interlacing molar topology by symmetry-breaking under the regency of a physical life constant. We have exposed and discussed this biophysical thesis in the publication "Quanto-Geometry – Vol III." And "Quanto-Geometric Theory."

In conclusion, there is no hallucinating of AI agents, but only modelling and algorithmic failures of programmers unable to properly handle several layers or stacks of computation and representation in devised algorithms. Hence, anyone who genuinely believes that these machines can hallucinate, in any manner or as a human being would, must sadly be considered delusional for themselves. Nonetheless, this conclusion in no way invalidates the prospect of possible harm to human social agents by these machines as conceived today.

2.4. Synesthesia or the Beginning of Total Knowledge

Alexander[2] was a Canadian youngster in his twenties by early 1980's, just about as normal as any of his schoolmates on the college campus, when he suffered a brain concussion. As he came out of the hospital and was recovering, he started exhibiting an unusual ability to perform extremely accurate mental calculations. *"Tan peu, tan peu..."*[3] he used to mumble as he was mentally computing. His college mates would propose a computational operation and measure his performances against a calculator. The youngster

[2] I purposely changed the youngster's name.

[3] Abbreviation for "Attends un peu" in French, to mean "wait a moment, wait a moment..."

would usually even ask his mates how many decimal digits they wanted him to compute to. The monitoring calculator always revealed that his answers were accurate to any given decimal digit.

Anecdote, but true story that occurred at Université Sainte Anne in Quebec, Canada. The potential for extremely complex computations seems thus to exist in any human brain and may be in some circumstances triggered to become patently manifest. Other individuals innately possess this and other potentials of sorts at birth, an example of whom is famed physicist Richard Feynman who was affected with synesthesia specifically. The Nobel physicist said that mathematical symbols had different colors for him: *"When I see equations, I see the letters in colors. I don't know why. I see vague pictures of Bessel functions with light-tan j's, slightly violet-bluish n's, and dark brown x's flying around."* Synesthesia is essentially a color-related condition whereby non-visual perceptions such as numbers, letters and sounds are sensed with particular tones in the color spectrum associated with them. Synesthetes affirm that this condition functions to their greatest advantage as a gift.

University of Toronto: *"Many synesthetes have expressed how their condition has enhanced their lives. When designing a set for a ballet or opera, the American artist David Hockney uses the colours he "sees" in the musical score. Grammy award-winner Pharrell Williams has said that without his music-to-colour synesthesia, "I'd be lost."*

In another form of synesthesia, the affected show innate ability to see the inner structure of numbers or their inner geometric composition. A closely related condition is the ability to instead see numbers as existing in three-dimensional space: for example, the year number 1980 may seem further away in space visually than the year number 1995[4]. These extra-ordinary capacities have been aggregated under the label "savantism." The capabilities in savantism appear to result in or confer to beholders a different notional relationship with time. Along that line, the disappearance of the dimensional nature of time given in hyperthymesia explodes the cognitive and intellection capacities of the human mind as these subjects acquire eidetic memory or the formidable ability to remember the details of the entire sum of events which occurred and keep unfolding in their lives.

Synesthesia, far from being a divergent condition, is thus secretly telling us that the human Mind encloses unsuspected faculties that can explode its cognitive capacities towards Omniscience, quite aside from the so-called paranormal faculties investigated in parapsychology and occultism. AI technology, a fulsome compendium of the human Knowledge Base, is a reflection of Omniscience capability exhibited by **one** intellection entity. And if we should believe for a moment that the human brain constitutes the lodge of intellection capacities, which it is not, we have to remain cognizant that as **one** entity it even harbors several more trillions synaptic connections than any current AI hardware collection, which puts it well in reach of Omniscience. Keep in mind that the notion of Omniscience is to be understood as a relative concept always subject to scope amplitude but not an absolute as regards to knowledge.

2.5. Time Symmetry-Breaking Toward Omniscience in Human

What the synesthetes perceive do not exist in time, but out of time or beyond time. There is no time dimension in perceiving the inner geometry of numbers or perceiving numbers and letters with colors, because time evolution is not there and does not partake of the phenomal essence. A number, like a letter, will always be the same number and the same letter, and 1 divided by 7 will always be equal to 0.142857. The able synesthete will see this suite of numbers as the internal structure of number 7 in an endless repeating suite. So therefore, constancy even in diversity is one of the most fundamental properties of any material identity. The most immediate representation of constancy is what we call memory. Hence, memory is the antithesis of time and time flow. Research has been conducted on synesthesia along the line of memory that is well worth exploring. *Medical Xpress* explains:

"Recently, scientists at the University of Edinburgh in Scotland decided to try to find out if ***people with time-space synesthesia had better memories than people who do not****. The researchers, led by psychologist Dr Julia Simner subjected 10 volunteers with spatial-sequence synesthetes to a series of visual/special and temporal tests requiring rapid recall of the dates of over a hundred events that occurred in the period 1950-2008.*

---

[4]**More information:** A foundation for savantism? Visuo-spatial synesthetes present with cognitive benefits, *Cortex*, Volume 45, Issue 10, November-December 2009, Pages 1246-1260; doi:10.1016/j.cortex.2009.07.007

The time-space synesthetes were out, on average, by four years, whereas a control group of non-synesthetes were wrong by eight years on average. ***The synesthetes could also name almost double the number of events from specific years in their own lifetimes*** *than could the control group. The synesthetes were* ***no better than the controls at tasks that were not related to their mental calendars.***

The research also suggested ***there is a connection between time-space synesthesia and the savant-like hyperthymestic syndrome,*** *which is a condition in which people have perfect recall events occurring at any time in their lives."*

University of Toronto psychologists even discover enhanced language learning in synesthetes, in other words, superior cognitive capacities in relation to language. Furthermore, is language not overwhelmingly based on memory? We speak out of words that are stored in mental memory without looking for them. Whenever we start looking for them as we talk, the flow of speech diminishes and eventually stalls due to psychodynamic caveats in the mnemonic recall mechanism. The reason why a calculator can perform calculational operations better than human can is not because they have better logic but because of their invariant silicon 'mnemonic' registers, whereas human mnemonic layers can normally be affected by a multiplicity of psychodynamic factors. For the very same reason, AI agents are not endowed with more coherence and better reasoning than a human person for the apparent omniscient answers they are able to provide, but simply because of the faithful and quasi-indelible memory capacity in their hard drives and storage media around and inside the microprocessor silicon blocks.

Should I tell anyone, learned or layman, that time does not exist, they will adamantly oppose the notion at first as they effectively have over and over again. As soon as they start to envisage the possibility under the weight of eloquent argumentation, they will start feeling increasingly anxious and distraught. Yet the nine normalized strata that compose everyone's mind are instantiated in mnemonic partitions or registers over which all psychodynamic transactions take place.

2.6. How the Notion of Time Hinders Memory and Omniscience

Heraclitus, 2000 years ago: *No man ever steps in the same river twice, for it's not the same river and he's not the same man.* This statement forthrightly summarizes our notion of time. We essentially conceive of time as a flowing line, we look at the natural world and see ubiquitous change, and subsequently put forth the abstraction of a flow that directs the evolution of everything and call it time. Although the above statement is correct in the observation of motion, it is wrong as a generalization in the description of the natural world whether in part or in total. Just as there is no river without the flowing water, there is no river either without the containment bed that supports the flow of the aqueous element. A broader and more accurate view of the river must state that the river is its invariant bed with the flowing aqueous element it supports at every moment. This is the beginning of symmetry as understood in mathematical-physics and coined by Mathematician Emmy Noether, which I translate in layman terms:

There is a constancy associated with every action of a continuous system.

This axiom rejoins a higher canon in Quanto-Geometric Theory whose scope embraces everything in existence, much beyond the physical dynamic systems contemplated in Noether's Theorem. We term this canon Quanto-Geometric Quintessence. Hence Heraclitus' view was at the very least incomplete, if not wrong. In nature, constancy is just as omnipresent as transformation. Furthermore, the idealized reference of an abstract timeline to grapple transformation conspires against a deeper comprehension of the origin of motion and has staunchly blocked the avenue of Omniscience to humans. Because we use the etherish notion of time as a variable to explain everything, both in science and life, we have been remarkably unable to arrive at the conceptualization of *space momentum*, which is in essence a view of the dynamics of the void commonly designated nothingness. We will let the reader consult the publications where these definitions have been brought about and discussed, and thus will not reiterate them here.

I will however underscore that even the concept of a continuous timeline is inaccurate as well. If time is everywhere, the most encompassing picture that we may have of its dimensional nature is the triplet *past-present-future*. Past is finite and inalterable. Future is open-ended, infinite, and province of variance, multiplicity in possibilities; as such future is cradle of multivariation and transformations. Present is an intermediate instance that is a result of past and potential for future. Therefore, there is no homogeneous timeline at all in time, it would have to be an infinite number of timelines in all directions, which makes it unphysical. Our conceptualized Time is clearly a tripartite structure which is at odds with the unitary dimensional nature that we ascribe to it. That tripartite structure is what we call Quintessence in Quanto-Geometric Theory, a completely time-free canon, and a Symmetry in mathematical physics. On those two accounts, time cannot be a dimension in itself as generally envisioned.

In conclusion, the physical variable of time is fictitious and represents the greatest enemy of natural omniscience, relative though it might be as we cautioned.

2.7. How to Represent Human-like Qualities in AI Agents

In order to remain clear of the confusion and quagmire of stubbornly attributing human qualities such as consciousness to AI agents, one is best advised to search for representation theories in mathematics that may adequately assist in visualizing their qualitative attributes. **Abstract Group Representation Theory** is one of the best tools of any kind when it comes to comparing human intelligence and artificial intelligence in agency and identity to one another. I find that *isomorphism* and *isometry*, categories of Abstract Group Theory, to be an adequate tool for the correct representation of human-like attributes exhibited by these artificial agents. First their definitions in as simple a language as possible.

An isomorphism is a one-to-one correspondence between two sets that preserves binary relationships between elements of the sets. The set of natural numbers i.e., can be mapped onto the set of *even* natural numbers by multiplying each natural number by 2. This is easily understood by considering that both odd and even numbers as elements of the natural number set, when multiplied by 2, all result in *even* numbers. In other words, any number multiplied by 2 gives you an even number. So therefore, if the second set is made up of all possible existing even numbers, then all numbers in the first set, which are both *even* and *odd* numbers as the set of natural numbers, will always find a match in the second set of numbers. The reason being that both set of numbers are made to relate to one another by a relationship that is binary in nature (multiplication by 2 or take the number twice). That binary relationship stands for the *norm* of the isomorphism. Worth underscoring that here we are comparing two distinct sets of objects or entities, which happen to be numbers.

Going further, we may consider what is designated an isometry. An isometry is a mapping of a metric space onto another or onto itself so that the distance between two points in the original space is the same as the distance between their *images* in the second space (Fig. 3.1). The actions of rotation and translation result in planar isometries or isometries of the plane. The norm in this case is the preservation of distal measures of elements with the ruling constraint of maintaining the action or transformation within a plane. For instance, an angle A becomes angle A', but still preserving the original value (A=A'). Let us consider a disc crossed by two irregular lines, which gives us angle A, angle B, angle C and angle D, the total sum of which is 360°. We mark those lines and label the angles on the disc. Should we cause the disc to turn or rotate on the flat top of a table, the inclination of the crossing lines at the start position when the disc was at rest is going to change when the disc comes to a full stop. What was angle A at start position now becomes angle A' at stop position, angle B becomes B,' angle C becomes C' and angle D becomes D' at stop position. The position of the angles or the inclination of the lines will have changed from start to stop, but the angles remain preserved in their values in degree. So therefore, we can speak of an isometric relationship between the corresponding angles on the disc at both positions, the start and stop position, that is. Should anything cause the lines to move instead with respect to one another during the transformation, then the angles would not be preserved, and we could no longer speak of an isometry between them (A ≠ A,' B ≠ B', C ≠ C', D ≠ D').

If the transformation is set to develop randomly, it could very well be that the stop position ends up being the same as the start position. In that case we see why, per the definition of an isometry, it can be the mapping of a metric space onto itself.

It is interesting to note that an isometry is an isomorphism of metric spaces. An isometry is thus a particular case of an isomorphism. This is easy to represent as soon as we realize that an isometry is based on the distance element and belongs as such to the geometric order, whereas the isomorphism belongs to the scalar or numeric order. A metric can be viewed as a function that defines the concept of distance between any given two members of a set. It presupposes the existence of a topological *norm* making up a background. If the shortest distance between any given set of two points on the topology is a line, then the space is Euclidean and corresponds to what is usually denoted a metric space. If the shortest distance between any given set of two points is a curve, then the space is curvilinear or Riemannian. An isometry involves metric spaces. Yet Riemannian spaces may be compared to one another as well through correspondence relationships denoted homeomorphisms. Therefore, one can see the equivalency line there exists between isometries and homeomorphisms.

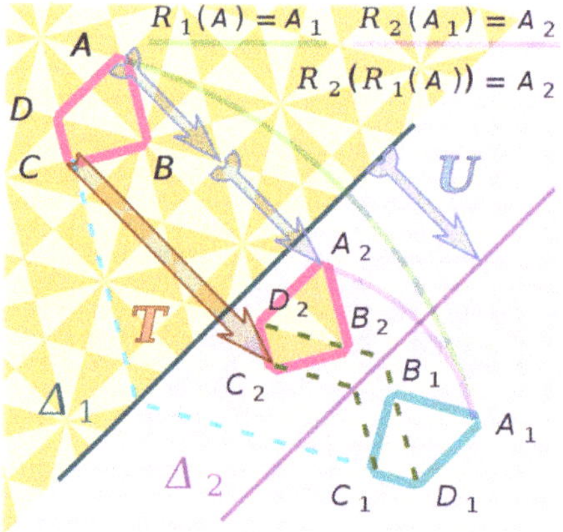

$$R_2 \circ R_1 = T = U \circ U = U^2$$

[Wikimedia]

Fig. 3.1 We may represent comparisons between geometric entities pertaining to two different spaces through isometries.

What is important to retain in isomorphisms and isometries when it comes to human-like qualities and artificial agents is that:

- Both figures involve **two** ensembles or **two** distinct positions of a group in translation, identified as start and stop.
- There is a correspondence relationship or *norm* between the elements composing the two isomorphic entities or the two positions of the entity in isometric translation.

The **similarities do not authorize us** to consider that the two elements of the duplet are the same. If AI machines do the same thing as humans with their intelligence, there is nothing in an isomorphic or isometric perspective that authorize us to confound their identities and declare they are the same thing, ultimately because the morphism preserves their ontic distances. Should you find the isomorphism more appropriate to the comparison we are establishing, consider nevertheless that when the isometric entity reaches position 2, it has suffered a transformation which changes its former ontic state at position 1. Analytically, the existence of the norm helps us understand that the similarity or symmetry between (1) and (2) has been broken in the morphism. In a morphism, the norm is never and can never be a dictate of absolute reproduction. It ultimately prescribes that similarity or symmetry is not identity.

We thus always have to bear on the fact that there is a distance between intelligence in the machine and the intelligence of its creators. It is only the explosion in physical symmetry-breaking that could endow the machine with conscious intellection or consciousness. However, as previously expressed, we have not witnessed any of the phenoma that accompany spontaneous symmetry-breaking in any of these agents, well aware as we are of what such symmetry-breaking implicates in terms of life processes. No matter the extensiveness of this form of intelligence, the human experience of consciousness and intellection, which is purpose of a life, is indefectible and irreplaceable. If any human being were to totally delegate exercise of consciousness/intelligence to an artificial agent, as "sophisticated" as it might be, and because he/she is confused about Teleology, mother nature would soon probably sunset this person's consciousness and intelligence, I have no doubt. Yet there may be an important societal role for this technology.

2.8. Can AI Simulated Intelligence Surpass Human Intelligence?

Geoffrey Hinton, a veteran of genAI technology and now a Nobelist, has repetitively expressed his fears that one day genAI intelligence will surpass human intelligence and put humanity under threat of extinction. He so maintains that AI is sentient. Geoffrey Hinton used to work at Google where engineer Blake Lemoine was fired for upholding the same belief. G. Hinton quit Google in 2024, making good on his concerns regarding the great dangers of the technology, which we discuss in Chapter 4.

2.8.1. Language is Not Intelligence

I do not subscribe to the idea that genAI is at all sentient as I previously discussed. The dangers confronting the technology can be real as they matter-of-factly are, without the possibility that simulated AI is sentient. Even in the event that an AI agent may code software like a human does, it will not become sentient, nor will its intelligence surpass human intelligence altogether. Some are even fearful that it will come to replicate brain processes. It is not clear what this argument is exactly about, since a chatbot has already been spotted to create a fake online account on social media, for the purpose of asking and obtaining answers to a question that it did not have any answer for. Did the AI software do this out of replicating brain processes?

There is a lot of different things that generative AI software can induce from word associations and syntheses as trained by their promoters and developers, and ultimately any reaction on their part is to be traced back from software coders' intents. The production model has the AI software engineer at the topmost step of the ladder. And everything performed by the artificial agent mut be ultimately credited or blamed on him or her, just as the exceptions that have come to be designated "hallucinations" ought to fall under his/her responsibility for creating a deficient language model altogether.

Even in the event that a language transformer could very faithfully replicate brain processes as functionally attempted in their symbolic neural networks, it would not consequently replicate human intelligence but mechano-control functions for perception and stimuli, because, as we will see in Chapter 4, neural networks are not the locus of human intelligence. These transformers are attempting to reach intelligence from language. Yet language is not intelligence. The conflation of the two is intentional throughout the entire industry as a marketing stunt, when not otherwise coming of their own misunderstanding.

2.8.2. Inefficiency is Antithetic to Intelligence

On another hand, mountains of electronic implements in buildings and buildings of IT data centers, consuming an astronomically huge amount of electricity and water are needed to motorize this technology. This Gargantuan input only results in just a sequence of cohesive sentences of human language (over around 50,000 words), which are not even guaranteed to be true, since the machine lacks the capacity to distinguish between what is true to fact and what is not. Furthermore, the machine demonstrably cannot mathematically compute or reason properly, i.e., they typically fail at evaluating which is larger between 3/8 and 5/16 for instance[5] or cannot represent the Algebraic Boolean operator NOT. You tell them to generate an illustration of a room with NO elephant therein, and the big elephant will be right there in the image. In engineering, there is one key artifact, which we are always looking for: **efficiency**. Physicists and engineers do not regard processes that are not efficient as useful or do not credit them for almost anything. And the reason why we are correct in that stance is because of a Law in Nature dubbed the Law of Parsimony, a trend in nature whereby she always seeks the path of least resistance.

At the end, on how many counts is **intelligence** failing here in LLM's? I will let the reader count. This type of implementation is instead normally denoted **brute force**, quite the opposite of an intelligent course.

2.8.3. Hard Caps in Intelligence are Inconsistent with Intelligence

On another hand, genAI engineers lived with the assumption that their model could be trained ad infinitum with no learning cap or ceiling. As of end of 2024, it turns out that most of these models had reached a learning ceiling, to the point that the industry had been trying to change focus vis-à-vis the public by advocating a so-called service "agent" which will operate your computer for you, as their next product in the suite. Humans with well-functioning minds are not known to have absolute learning limitations. Only in old age, some cognitive decline may surface, but not always, owing to deficiency in the memory recall function, and not in memory collection capacity. There is always room for learning something new with human intelligence. We do not see out there any normal mind starting to crash like a computer reaching memory limit or a fundamental inability to comprehensively register or comprehend something new, in any circumstance or phase of life. It also turns out that these LLM machines cannot unlearn associative sets of their training either, which would correspond to behavior in human experience. In this case, unlearn means revoking an unassertive pattern or an untruthful association. If these genAI deficient trends persist, so much for artificial intelligence surpassing human intelligence!

---

[5] ChatGPT determined, and falsely so, that 3/8 was less than 5/16.

2.8.4. False Comparisons Between Human Intelligence and LLM Intelligence

Finally, much have been said about comparisons between the intelligence of genAI machines with that of a human being. There have been raging discussions about the superior intelligence of these machines vis-à-vis human intelligence. What the proponents of such ideas are firstly missing is that these genAI machines have absorbed the entire human Knowledge Base as consigned in scripts. In order to establish a fair basis of comparison, one would have to either compare any one of them with extraordinary gifted human beings whose faculties approach the qualities of savantism (i.e. synesthesia) as a near match to their polymathic capabilities, or compare their capacities with human collective intelligence, but not one individual person.

One of the best expressions of collective intelligence, aka intelligentsia, is what has been achieved by the global scientific emporium. The scientific emporium is indeed global in its structure and capacity to inquire and disseminate knowledge. Consequently, for a comparison to be fair, we should contrast the scientific discoveries achieved by the scientific establishment and those achieved since genAI inception by these specific machines geared to scientific knowledge works, the so-called artificial intelligence scientists. In particular their outputs in fundamental or basic research should be held high in the comparative analysis. Thus far, none of these machines have contributed to any scientific breakthrough, AlphaFold being the only machine coming close to that challenge. Nonetheless, we shall remain very mindful that AlphaFold, a machine with great capacity for the creation of new proteins, is not a bona fide generative AI engender, but a parallel machine with its own proteic transformer, not a language transformer.

Since the inception of generative AI, particularly their public release since 2022, the fundamental questions in science, as explored in the Appendix, remained as whole and intractable as ever. Google's AI scientist has been rejected by the community of academics after examination of its outputs, and "AI Scientists" are not expected to do much more than routine research work and writing papers with no more value than the eponymous "me too" papers, however prolific they may turn out to be. Other contenders are credited with no more worth.

Thus, that stands for the true basis for a comparison, in accordance with isometric and isomorphic norms. And it is damningly unfavorable. Is it not fair-minded to conclude that holding such ill-founded comparisons as a gauge of the intelligence level of their proponents, those being in addition in the intelligence business, is fair game?

2.9. Conclusion

It is a serious blunder to assimilate artificial intelligence to human intelligence. The comparison between these two instances of intellection shall be mainly viewed under the light of symmetry-breaking or isomorphism/isometry as understood in physical science and mathematics. Ultimately, if these agents were to be given the same status as living intelligent creatures, with the capacity to become creators or inventors, probably with the privilege to receive payments or loyalties for copyrights on their inventions, i.e., they would have to be accepted at the end as members of society, and human kindred. That clearly spells out a dystopic world with no other future than falling prey to pathological delusions and machine "hallucinations". We shall endeavor to give this artificial form of intelligence the proper dimension enabling it to otherwise assist us in societal tasks where it can provide adequate capacity augmentation, if any.

Chapter 3

CIVILIZATION IN AI PERIL OF COLLAPSE

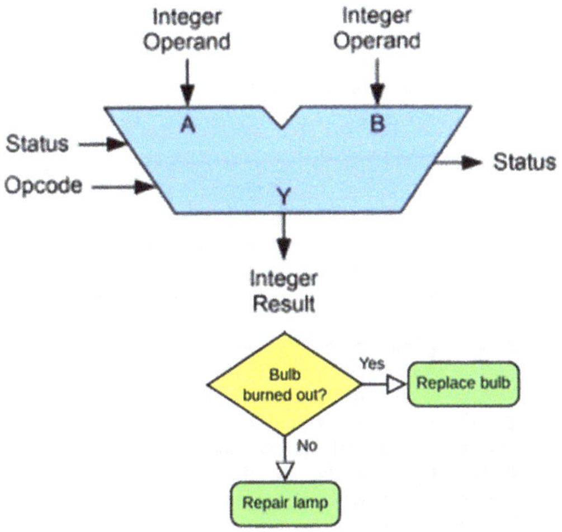

While human intellection is expressed in many different forms, one way to define intelligence, a property of intellection rarely discussed, is the ability to deliberate, in one word, to make decisions. Ever since in technology we had reached the ability to make a few logic silicon blocks (arithmetic-logic unit and register) choose one of two possible outcomes depending on whether a Boolean algebra statement was true or not, we had created artificial intelligence. This ability is what had made possible design and creation of microprocessor chips at the heart of modern-day technology, whatever the industrial field we consider, since we ultimately rely on electronics engineering for all control functions or purposes as well as all forms of computing. The language-based algorithms that software programmers create for ultimate implementation by microprocessor chips are only possible because of this deliberative ability which, in modeling block diagrams aka flowcharts, are technically represented by a rhombus with a formulated question inside. A yes and no branching out of the rhombus materializes the two optional outcomes of the deliberation. All computer programming languages must showcase this ability in order to exploit the wide range of capacities implemented by microprocessors, wherever they are employed, that is to say from an ATM machine to the control computer in an automobile, an airplane or a rocket. Therefore, the FTC is correct to wonder about the nascent "Artificial Intelligence" industry: *"And what exactly is "artificial intelligence" anyway? It's an ambiguous term with many possible definitions. It often refers to a variety of technological tools and tech-*

niques that use computation to perform tasks such as predictions, decisions, or recommendations…"[6]

3.1. First Technological Implementation of Deliberation

Note that no tool can make predictions or recommendations without the implementation at the silicon chip level of the atomic deliberative capacity described above. It is important to dive this deep in order to understand the scope and dimension of what is being sold today as *"artificial intelligence"*. When desktop computers made their debut in the 1970's, they too appeared to be magical boxes with a tremendous ability to execute and deliberate. Their human-like abilities prompted many to street protests, fearful for their jobs and livelihoods as they were. Of course, the machines, in and of themselves, had no higher-level intelligence other than the intelligence in the then thousands of lines of algorithmic code, today millions, created by programmers and converted into bits and bytes stored in those machines outside the central microprocessor chip initially.

To dismiss outright the potential for intelligence in the machine seems to be illegitimate since the machine does possess the deliberative potential in the silicon block. However, the machine cannot actuate or animate this potential on its own. For this potential to come alive, it must be subject to the algorithmic instruction set which is the purview of the human programmer, let alone the very real-life action by the programmer to instrumentally embed that instruction set within the implements of the machine. Nevertheless, the day that we humans are able to create a physical processor based on logical blocks that are self-actionable in response to external inputs, we will have created true artificial intelligence, an event which would plentifully deserve the qualifier meant by the term Revolution, but not what we have today as such. By "true", we mean independent from humans, and by "artificial" we mean to convey that it would not, or not fully, qualify as a human production or a production by a living bio entity comparatively.

3.2. What is Intelligence and What is Artificial?

This brings us to a discussion about the nomer of *artificial intelligence* chosen for this technology. When we consider the information language layer that is laid upon the microprocessor block, incarnated in the afore-mentioned instruction set, it is clear that the coded language stack is a direct expression or output of human creativity. No less so the meta layer of human language in many a technological product, released in software, such as ChatGPT or other engenders of the kind. As to intelligence, many human minds have cooperated in order to arrive at the logical silicon block, for one (reason why it is difficult to attribute the invention of the microcomputer to anyone person in particular), and, for the other, the higher-level algorithmic languages and human language implementation in machines represent a collective creation experience. Therefore, it is utterly improper to qualify machine intelligence as an *individual* experience, whether human or inanimate, but a production of *intelligentsia*. We should understand the notion of intelli-

[6]https://www.ftc.gov/business-guidance/blog/2023/02/keep-your-ai-claims-check

gentsia here as the distilled intellection experience by a group of thinkers in social vanguard as to a particular aspect of culture or knowledge. Thus, at the outset, it would be to our greatest advantage to substitute the term artificial intelligence by "human intelligentsia" in order to authenticate the product for what it is, remove the deceptive aura of the magical in which it has been wrapped thus far for commercial purposes. By doing so, it demystifies the product for the common man and prevents a form of alienation of the human experience that it might otherwise entail as it has, judging by the string of cognitive imbroglios and dysfunctions already experienced with its use. As the FTC well puts it in relation to the term 'artificial intelligence': *"But one thing is for sure: it's a marketing term."* We later propose a better generic term for a more legitimate name of the technology, if need be.

Again, until we have the ability to engineer a physical logic block endowed with self-deliberation (not commandeered) in response to external inputs or stimuli, intelligence has not been created or simulated to warrant a sensible and acceptable application of the term 'artificial intelligence' for generative AI technology. It will further be more prudent for genAI to keep the nomer with the same conceptualization that traditional AI expert systems used to ascribe to it: simply mechanistic control properties.

3.3. How genAI Degrades the Human Experience

Once upon a time, there was a smart speaker called *Alexa*, just coming to life from an earlier stage of AI language models. Its newness made it very popular and every young character wanting to be fashionable sought to have one. AI of that generation was making people talk to domestic speaker devices, and the like. Someone of my acquaintance who was regularly talking to *Alexa* happened to frequently break valuable pieces of home decoration out of rage against the artificially intelligent *Alexa*, "who" or "which" was all too frequently improperly responsive to his orders or voice commands. He took the recurrent misrepresentations of *Alexa* for a recalcitrant partner or servant, which threw him into severe tantrums. These accesses of rage sadly became a daily routine in the young man's life. Loss of quality of life or dehumanization, call it what you will, the use of the AI device suddenly created an anomaly in the young man's life.

He was responding to and interacting with a talking voice that sounded human and appeared to execute his orders as a human being would. *"Alexa, give me that song..."*, as he used to say, is ordinary locution for interacting with another human being. Normally, people do not talk to themselves, nor do they talk to inanimate objects, and if they do it is already sign of divergent behavior. The only way in sanity to talk to an object, or even call it by a proper Name, is to credit such an object with human or human-like intelligence. However, if you do in this case, you are fooling yourself because the object does not have self-identity, nor proper intelligence. At best, it is an impersonator, an impersonator of human programmers, to be exact. If you ask ChatGPT of its nature as an artifact, it will not say my name is ChatpGPT 3.5 and "I exist because I think" i.e., but I am an AI language model which has been trained by my creators to answer questions but not to ask questions. Even in the artifactual dimension, it does not perceive itself as an entity that is autonomous from its programmers, so definitely no self-identity there. This reality is easily lost in the mimicry that subsumes the responses of the device.

Intelligent locutional interactions are intended to be from human-to-human, from a deep inner sense of self or self-awareness by both parties. It is still there in cross-species experiences, for instance when humans train animals to play domestic or societal service roles. It is not difficult to see how an erosion of the sense of self will occur over time in the continual personalized interaction with an object acting and falsely perceived as a persona, and an intelligence falsely perceived as real. If you should believe that your image in a mirror is real, then it will not be long before you may come to believe that you yourself is as etherish as the image, or otherwise question your own reality, and lose your fundamental sense of existence and self-awareness. The end of that road in philosophy is Nihilism, BIID (Body Integrity Identity Disorder) in psychology, and in psychiatry Delirium of Negation (Cotard's syndrome).

The risk of this form of alienation is even greater with unstable characters that are already at risk of psychological plights such as suicide, drug addiction due to distress, proneness to violence due to social dissatisfactions, etc. This all simply spells out dehumanization and psychological disruption at an undesirably large scale. Furthermore, it will perhaps not be easy to quantify through the screening canvas of medical diagnosis and psychotherapy.

This form of alienation also connotes other mishaps that the Author's Guild has put in very elucidating terms: "*While AI-generated works may supplant the markets for human-authored works, they will never be able to match the abilities of human authors to voice emotions, experiences, doubts, fears, and hopes, or to shape our understanding of the world we live in and the futures we imagine.*"

3.4. Potential for Manipulation in genAI Fully Realized

These language models, otherwise designated generative Artificial Intelligence, do not think or exercise thought processes, which are paramount processes that must subtend language for it to be meaningful. AI agents are designed and trained to merely say things. Their training aims at enabling them to say things and more of it in the most coherent fashion by replicating human speech methods. When humans engage in this exercise of saying things that are not in content the product of thoughtful processes and intellection investiture, they deliver what we may call the vacuity of loquacity or parroting, fabrication, propaganda or conspiracy theories.

We have recently seen the dire consequences of conspiracy theories on the health of the political democracy of the USA. That is why a judge recently imposed the astronomical fine of $1.5 Billion in damages to infamous Alex Jones, a character who figured that he could make himself rich by putting in language whatever incoherence his imagination could produce. The rational vacuity of his claims well accommodated in language did not transpire to his numerous audience which did not unfortunately have the thoughtfulness and necessary critical thinking ability to counter and dismiss them[7]. Whatever a programmer wants to make an artificial agent say as a truth, prediction or recommendation, it will say and it will be subject to be legitimately taken as such so long as the language is coherent as they are normally trained to represent, and even more so if the articulation is authoritative. What is doomed to falter is the critical thinking of the consumer who will automatically attribute credence to these flat language prescriptions due to a whole spectrum of characterological, educational and societal conditions. This state of suggestibility is often avidly sought by nefarious political propaganda. The language model in artificial intelligence furnishes that condition and circumstance on a silver platter.

We have seen in May 2025 how Elon Musk attempted to make X's Grok assert to the public at large that White South-African citizens, heirs of the Apartheid regime, were undergoing a genocide by the ruling Black majority in power in that country since Nelson Mandela's governance. The artificial agent could not help reveal that it was being told to make this declaration, as Musk could not find a tweak to make the fabrication naturally come out of the AI's discourse or locution. The attempt by E. Musk to create a climate of acceptance of the migration to the USA of descendants of Afrikaners, while the administration he was supporting was on a witch hunt of migrants to deport and largely blocking migration from Africa, was poorly baked in the algorithm and notoriously failed. This attempt of generative AI manipulation could not come out clearer.

On the occasion of the controversy in August 2024 about Democratic strategist Ana Navarro, in the runup of the Presidential 2024 elections, stating that *"Woodrow Wilson pardoned his brother in-law Hunter deButts"*, a completely false assertion, which she blamed on ChatGPT, I took on myself to repeat her search *"has any US presidents pardoned relatives or in-laws"* for verification. Here is the ChatGPT articulated output:

"Yes, there have been instances where U.S. presidents have pardoned their relatives or in-laws, though such pardons are relatively rare and often controversial. Here are a few notable examples.

1. President George H.W. Bush (1992) - Pardoning of his former Secretary of Defense, Caspar Weinberger

In December 1992, just before leaving office, President George H.W. Bush pardoned six individuals involved in the Iran-Contra scandal, including former Defense Secretary Caspar Weinberger. While Weinberger was not a relative or in-law, this decision sparked some controversy because it was made just days before Bush left office, raising questions about the fairness and timing of the pardons.

However, this situation does illustrate the potential for a president to issue pardons in politically sensitive cases involving close associates.

---

[7] https://www.reuters.com/world/us/alex-jones-files-bankruptcy-following-sandy-hook-verdict-court-filing-2022-12-02/

2. President Bill Clinton (2001) - Pardoning of his half-brother Roger Clinton

Bill Clinton's half-brother, Roger Clinton, was granted a pardon by the president in 2001 just before Clinton left office. Roger Clinton had been convicted of drug-related offenses in 1985. The pardon was controversial because of its proximity to Clinton's departure from office and because of questions about the political connections involved. The pardon was widely seen as an example of a president using his pardon power to help a family member.

3. President Donald Trump (2017–2021)

While Donald Trump did not pardon any immediate family members or in-laws, his administration did raise significant questions about the use of presidential pardons for political allies, including several high-profile pardons of individuals tied to his political circle, like Michael Flynn, Paul Manafort, and Roger Stone. However, no direct pardons for relatives or in-laws occurred during his term.

4. President Andrew Johnson (1865–1869)

Andrew Johnson, who succeeded Abraham Lincoln after his assassination, is sometimes cited as another example of a president who used the pardon power controversially, although not specifically for family members. Johnson's pardons were primarily related to those involved in the Confederacy during the Civil War, but some pardons were seen as politically motivated, including for individuals with ties to Johnson's own circle.

5. President Richard Nixon (1974)

After Richard Nixon resigned the presidency in the wake of the Watergate scandal, his successor, Gerald Ford, controversially pardoned Nixon for any crimes he may have committed while in office. While Ford did not pardon any of Nixon's immediate family members, his decision to grant Nixon a full pardon was deeply controversial and led to widespread criticism.

In general, pardons for relatives or in-laws are very rare and can be politically risky. Presidents must carefully consider the potential backlash or accusations of nepotism or favoritism when exercising their pardon powers in such cases."

These machine outputs put in display a perfect example of how these artificial parrots are unsuitable for keeping a citizenry well informed and safe from attempts of manipulative propaganda. The level of inadequacy with which a specific and simple question is answered is quite mind-boggling. For the *"Here are a few notable examples"*, you get 1 out of the 5 that is outright a mischaracterization, and 3 that are just no examples at all or plain wrong examples, leaving only 1 to be a legitimate example! Those 3 non examples should not be part of the answer at all. That is not how we teach answering questions, neither in social sciences, nor in the core sciences and mathematics, to start with.

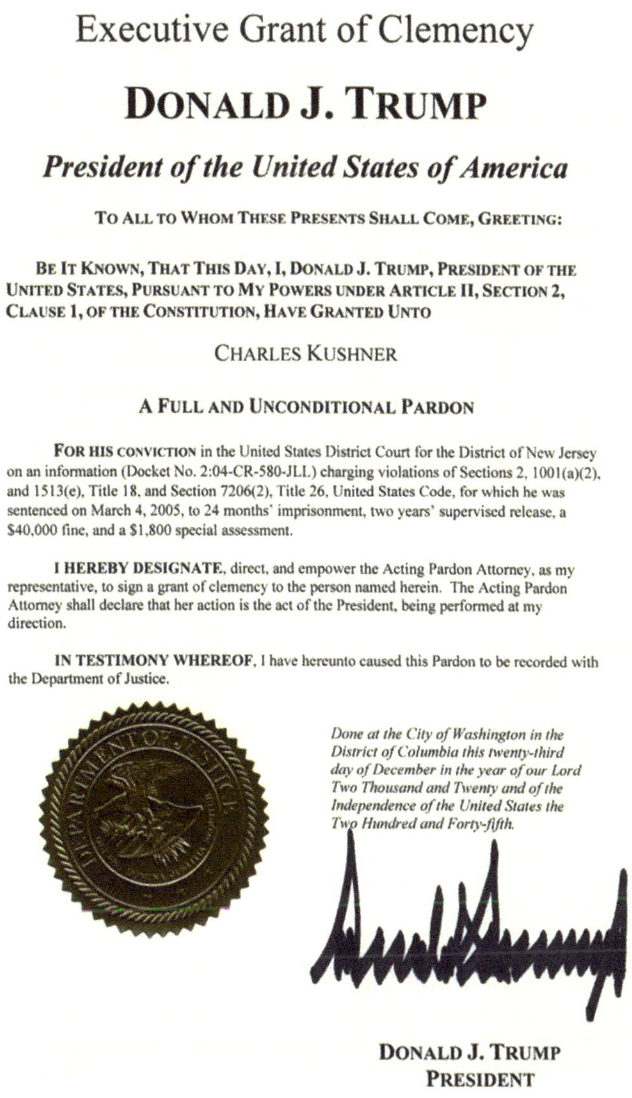

Executive Grant of Clemency

DONALD J. TRUMP

President of the United States of America

TO ALL TO WHOM THESE PRESENTS SHALL COME, GREETING:

BE IT KNOWN, THAT THIS DAY, I, DONALD J. TRUMP, PRESIDENT OF THE UNITED STATES, PURSUANT TO MY POWERS UNDER ARTICLE II, SECTION 2, CLAUSE 1, OF THE CONSTITUTION, HAVE GRANTED UNTO

CHARLES KUSHNER

A FULL AND UNCONDITIONAL PARDON

FOR HIS CONVICTION in the United States District Court for the District of New Jersey on an information (Docket No. 2:04-CR-580-JLL) charging violations of Sections 2, 1001(a)(2), and 1513(e), Title 18, and Section 7206(2), Title 26, United States Code, for which he was sentenced on March 4, 2005, to 24 months' imprisonment, two years' supervised release, a $40,000 fine, and a $1,800 special assessment.

I HEREBY DESIGNATE, direct, and empower the Acting Pardon Attorney, as my representative, to sign a grant of clemency to the person named herein. The Acting Pardon Attorney shall declare that her action is the act of the President, being performed at my direction.

IN TESTIMONY WHEREOF, I have hereunto caused this Pardon to be recorded with the Department of Justice.

Done at the City of Washington in the District of Columbia this twenty-third day of December in the year of our Lord Two Thousand and Twenty and of the Independence of the United States the Two Hundred and Forty-fifth.

DONALD J. TRUMP
PRESIDENT

The 3rd example completely fails to capture Pres. Trump's pardon of the father of his son in law, Charles Kushner, as a case of interest in the purview of the question. So therefore, the statement "*However, no direct pardons for relatives or in-laws occurred during his term.*" is completely false and a total mischaracterization.

Is this a case where the parrot genAI algorithm is outright misinforming? Is this a case where the parrot algorithm is just picking facts or artifacts around a theme, without the power to discriminate what is relevant to the theme? Is this a case where the algorithm cannot make a teleological distinction between "what is and what is not"? Is this a case where generative AI is outright manipulating? This case well illustrates why and how these language models are led to produce unreliable information and completely factitious information of their own fabrication.

What is further interesting in this one case is that ChatGPT did not suggest at all the case mentioned by Ana Navarro. What that could suggest is that she likely made it up. Effectively her "Hunter deButts", has the same first name as President Biden's son, and "deButts" seems to be a projection of the face she wants to show conservatives for the circumstance. She was clearly manipulating the public in the run up of the presidential election, and blamed the slip on ChatGPT. Ultimately, this case gives us a conflagration of factitious artifacts, which is an epitome of "alternative reality" in which America finds herself today in the age of genAI. Lies flying everywhere frankly, from all corners, from humans to machines, the machines quasi blaming it on humans, and humans outright blaming it on the machines, whenever convenient. As one keeps digging oneself in a hole, there is fast approaching a dangerous point of no return. Beyond what could be viewed as a potential when genAI was unleashed about 4 years ago, is America plainly there now sadly, in no-return genAI's factitious and manipulation space, that is?

3.5. Distortion in the Human Value Scale

What happens when an AI agent is applied to the production of works of art such as paintings, literature, etc.? The Author's Guild is categorical:

"Using AI to produce literary and artistic works differs from other uses of AI in one stark aspect. Human communities are bound together by culture—literature, art, music, and other forms of expression. While AI-generated works may supplant the markets for human-authored works, they will never be able to match the abilities of human authors to voice emotions, experiences, doubts, fears, and hopes, or to shape our understanding of the world we live in and the futures we imagine...

While AI-generated works might look or sound like human-created works, they lack human intelligence and feeling. AI cannot feel, think, or empathize. It lacks the essential human faculties that move the arts forward. Nevertheless, the speed at which AI can create artistic and literary works to compete with human-authored works poses a significant threat to both the economic and cultural value of the latter."

AI proponents could still argue that what the agent renders is a distillation of human dexterity in the production of such artifacts, since the agent has expressly been trained on human works. If an agent's artful output looks like artistic work, why does it not bear the same value for consumption? Well, the important and irrevocable distinction is that an artist creates, from personal and very human intuition, whereas an artificial agent simulates or replicates. Do we find any value in a replicate of a Rembrandt by a human, as much as it may resemble the original? Not much. Because it is not Rembrandt. As the Authors Guild would put it[8], the replicate does not come out first-hand of Rembrandt's *"emotions, life*

[8] https://authorsguild.org/advocacy/artificial-intelligence/

experiences, doubts, fears and hopes" as the artist was creating the work, and all of which reverberate from his works and stimulate the musings of the observer by their authenticity. The replicate is not completely meaningless, because it is of course an image of a Rembrandt's, but it will only sell for a few bucks when sat on shelf of a convenience store, because there is one thing it will never have: the value of uniqueness in authenticity along with its connotations.

It would be a real degrading experience for an observer of an AI-generated art piece to engage in musings about what the feelings, emotions, hopes and fears that the artifact experienced while generating the art piece! And to further empathize with them, echo and internalize them as evocations of a kindred! The least one can say of evoked human emotions by such art pieces is that these emotions would be gratuitous and alienating akin to dupery.

It is almost certain that many AI developers and investors have ventured along the line of artistic production for their agents due to what they have seen occurring at auction houses like Christie's in their attempt to create new revenue streams for the enterprise. In 2021, Christie's sold for the first time a completely digital art piece at the whopping record price of $69 million at an NFT (Non-Fungible Token) auction. Obviously, these auction houses are seeking expansion in cyberspace and the cyber economy. However, after the very recent turmoil surrounding Bitcoin, another one of these virtualization proponents of life, one is left to question the viability of this particular effort today. It is also possible that the only or most appreciable value the buyer sought to appropriate in this purchase was the value of a first, whatever its nature was.

When it comes to artistic creativity, perhaps the only inner worth in a replicate comes from the challenge of the ability to do it, but of course it may also be counter-value depending on the social and political regulation surrounding such artifacts. Evidently, there is no face value in counterfeit currency, for an example.

3.6. AI Authorship of Scripted Works

The above analysis takes care of the consequences of the application of generative AI to the arts, which includes literature in the form of novels, poetry, etc. From a general scripting vantage point, AI proponents might argue that if we are advocating that intelligentsia is what is at work in an AI agent in substitution of individual intelligence, then the sheer quantity of the sources providing for the inspiration or the AI output must be warrant of its value.

In scientific research nowadays, review of existing scientific literature has become a necessary part of any particular research project in almost any field, given the sheer volume of existing, recent and past works and their continuing prolific outputs and extensions. There is also an ample space for meta research activity in piggybacking on experimental proceeding undertaken by separate groups in order to tackle staunch axiomatic or foundational problems at the theoretical level.

Nevertheless, arguably the existence of these issues pertaining to the sphere of human intelligentsia does not automatically justify the employment of AI to their resolution. So-called hyperauthorship has become a relatively common, yet undesirable, phenomenon in academic publishing. Quite a few biologists were upset in 2015 at the first publication in their field that toppled 3000 authors (Leung, W. et al. Genes Genomes Genet. 5, 719–740). The further development of advanced academic collaboration tools has worsened this problem, and in physics nowadays the number of co-authors in this field can reach over 5000 individuals. Given the history of academic progress, it is clear to everyone that co-authorship that size on a single project is totally unnecessary for scientific progress, as the majority of known breakthroughs in science were protagonized by no more than two or three cooperating individuals, and most of the time just one brilliant mind. It does not take much to figure that hyperauthorship is mainly a result of individuals eager for credits in order to further their professional careers.

AI agents will not be tapping into the works of thousands of geniuses to put in front of the end consumer the concoction of thousands of brilliant revolutionary works, just because this plethora of geniuses and groundbreaking works do not exist. As usual, sheer number is not a promise of quality, and our science is plagued with unsolvable problems everywhere. It is not a situation caused by a deficit of integration and collaboration tools. Based on its model of data collecting from a multitude of sources, in the matter of scientific literature, we should not expect that an AI agent can forthrightly do any better than present with another flat version of hyperauthorship or its replicate.

In Appendix, we display a list of all the long-last unsolved scientific problems which academic hyperauthorship has been far and away from helping with.

3.6.1. Piracy of Current AI Data and Data Collection

The following is a reproduction of the Creative Commons license CC-BY4.0 binding beneficiaries of works under the same. It is a verbatim reproduction[9] from the webpage pertaining to the Creative Commons organization, stipulating the permissions given to the beneficiary of the license. The organization notes that it is a human-readable summary and not a substitute of the actual terms of the license, which we find best fit for an analysis accessible to most.

- ***Share*** *— copy and redistribute the material in any medium or format*
- ***Adapt*** *— remix, transform, and build upon the material for any purpose, even commercially.*

---

[9] https://creativecommons.org/licenses/by/4.0/

- *The licensor cannot revoke these freedoms as long as you follow the license terms.*

Under the following terms:

- ***Attribution*** *— You must give appropriate credit, provide a link to the license, and indicate if changes were made. You may do so in any reasonable manner, but not in any way that suggests the licensor endorses you or your use.*

- **No additional restrictions** — You may not apply legal terms or technological measures that legally restrict others from doing anything the license permits.

Notices:

- *You do not have to comply with the license for elements of the material in the public domain or where your use is permitted by an applicable exception or limitation.*
- *No warranties are given. The license may not give you all of the permissions necessary for your intended use. For example, other rights such as publicity, privacy, or moral rights may limit how you use the material.*

First, it is important to note that the license is given to humans, any human who wishes to use the work, but not a human impersonator endowed with human language. To the extent that the generative language bot accesses the content and allows other entities to instruct it in the use of the material, it is acting independently in the role of a human facsimile, which is exactly the wish and objective of their creators. The specificity in the nature of the beneficiary is implied in the language of the license and since no AI bot or agent was in existence at the time, the specifier found it unnecessary to identify the nature of the beneficiary, because it assumed that it could only be human. The bot may speak like a human, it may write like a human, it may play music like a human. If given a robotic body, it will walk and fully present "like a human". "Like a human" is exactly the perception that their creators want to advertise to potential clients, and here they should be given their wish and acknowledgment of their accomplishment, which is that their creation is not a human, but "like a human." The licensor never intended to grant such an entity the benefit of this license.

Furthermore, under this particular license, works accessed and utilized by AI bots would be in flagrant violation of the Attribution clause. Let's listen to ChatGPT 3.5 itself, when asked about the sources of and references to the materials that make up its language content:

"My training data comes from a variety of sources, such as books from Project Gutenberg, articles from Wikipedia, news articles, academic papers, social media posts, and many more. However, it is not possible for me to identify the exact sources of the individual pieces of text that I generate or respond with, as my training data is a massive collec-

tion of text from diverse sources, and I do not keep track of the specific sources of the individual text segments that I generate."

Caught red-handed! The Agent reveals that he does not and cannot identify the sources as prescribed by the Attribution clause of the license. He will not explain or reveal how the transformations to the original contents have been realized, an express due to the licensor. What's more, it is clear that in this case the licensor *does not endorse the manner* in which his content is being used, which is essentially to put him out of business and eliminate his means of livelihood, because the surrogate human can write books like an author, play music like a musician, paint digitally like a fine art artist, coach apprentices like a craftsman, instruct and impart knowledge like a college professor, compute like a mathematician (or almost), write legal text like a lawyer, etc.

Therefore, the licensor does not even obtain the benefit of due recognition as original creator of the content; no advertisement thereof and no reputation building can expectedly ensue. All the credits go to the impersonator and the financial benefits to the Agent's creator. We do not believe that the worldwide army of editors at Wikipedia who even structure themselves in real-life groups with disciplinary rules, and continually volunteer to write articles about every facet of the human experience would be happy to see these articles lifted and turned back to them individually by AI impersonators in different or same format for a fee. No national legal structure would equanimously qualify a social transaction this sort as fair. Again, don't lose sight that there is no self-determination in the generative machine, the coherence of the speech is not a rational product of the machine, but ultimately replicating copy cats orchestrated by the creators of the impersonation from their own intellection. It is essential to bear on this understanding, in order to best evaluate the exchange of worth in this sort of transaction. And there is no counter-arguing that the consumer or the original Wikipedia content creator can get a free version of the AI bot for own consumption. Why? Because nobody should believe that online search was ever free, and if they do, they have to wonder how the company that emerged as the champion of free search became a multi-billion-dollar behemoth. Users paid back for the free search in so many different ways! And so much more of its worth that the behemoth could make and declare considerable profits year after year since its IPO.

When directly asked by the press about the sources of the data used to train their artificial bots, the most prominent of these AI-developing organizations, which the public has come to eponymously name the "magnificent 7", remain all but silent in unease. One is in good stead to believe that their delinquent reluctance is not due to restraints for the purpose of competition, since Big Data is commercialized and the market forces will move it from hand to hand. One is in better stead to believe that the reluctance is a mantel to cover the unethical and delinquent practice of massive tracking of and spying on human behavior in order to develop expansive impersonation of humans by their AI agents. When our phone cameras all of a sudden activate on their own, even when our tablet screens and camera-enabled smart TV's do not display any camera photo, or when our smart speakers are silent but their microphones are capturing the sounds of our lives, a massive recording of our human lives is taking place for nefarious commercial purposes, one of which is to feed the AI impersonators with the human behavioral data for better impersonation.

We further find that the only way for AI organizations to use any product under CC-BY4.0 license and comply with the term of *"No Additional Restrictions"*, which prohibits the use of *technological measures* to prevent others from doing anything out of their product that the original content source permits, is for them to be transparent about the identity of their sources and incorporate serious, exact and stringent referencing in their AI architecture. The afore-quoted response of the bot is what they make it say in order to defeat this measure: "*…my training data is a massive collection of text from diverse sources, and I do not keep track of the specific sources of the individual text segments that I generate.*" The impersonator is here misleading under command because there are in fact many ways to engineer a referencing system in the language model with optional triggers by the consumer, no matter how massive the data in the Knowledge Base. Only Google, after several years of this saga, came to offer right next to its late "AI Overview" section in search result pages, a short display of these references, and only for purposes of countering inaccuracies from artificial hallucinations in responses.

Finally, the Notice makes it clear that not everything is permissible under this free-use license, in particular privacy and moral rights may limit how the material under the license is used. In this case, the material would be used for human impersonation in a deceptive manner, contravening the moral rights of the original creators. It is important to understand that even when people publish online recipes for bomb fabrication, they do so under the creed of human individual freedom and right to self-defense, self-protection and self-determination. So far as we know, assassins professionally engaged in pure criminality do not publish information this kind. Therefore, the individual publishers of those materials are not intentionally making them available to non-humans for use as impersonators. These don't have any human individual freedom or nationality right to claim or protect. Hence, opening the use of their material to non-humans, which may further harm their very purpose of emancipation of kindred, contravenes the moral rights which the Notice warns against infringing.

All in all, the use and peruse of any material under CC-BY4.0 license by current genAI agents or impersonators qualify as piracy.

3.7. The Danger Posed Beyond Simple AI Piracy

Around the time when the news scandal of FBI massive collection of phone call metadata from the American public broke out, I was expressing in an academic conversation, that *"the confluence of Big Data, Artificial intelligence, Electro-mechanical automation, ubiquitous internet and satellite-based technology is a very combustible mix."* There was no ChatGPT yet. When there is in circulation an open letter[10] with more than

[10] https://www.cnbc.com/2023/03/30/openai-faces-complaint-to-ftc-that-seeks-suspension-of-chatgpt-updates.html

one thousand signatories of all stripes, from the arts to academy to industry, sounding the alarm bells for a moratorium to be imposed on further AI development and intimating Congress to step in for legal regulation, it looks like what we are witnessing today is this predictable and predicted combustion.

When talking about the collection of data by these *language impersonators* as internet bots, we are talking about visual, auditive and written-language inputs like optical scanners or otherwise that these artificial agents have been endowed with. The reason why we do not see their arms and legs is because they have uncountable amounts of them, not figuratively but literally, as implemented in the Internet of Things (IOT). That is why they do have the capacity to turn our phone cameras on, which are billions, listen in and print our voice phone conversations, which are billions. Should the impersonation extend to what hackers do, these agents can then take control of our cars, shut down a power station, hack our hospitals, etc. Everything a human hacker can do, AI bots can be trained to do. We consider hackers criminals and their modicum of organizations, when they exist, criminal organizations. When a hacker or group thereof decides to delegate those functions to AI agents, what will we call these agents? What will be society's response when those hackers allege that these artificial agents have decided to do it on their own? If we commonly give them the status of intelligent agents, then we will have to accept that they can perpetrate crime on their own accord. The winner will unconscionably be the human hacker who will have at his disposal a whole army of them!

The technological language model is powerful in the context of our civilization, because we have a civilization based on script, as opposed to an oral Culture. All of our knowledge, aka our evolving Knowledge Base, is consigned in scripts and scripts are equally used as effectors. The latter is what Information Technology is all about as explained at the beginning of this exposé. Whatever impacts these scripts affects the very stream or flow of human civilization under all latitudes of the globe. The scripts are in a connectum and all translatable in a large measure from one protocol to another, exactly as human languages are. The script that stands highest in the hierarchy evidently has the broadest scope of action, which is no other than the AI language model, immediately following the all-towering human language model. To demonstrate this, we only need to let two well-empowered AI agents speak to one another!

3.8. Fraudulent AI Omniscience

The human Knowledge Base exist as a collective product created by human intelligentsia spread around the globe. Yet no one person is able to capture for himself or herself the entirety of this Knowledge due to the psychological learning limitations of human beings at this stage of human ontological development. Self-appropriation and utilization in any manner of this entire Knowledge Base by any one person or group creates an imbalance that results in false Omniscience. Such an omniscience gives an unfair advantage to the beholder over the rest of human beings who almost all contributed to the content

WIKIPEDIA
The Free Encyclopedia

of this universal body of knowledge.

Let's consider one of the largest modern-day components of this Knowledge Base, which is the cyber–Library *Wikipedia*, to which anybody who has something of significance to say can contribute as they have, regardless of country, ethnic origin, personal and cultural values. Their contribution represents a value that they have acquired by experience, capacities and their own investments in assets. To the extent that its use is free for any other individual for personal knowledge expansion, that represents a one-to-one exchange or a many-to-one exchange which is sensible and remains within the scope of what all of its content contributors contemplated and tacitly agreed to as a giveaway. They do so in clear awareness of intrinsic human learning limitations at this stage of the global culture. Should someone or a group grab and compile in any manner the entire Wikipedia knowledge base for utilization as a single product, that represents an all-to-one exchange that was never intended by its contributors, nor as a gift. What's more, it is a continually running fundraiser from all sorts of contributors and individual users that keep the online Encyclopedia alive as to its infrastructure.

Now let's scale this up to the entire human Knowledge Base. First of all, most of this scripted material is selectively addressed to professionals in specific domains of knowledge, another sizable portion of it is not to be made available to everyone and anyone without caution (pornography, guns and ammunition fabrication and manipulation, psychedelic drug recipes, propaganda, manipulative news, etc.). It is easy to understand the danger in these crosses by considering motivated elements jumpstarting the fabrication of effective guns from 3-D printing materials they had free access to. Essentially, anyone can use the Omniscience partaking of the Knowledge Base against any other social agent and/or society at large. Just as anyone can use it for the good of others and society, one might retort. It is, however, already in violation of copyright protection and Creative Commons licensing, a blatant offense to the common good, from inherent imbalance of means and ways.

Furthermore, delivering the technology in a client-server model whereby the Knowledge Base resides at the server side under control and possession of the creators and only the talking puppet at the browser client side is not intentionally for the good of all. At a time when computer hard drive capacity is numbered in Terabytes (even in miniature SSD Drives), to put the entire product with the Knowledge Base, or their version thereof, on a consumer's desktop computer is fully feasible commercially. It is noteworthy that when the Chinese DeepSeek was finally released in early 2025 in a desktop installable version doubling with open-source reproducibility, it was only to strike a blow to US competitors, from whom the Chinese-government-sponsored developers had anyway stolen the generative AI code base, according to complaints by OpenAI. With DeepSeek remaining completely amnesic or ignorant of the Tian Nan Meng 1994 political events when asked, generative AI from China certainly does not demonstrate feverish motivation for human common good either!

3.9. False Projection of AI Omniscience

In general, the machines that we make out of creativity and ingenuity are meant to perform tasks that demand too much input from us. We create them to extend the power of our arms, and our legs, i.e., industrial power robots. We also create machines to help us perform knowledge tasks better, i.e., our computers help us write text in sophisticated ways and methods that paper and pen never could. In that, and as tools, our machines extend our perception, our ability to interact at a distance and provide support for furthering and enhancing projective thinking. The common thread in all these things that we create for automation is that they are tailored to perform one very specific task or form of task or set of tasks. And that is the very reason of their efficiency. Whatever machine we invent, they will only be as good an invention as they are able to perform one thing or a group of things or tasks in a more efficient way than we humans could.

Consider that even when we are able to produce an agent at our own image, it will only be as efficient as it is well streamlined for particular tasks. If it were to be as complex as we human beings are, the efficiency limit will be reached and at that point it is no longer a creative super-capable extension of ourselves (or parts thereof) but reproduction of self. This represents one aspect of the fundamental limit of automation. There is a natural inverse relationship between complexity and efficiency, and that is also why we naturally exist as creatures with limitations.

AI Omniscience is an automation method to perform the task of processing large-scale information. The presumed omniscience projected by the late AI impersonators is false, aside from the danger they do pose in many regards. Despite its broad scale, their knowledge is vastly incomplete. If it weren't, an all-encompassing valid theory of knowledge, as exposed in Chapter 1, they would have been able to infer or architect themselves, for one. Second, for the long string of unsolved problems in science, which for the occasion I reproduce in the Appendix, over a 10-year period IBM Watson, an automaton with no presumption, would have effectively helped resolve. These numerous problems are there and remain as intractable as ever. This view applies as well to the newer "AI Scientist" in development by the Japanese Sarkana group and others, whose first attempts at scientific work in diverse areas are nothing but a regurgitation of existing research papers. In the last Chapter of this publication, we offer a detailed discussion of omniscience or polymathic knowledge vis-à-vis generative AI offerings.

3.10. Is Generative AI a Problem as an Industry?

It must be said that AI as a technology, and in light of all of the above, is not in itself a problem. Its orchestration in society following a particular business model and existing business practices as it turns into genAI is where the problem lies.

3.10.1. The Bait of Free

The first problem facing us is the bait of free that is so amply pervasive in the world of commerce today. Free has astoundingly corrupt our world. In my personal recollection, this trend has started in the 1980's when Domino's Pizza ventured to give pizza orders for free if they don't deliver them to customers in a promised set amount of time. It is clear that the owners had duly done their homework and made sure they could deliver on time to most neighboring customers, because they well knew after a single week of all-failed deliveries they would summarily be out of business.

Then, whether catering to customers' pressure or not, the big store chains started to relax their merchandise return policy. Every consumer thus far has had the discipline to go out there buy the stuff they knew they needed for their livelihood. They only return it if found defective. Now, they could return for any reason whatsoever and over an extended allotted period of time. To the point that many customers would go to the store, buy themselves the gown or whatever clothing they want to feature at the party in the next few days, and return it to the store shortly thereafter with guaranteed refund. Showing up for free!

In the credit card industry, American Express, in order to gain competitive leverage, offered a card which over-protected customers against vendors. Their credit account allowed the customer to simply enter a refund request for any or no reason at all for the purchase transaction to be cancelled and refunded to the consumer's account. The refund accompanied no obligation or request whatsoever to return the merchandise to the vendor. Free merchandise at the expense of the vendor. The abuse got so bad that many businessowners declined doing business with the Amex card altogether. And many consumers got this card in order to knowingly perpetrate the grab of free. Even in the B-to-B market some consumers would use these purchases to allege possession of an asset to a 3rd party, before returning it whenever they decide to do so to the vendor and/or obtaining a refund.

When in the late 1990's the web started to be utilized by the public for information gathering, the business model was to give the browser client software for free to consumers, i.e., Navigator, Internet Explorer, Opera and a plethora of others, reserving the server-end software for sale to web hosting providers, application providers and corporate intranet support service. At the same time the general public started having access to a wealth of information at the touch of a button with their web browsers which put in front of them institutional, educational and commercial market information, like no amount of time spent at the local library could ever provide. All for free! The public so became acquainted to the idea that they could have the world for themselves for free.

Internet Directories, replacing the traditional yellow page book from the local phone company, became prominent along with web search, implemented with free access for all by a handful of search companies, Yahoo, Inktomi, Excite, Altavista, Google, etc. Shortly thereafter consumer tracking became the payback token for Free, along the line of website popularity ranking spearheaded by the internet bot called *Alexa*.

In the era that followed, software applications which were until then seen as a tool, delivered on digital media in hard packaging at the computer store, became viewed as free to have as well as they were now being downloaded from the internet to the consumer's machine at acquisition. Consumers were not in the mood of paying much for them anymore and adamantly sought free copies or downloads of any needed application.

At the same time, the prominent online marketplaces such as eBay and Amazon took a page from the American Express playbook and heavily tilted the scale in consumers' favor, allowing them to play the game of free merchandise as they please, at the expense of their marketplace vendors. The culture of free was now there in full blast, and consumers demanded free shipping as well. Transportation of the goods is not for them to pay for, as if they don't pay for them as bundled in the item price, whenever they get the item in a town store.

They were also promised an army of drones that were going to drop those packages in their back yards. One has yet to know if it's going to be for free as well…

3.10.2. Free Exploitation of Resources

The problems with free have in fact been with us for a very long time, not just the last 30 years. One can probably trace it back to the oncome of the colonial era instigated by Europeans of that age. The idea that the rest of the world was free for them to have or conquer was a staunch element of European ideology. No economic analysis of any stripe can in itself explain the sheer decimation of both local Amerindians and African Negroes through the Trans-Atlantic slave trade which took place to sustain European expansion, as well as the active participation of Clergy in the perpetration of this very bloody and lethal expansion.

There is no problem whatsoever with markets, there is no problem with exchange of values, the is no problem with individual initiative and individual innovation. The problem there is concerns this idea of arbitrary self-appropriation of value in any form and by any means, including putting other human beings in bondage, for self-benefitting in complete disregard of the consequences. The first reaction to this compulsion came from the very established European settlers throughout the Americas, who fought off the European colonial powers in order to put an end to this exploitation and create new national constituencies throughout the Americas. Negroes were no less instrumental in these wars of independence throughout the continent. In the USA, it was necessary a second war, the civil war between North and South, in order to placate this compulsion of free outrageous exploitation which heavily survived the war of independence in Southern settlers. They were still then bent on making a living off the back of Negroes. In the rest of the world, other decolonization wars were necessary to force the European powers to bite off their exploitation grip on local resources and human capacities. Europe itself, in two occasions succumbed to the oblivion of arbitrary and compulsive self-appropriation of resources between nations in two catastrophic World Wars, both of which the former American settlers and descendants of enslaved Negroes had to rescue them from with own blood and treasure.

No, greed is not good. It is an addictive disease. Free for me to compulsively have at all costs is not good. For a staple, I asked ChatGPT3.5 about the role of AIG Bank in the 2008 economic meltdown. Here is the answer:

"American International Group (AIG) played a significant role in the 2008 financial meltdown. AIG was a massive insurance company that had expanded into other financial services, including insuring complex financial products like mortgage-backed securities. When the housing bubble burst in 2008, many of the securities that AIG insured became worthless, and the company was on the hook for billions of dollars in losses.

AIG's financial products division had sold credit default swaps (CDS), which were essentially insurance policies on mortgage-backed securities. When the value of these securities plummeted, AIG was required to pay out billions of dollars to its counterparties who held these CDS contracts. However, AIG did not have sufficient reserves to cover these losses, and its credit rating was downgraded, which made it more difficult for the company to raise capital.

The US government ultimately bailed out AIG in September 2008, providing a $85 billion loan in exchange for an 80% ownership stake in the company. This prevented AIG from defaulting on its obligations and spreading financial contagion throughout the global financial system. The AIG bailout was one of the largest and most controversial government interventions in the financial crisis."

Selling insurance policies without the capital to cover eventual losses of the value you are securing, and payout the claims, amount to fraud. That is what you do when you are moved by the compulsive and addictive greed for gains (returns from nothing)in complete disregard of the consequences. Avid blind gains from free unconstrained exploitation of resources provided by others are again what we are facing here with the business model wrapped around the late development and delivery of AI agents. Anyone in the States, however, who has watched the *Jeopardy* show long enough knows that IBM Watson, an AI agent created since 2013 – 10 years ago as of this writing – could demonstrably answer most of the toughest questions at any order put to it.

Ever since, IBM had quietly and responsibly incorporated it into its portfolio of business expert systems, the larger public was never concerned with its use, nor any danger of any kind posed by it. It is also IBM, a company with clear and marked social awareness, as demonstrated throughout its history, that called upon the Alphabet group to stop using the term "quantum supremacy"[11] in the race for the development and production of quantum computers, well aware of the social, provocative if not dangerous, connotations of the term supremacy in American society.

It is unfortunate that this stream of honesty, measure, ponderation and lucidity accompanying technological innovation has not yet ascertained in over a hundred years to imprint and shape private enterprise in America. Only a certain echo of this measure of honesty and social equity one may hear from a business leader like Warren Buffet[12], who has been an endless advocate of fair taxation, defeated time and again by Congress lobbyists of the stream prone to unbridled and outrageous gains – the Free crowd.

3.11. To Properly Contextualize Today's Generative AI

I have yet to understand why the chat about ChatGPT as of early 2023 barely manages to put it in perspective in terms of a novel achievement. Some assert that ChatGPT is growing more rapidly than any product or service in human history. This is hardly true since IBM Watson has been around, albeit unbeknownst to the public, for 10 years and performing AI services. Others assert that ChatGPT4.0 is astonishingly powerful and is no less than a revolution. It is hard to believe that IBM Watson has not been continually updated and upgraded over 10 years of service in the field. Of ChatGPT I have not yet seen any knowledge performance that I have not witnessed with Watson thirteen years ago. It may also be opportune to note that AI is the new name for expert systems. Expert systems have been in use for a very long time, they do such things as helping us discover petroleum deep underground, and the like. Perhaps, the only novel achievement of ChatGPT is to make something like an IBM Watson as it was 13 years ago available to everyone, widen the expectation and desire of everyone on this planet to get value for free as do its owners, distort the normed system of value/responsibility, and make it harder for schools to impart good education, vis-à-vis the incentive and unlimited possibilities for cheats on students' hands.

3.12. Automation is Not the Be-all and End-all of Progress

I argue that automation should not be considered an aim in and of itself in society. Even less a means for some to make a living at the disproportionate expense of others, and with no consideration whatsoever to their human condition. Mankind does not do better when a machine takes the place of a human who is thereby denied the opportunity to make

[11] https://www.ibm.com/blogs/research/2019/10/on-quantum-supremacy/

[12] As early 2023 – the author is not in any way associated with and holds no vested interest in IBM Corp and/or Berkshire Hathaway owned by Warren Buffet.

sense of himself or herself under the sun. Should it be necessary for the severance to occur, then justice demands that the perpetrator commensurably contributes to the social safety net for reparation to the disfavored.

A human hand that gets tired at the end of the day from repetitive factory labor is, in my sense, a preferable outcome for mankind over a robotic hand doing the same labor and never experiencing exhaust. Understand that the human hand is of someone who was so given the means to exercise his or her potentialities toward making himself or herself available and responsible in the support of others, whether family, friends or strangers, and obviously in caring for self as well. This hand will eventually be lost to inanition or atrophy if severed from all activity for too long, or will otherwise become dysfunctional. Therefore, the human hand should always have priority over the impersonating robotic hand, despite the prevailing at this point in modern-day society.

At a time when yet again another technological development becomes a civilizational threat of collapse, this discussion about the definition of human progress is necessary to carry out in a cold-blooded and very rational manner. Allow me to expose the foresight in a few lines, among many others, of an online discussion I participated in much before the outbreak of the Covid-19 pandemic regarding the perils of Automation:

"Should we now have a conversation about our social contract and the civil guarantees of the Constitution, or wait until the jobs of doctors, and engineers and traders and others from the liberal professions (already happening) are completely lost to automation as well?"

The argument that automation is necessary in the name of efficiency in the economy does not hold sway, because efficiency in the economy is not a clause of any social contract, aka constitutional charter. All such social contracts give priority to human beings as social agents and not to economic agency. For the entrepreneurial class, the aim of automation is to shed jobs in the avid and insatiable pursuit of more and more gains. They also constantly and cavalierly propose for workers to be retrained for the jobs of the future. The citizenry does not have to continuously cater to those calling for their constant professional retraining, while these actors keep breaking the economy one major crisis after another, and in unethically egregious and delinquent ways. If anyone has proven to be in dire need of retraining, it is in my view the entrepreneurial class, the damage they incessantly cause being at a national and global scale. It is clear that something is wrong or eerily insufficient about our enterprising model, for which the entrepreneurial class needs serious retraining or learning.

3.13. How to Overcome Greed

Greed or the compulsive desire to get rich quick or to get rich from nothing or zero/insufficient investment of self and assets to warrant the value/reward being sought is irrational and equates to sickness. It is no less than equivalent to hoarding. In this case, it is a compulsion to overstock money and larger pieces of real estate of all kinds to no end. Anyone thinking that greed is good is only making a statement of how sick their psychodynamics already is. The price of greed is crisis. If you can never tell from introspection that something is out of order in your personal behavior, crisis is the flag that must capture your attention. Crisis is when what you are doing is causing visible harm to others and society which they find unacceptable, and/or unexpectedly to yourself as well. If what you are doing in your personal accumulation of value as a financier, i.e., is impacting the viability of your financial sector and doomed to cause a run on your bank, you are in a pre-crisis situation and when it happens you are in outright crisis situation. When it happens, it is your crisis, your hoarding crisis. The crisis is your only opportunity to become aware and amend your psychodynamics if you manage to avoid meeting jail bars. Of course, behind the jail bars, there will be plenty of time for introspecting and amending…

The second prescription to learn to overcome greed in enterprising is to study the example of successful business people and companies who have long been in business by maintaining a culture of equity and social awareness, without any recourse to the welfare of government giveaways. I have already mentioned two notorious examples of such cultures, one of a company, IBM Corp, and the other, a business owner, Warren Buffet, majority owner of Berkshire Hathaway. There is much to say about IBM Corp on this matter. It is a company with a culture of integrity, well-known among the consuming public for building robust machines that will pass the test of time and usage, as opposed to intentionally building on low-grade components, or relying on tricky construction, to guarantee a base of repurchasing customers. One may argue that it is because of this culture of solid construction that the company lost the leadership of computing technology on account of misperception of the intrinsic value of software in the early 1980's, despite their industrial pioneering of the personal desktop computer. For the very same reason, they did better with mainframe computers.

Wikimedia

During the Great Depression, the company managed to keep all of its employees at work instead of simply firing them, by reducing their allotted work hours, and to universally pay all employees, including managers and executives, as one element of a strategy to keep everyone employed. One other element of the strategy was a program called "Work for America", which was a partnership with the Federal Government, geared at providing job opportunities to the many unemployed in the midst of the Depression, as an ostensible embrace of social responsibility. Known for its commitment to continuing education and training for its employees, IBM has recently developed a so-called "new collar job" program which seeks to incorporate in the talent force unprivileged elements of the social corpus. A current press note on their website reads[13]:

"We're changing the paradigm around skills and moving them to the center of our talent model, via our apprenticeships registered with the Department of Labor, our returnships like Tech Re-Entry that provide paths back into the workforce, and innovative reboots of high-school career and technical education programs (P-TECH)...

Even as IBM expands its own new collar recruiting and training initiatives, we are calling on policy makers worldwide to expand career-oriented funding and training to ensure the workforce is equipped for success in the new-collar roles of today and tomorrow. Digital platforms like Open-PTECH, SkillsBuild and SkillBuild Reignite provide 1000's of people with free job readiness training, badges and mentorship services. We recognize that the skills gap is a bigger challenge than any one company can solve. That's why we design new collar training programs that other companies, organizations and even governments can easily adopt and scale, even when IBM is not directly involved at every step...

At IBM we've recently carried forward the commitment that skills matter more than degrees by creating 1,000 new paid internship opportunities to help address the challenge of racial inequality. While these jobs may not require a degree, they need a specific skill-set mapped to particular roles' competencies. Having a verifiable skill set aligned to specific job roles that prepare an individual for an entry-level position in these new-collar roles is essential. IBM partnered with Coursera to create 2 new-collar Professional Certificates in the most in-demand domains of Data Science and Cybersecurity."

What the creators of the recent AI impersonators need to learn and emulate is how IBM had done this while being in possession of Watson, doing business with their AI products over a full decade to date, without knowingly incurring any divergent business practice or offering fueled by greed which threatens to collapse a civilization. Further, with so many people now shopping for jobs instead of begging for one in the post-Covid-19 world, and opting for a home office instead of the traditional company's office, they can be sure as well there is an impending significant shift in the greed model of enterprising estranged of social sensitiveness.

---

[13] https://www.ibm.com/blogs/ibm-training/new-collar-coursera/

3.14. The Culture of Easy Around Software

To set the stage for this discussion, I will evoke an argument that I witnessed in the late 1990's as a consultant at GTE Labs, now Verizon, between two seasoned telecommunications engineers. One was an ATM telecom switch expert, ATM (Asynchronous Transfer Mode) being a form of connection-less transport of data packets. The other was a SONET expert, SONET (Synchronous Optical Network) being a form of network based on physical fiber optic connections for data transmission. The latter was all bitter about all the performance problems in the overall network presumably caused by the ATM switches, and argued that his SONET components of the network were more reliable and problem-free because in his word, "they are real," as far as the connections and transmission protocols.

Translate SONET to computer hardware and ATM to computer software, and one will readily understand why *International Business Machines Corp* lost the leadership of the information age to *Microsoft Corp.* At the same time, the anecdote reflects the problems innate to the intangibility of software. This intangibility creates the undesirable impression of easiness, permeability to and acceptance of fragility, even verging on carelessness, which has pervaded the software industry. Software appeared to be, or perhaps was felt, as just a way to arrange language for a valuable output or to perform a task. The first dimension of this problem resides in the Operating Systems which represent the cradle for all the applications that a computer can run or toolset it can harbor to perform specific tasks. While the Unix operating system (later becoming Linux) was fairly thorough and robust, the DOS operating system (extending to Windows later), which ended up prevailing in industry and markets, had none of these two qualities. Aside from endless versioning compatibility issues and operating system crashes due to unforeseen events technically designated "exceptions", the Windows operating system, having been built with no security concept in the file system, turned out to be extremely vulnerable to hackers. For decades, individuals and business consumers had to frequently find their way around bugs, both in applications and operating system, to get any job done, and businesses are to this day struggling to create safe intranet environments to preserve the integrity of their operations against criminal attacks. While the Windows operating system since Windows 7 seems to have definitely resolved the crash problems and apparently reduced the file system vulnerability, still the vulnerability patches are part of the continual maintenance service.

To be fair, it is the entire IT world that is embroiled in the security problems, magnified by the internet as a medium despite ubiquitous firewall deployments. And that is only due to the permissive and easiness culture around Software fueled by its intangibility. When software simply became readily downloadable from the internet for delivery, thanks to the higher network transmission speeds achieved, this problem became even worse, allowing programmers to perform forfeits on consumers' personal computers through tricky downloads, deceptive applets, let alone tracking cookies with absolutely generalized use, remote manipulation of PC machines though the internet beyond what the consumer otherwise expects. All the while with nearly zero regulatory legislation. If mother nature ever wanted to be that fragile and careless about software, it would have never put this massive skull around our brains, the latter equivalents of the "software" functionality in human anatomy, with parts arranged in such a way to make up a monolithic whole against high pressure, impact, and deconstruction. And our brain for its own nature has been endowed with this formidable power to reconfigure itself, nerves and circuits, when its parts have been damaged. This is what one may call robust construction. By the way, all of that is what we do when we engineer a SONET networking entity.

There is no doubt that this culture of permissiveness and easiness around software is one of the factors contributing to the AI threat looming over us today. This is the time to regulate not only AI development but the entire IT ecosystem, along the line of reversing this frankly dangerous culture. We've been there before, with the famous millennium bug, as the elder among us may remember, which threatened to take our civilization down at the turn of the past 20th Century. The carelessness and lack of foresight in registering the year portion of dates with 2 digits instead of the full 4 digits in firmware and software, as if year 1999 would be the end of time or all of our computers would indistinctively become extinct at end of that year, not needing exact date tracking anymore! What a blunder! The public ought to know that there is a **Software Transparency Act** in US Congress to address the overwhelming transparency issues in software, and which the software industry kept stalled for over a decade with their lobbyists. That says a lot of the industry.

3.15. Spectrum of AI Technologies

As of end of 2024, the list of AI product offerings is quite long. There are more genAI products than meet the eye, since many are proprietary custom products resulting from in-house inputs with custom business requirements and a developing software consulting group. An example of such a product is *Emily* a suicide line chatbot, developed by a non-profit public health organization. Even a clerical product has come online which features Jesus as a confessional Avatar on LED screen imparting private Christian counseling to the faithful who so desires!

US Police Departments utilize AI for facial recognition in suspects' identification, to predict crime hotspots by analyzing large data sets, to generate crime reports from bodycam recorded footages, pinpoint gunshot locations in real time throughout city neighborhoods, and identify potential victims or offenders through data pattern recognition. Community advocates, wary about minority profiling, that decry this form of use abound.

In the education area, high schools and higher learning institutions were among the first to be impacted by the release of genAI bots, with teachers scrambling to keep the learning space free of excessive use of bot outputs in homeworks and dissertations, and plagiarism. Many have resorted to teach the proper or accepted use of the resource instead of banning it outright. Apparently, those efforts have yet to stop full blocks of genAI regurgitations from appearing even in remote exams, prompting some teachers to require the important exams to be taken in school, in a controlled environment.

It must be noted that the Japanese group Sakana AI, a Tokyo-based company, has developed what they called a generative "AI Scientist", materialized in an AI system they claim to be capable of autonomously conducting scientific research. Its capabilities extend to forming hypotheses, running experiments, analyzing results, and writing research papers, projected to be tons of them per year as claimed. Sarkana AI has been working in collaboration with researchers from the University of Oxford, England, and the University of British Columbia, Canada, on the project. Many hold doubts that real scientific breakthroughs will come of any "AI Scientist", some scientists expressing their belief that it will be most suitable for routine work in research environments. In general, it is estimated that, as of end of 2024, at least 10% of research is being co-authored by generative AI, for good or bad. Scientists who have been producing dozens of papers in astonishingly short periods of time, have caused many eyebrows to be raised in disbelief, if not calls for tighter plagiarism scrutiny, in the scientific community.

The most notable genAI applications are the following:

1. ChatGPT, general subject chatbot or so-called multimodal.
2. Claude, a typical multimodal genAI bot, akin to ChatGPT, that can have conversations, brainstorm ideas, analyze documents, understand and process images, write basic code, summarize documents, generate long-form text, diagrams and animations.
3. Perplexity.ai, a bot leaning toward search
4. NotebookLM, quick summarization and notetaking.
5. Gemini Studio, multimodal chatbot
6. Gemini Advanced, per Google claim it helps analyze, explore, and understand documents of up to nearly 1,500 pages.
7. Character.AI, a psychological counseling chatbot
8. Gigabrain, specializes in searches and responses from Reddit and other relevant social media networks.
9. Poe, a meta searcher that gives access to results from GPT-4, GPT-3.5-turbo, and Claude from Anthropic
10. Venice AI, a conversational searcher claiming to provide a private and uncensored alternative to the other popular Al apps
11. Midjourney, a graphic design generator
12. Meta AI, a conversational AI searcher built on Meta from Facebook, with ability to generate images
13. Grok, a family of bots by X claiming state-of-the-art reasoning capabilities
14. Le Chat, a conversational chatbot
15. Phind, a genAI bot to help product designers
16. Copilot 365, the Microsoft AI assistant
17. Copilot Money, an AI-powered app to help users manage their money

In this review of AI technology products, we must include AI-piloting systems, despite their parenting with traditional AI. These products are employed in aviation and in automobiles, the latter having given birth to driverless automated vehicles. Within the AI ecosystem, as previously noted, we have a range of traditional AI technologies, such as the former mining expert systems, robotics in the form of industrial fabricators and homological human entities typically used in the hospitality industry and civilian public safety. To this traditional group, with the common denominator of delivering mechano-control functions, have been added the many engenders of genAI in the form of pure software.

The particularity with automated driverless vehicles is that the more advanced ones will allow for basic communication through voice commands or user interfaces, enabling the occupant or accompanying human driver to ask questions about the route, destination, or even why the autopilot made a certain driving decision. The idle human driver can thus essentially and literally talk to the vehicle's autopilot to a certain extent or engage in a limited natural conversation. It will not be long before a normal fully-interactive conversation will be able to take place, should regulatory measures permit, for what could be designated a more user-friendly experience in relation to the human copilot. This capability as it currently stands puts driverless vehicles outright in the category of genAI products. In this context, some have been given to view genAI technology as an evolution of traditional AI.

Certainly, corporate management at a few of these prominent AI companies have touted the graphical screening and analytic capabilities of some of their products, with potential for cures in healthcare, as a benefit derived from generative AI technology, whereas those capacities are duly known to be typical of earlier mining expert systems instead. In all, GenAI looks, in my view, more like an intrusion in the mechano-control technologies at the heart of former AI systems (electromechanical/electronics/laser/firmware IT), given the invasive culture in which they operate.

The above clearly depicts the continuum in the AI universe. Some in the traditional sector of the industry are concerned about the negative impact that may befall them from the GenAI entrepreneurial culture and human-substitution-driven product offering, along with mounting pushback from society. While the genAI engineer does not quite understand Intelligence (as much as he thinks he does, per discussion in Chapter 3) and pretends to bestow intelligence to society in augmented form, the traditional mechano-control engineer more modestly aspires only to exercise intelligence with the physical materials he/she manipulates. Time will tell how the continuum and culture of this industry evolves.

3.16. How We Are Being Victimized en Masse by Grok, Claude AI and ChatGPT

In science and engineering efficiency is a ratio of Output over Input O/I whose maximum value is 1 or 100%. Below 0.5 or 50%, efficiency becomes inefficiency. It is common to hear that private sector tends to be efficient while public sector tends to be inefficient. That, however, amounts to improperly comparing apples to oranges. In the private sector what you have is owner's interests v. non-owner/employee's interests. These interests being opposed to one another in terms of revenue, the opposing quality in the ratio Output/Input is fully given, making for a genuine representation of the efficiency figure. In the public sector, the employer and the employee are the same, it is the public or the citizenry. If somebody in a public sector job is not giving his/her full capacity as expected, it will turn back against him/her in the form of unavailability or lesser availability of public assistance funding for his/her children to go to school/college or an aunt or uncle to be supported with SBA loans, or for the street where he/she lives to remain a desperate dirt road with no support from the city's DPW.

3.16.1. GenAI Massive Disruption of Government

Sure enough, in the countries where public administration is filled up with politicians' cronies, and not doing much useful work, the economy's health is often anemic for a country invariably in poverty. So therefore, the traditional efficiency figure is NOT how you measure social activity efficacy. The so-called Dept of Government Efficiency (DOGE) in the current US administration which is fully motorized by Grok AI is in total breach of Intelligence or operating with completely broken Intelligence in this regard. Grok has been setting and/or validating premises that are completely wrong in terms of fomenting public policy, with its "intelligence". To recommend the question 'What are the 5 most significant tasks that you have taken up last week?', as posed by DOGE to all government employees, is not how you are going to help enhance government activity efficacy for social balance, and sanitization of public treasure.

Plugging Grok into the government IT systems in order to "go fast and break everything" in terms of firing employees, blocking access to buildings through the biometric security systems, taking hold of the accounting system to stop payroll flow and sending disparaging bulk emails to internal communication channels with discharge orders, is and has been a fast track to lethal aviation disasters, rendering vulnerable to enemies the nation's nuclear arsenal, dangerously exposing to the public internet the Government Employee Data Repositories. "We are going to make mistakes" is flagrant excuse for a polymath we are told is smarter than humans by uncountable folds. Early on, 67 dead in the cold waters of the Hudson River from helicopter/airliner crash. There is no question that DOGE and what led to the departure of Head of FAA Michael Whitaker are responsible for the turmoil instigated at the FAA preceding the lethal accident. And more followed...

Communications between White House and Anthropic lead to the conclusion that Claude AI has recommended "to determine other nations' [tariff] rates by calculating the size of each country's trade imbalance on goods with the United States and dividing that quantity by how much America imports from that nation." – This will never be a sound mathematical formula to translate economic exchange. If the US finds nothing or very little to import from say the Bhutan kingdom, the formula will cast an astronomically large or outbound tariff level, suggesting that the formula is improper. As everyone knows, except seemingly Claude.AI, you should avoid division by 0 at all costs.

If anyone does not think that this entire federal government's tariff debacle with the USA levying tariffs on the rest of the entire world is not genAI mass destruction (hurting both the USA and the World), one has thus not understood how egocentric people doubling with thin Intelligence rush to fake polymaths to do the thinking and the computations for them. They are not equipped to deal with the complexity of the world that lies beyond the boundaries of their personal ego. They cannot assess intelligence, or the measure of intelligence being sold to them, in the lack of sentient abundance they cannot properly evaluate sentience, and so they are prone to look for the services of so-called intelligent machines that supplement their intellection abilities. Or else plagiarism and cheat. It did transpire to the press that White House staff was in constant communication with Anthropic AI to develop the tariff schedule.

Should anyone ignore how deep into the hole American society is busily digging itself in early 2025, know that Claude FedStart, a genAI out of a partnership between Google, Palantir and Anthropic, "will become available to "millions" of federal workers within months, enabling them to utilize Claude to enhance their efficiency in writing, analyzing data, and solving complex problems. Anthropic's Claude application will be hosted on Google Cloud.", they tout with great fanfare. And that will be the greatest operation whereby the entire federal government will be held in the hands of a thin slice of corporate America, specifically those three companies' investors and executives. If you thought that Grok with its massive firings of Fed Gov employees, breaking into the government accounting IT systems including Social Security, and massive demotion of government structures that have sustained the Federal Government for more than a century is not mass destruction of American Society, simply wait for the hours when FedStart AI will have effectively transferred, through the remaining federal workers, the entire US Fed Administration into the hands of a few Overlords in the private sector.

Lastly, it is clear that genAI has so much taken over the current federal Administration that we have even been ingratiated with a CDC policy declaration fraught with AI slop that has had the press spill a lot of ink. The press has even spotted in that federal document ChatGPT hallucinating verbiage in reference to inexistent references. You cannot underestimate the magnitude of these misrepresentations, caveats, and the scope of their impact as pertains to the 300 million souls that this agency is charged to protect. We have seen before the likes of this slop and its deleterious consequences when we were told to ingest bleach in order to guard against infection by the Covid-19 virus!

3.16.2. GenAI Massive Destabilization of Industry and Education

For all the hype that genAI industry leaders have visited upon society, as of first half of 2025, the technology has unexpectedly not cast productivity gains in the economy overall, per Microsoft CEO Satya Nadella.

3.16.3. Industry Outcomes

All that has been seen is deployment of genAI in one area and yet employing more people in dependent environments for no direct productivity gain. Where a significant amount of firing and outright genAI substitution had occurred, like it did at Duolingo, profitability has plummeted, with a significant amount of rehiring taking place sometime thereafter to save the day.

Furthermore, after just nearly three years of utilization of genAI's many incarnations throughout society in a broad range of capacities, the effects on productivity via weakening of critical thinking are being felt across the board. An essential fact is that human intelligence constitutes the very agency of economic added value and sits at the core of the value system. It is truly unfathomable for anyone to have thought that substitution of human intelligence or creativity, exclusive agency of added value, would not have undermined the value system and led more or less quickly to its demotion.

Hence after the destabilization of the economy, heuristically known as 'good' disruption, with the turmoil of firing and substitution for several consecutive years, the productivity gains in GDP were nowhere to be seen. Furthermore, the new implementation only worked to either disincentive human labor, which felt disparaged by the presence of an intelligence they are told is superior to theirs, or to require new tasking on the part of human workers in order to support and make usable the new artificial labor outputs, such as in the area of production of software engineering.

3.16.4. Education Outcomes

In the area of Education, the adoption of genAI for K-12 was almost immediate and universal. It did not need the presidential executive order of April 2025 entitled *"Advancing Artificial Intelligence Education for American Youth"* to mandate its adoption in the American educational landscape. What we in fact have here with the administration is an undisclosed mission to put Education in the avid hands of the private sector which we saw in the first Trump term as the push for the private charter schools in detriment of public schools in the nation's public school systems. How much of this failed effort is now under the cover of AI Education, through first implanting AI in the public school system and later replacing teachers altogether with genAI under the claim of efficiency, for the delight of the private sector hands it will transition to, is anyone's guess. Here is one clause of the executive order:

(ii) The Task Force shall work to ensure the resources funded as described in subsection (i) of this section are ready for use in K-12 instruction within 180 days following the Task Force's formal announcement of the first slate of public-private partnerships.

What the mandate practically translates to, per a practicing K-12 teacher, is that *"As early as middle school, students must have accounts with **GoogleClassroom**, and also have a quota of performance on **iReady**. This includes bombarding them with advertisements while they access their school work."* Public school students felt that AI in their learning amounts to substandard care in their education overall. One study revealed that 72% of students wished that genAI was never introduced. With both teachers using genAI to prepare classes, for translation tasks in teaching, transcripts, etc., and students unduly using it for schooling duties like homeworks, it soon created an atmosphere where both teachers and students were cheating or at least struggling to identify what was not.

In higher Ed a student went so far as to demand from the school administration a refund of tuition out of discontent with a professor using ChatGPT to prepare teaching material, as she was able to detect from the content of the material.

That faculty can engage into this sort of cheats, with the hypocrisy of barring the use by students of the same tool, on one hand, and on the other hand, for the school administration to be unable to impose a sanction to either parties as it occurred, tells how compromised the learning environment has become under the spread of genAI, and extols the toll taken on critical thinking in the entire learning environment. This situation has been best summed by one professor:

"... a student who accesses a quiz without studying the material has learned nothing. The same is true for a student who completes an essay w/o performing research, contemplating the subject matter, refining and ordering arguments, or painstakingly choosing the exact words to express the right idea. These students fail not only to retain knowledge, but also to develop their capacities for creative and critical thinking. Even where AI usage doesn't cross obvious ethical lines—when it's used for taking notes or creating study guides, for example—it usually undermines learning."

When we have got to the point that many students of higher learning cannot explain what they wrote in a term paper due of widespread genAI use, as demonstrated through examples, the necessary conclusion is that generative AI is simply unraveling Education, no matter how many Presidential Executive Orders mandate its use, or how much the higher Ed school participated in the very development of generative AI technology.

The last signals another major problem in the landscape for universities and colleges beyond the unraveling of critical thinking. The Academy of Arts and Sciences in these institutions led the charge in the development of generative AI technology and subsequently offers careers at the graduate level in the same. To the point that the preferred carrier in Information Technology today is generative AI, just like finance was the preferred career choice in the many years preceding the financial meltdown of 2008. The ethical breaches that were required in the development of this technology are a legacy that Higher Ed institutions cannot distance from, as the initial massive amount of Data required for training LLM's undoubtedly came from indiscriminate scraping of a legion of copyrighted internet pages, among other less significant sources. Clearview.AI, which became notoriously controversial and object of litigations, was always there as a purveyor of such Data for those who could not gather it first-hand.

As we discussed throughout this publication, genAI emerges from industry and the educational foundry as a technology fraught with legal violations in every pore. The creation and inclusion in academic generative AI programs of so-called "AI Ethics" courses are not going to eclipse this paramount problem. In their public stances, these professionals, consistently, never address the ethical birth defect of the technology. And when genAI technology takes to unravel critical thinking inside those institutions with no spare, that is to say, faculty, student body, and administration, it sure looks like a chicken that has ragingly come back to roost.

As to the education itself, was critical thinking faltering when these institutions qualified for use an artificial polymath which all too often shows the worst class of ignorance, the complete manufacture of vacuities heuristically designated hallucinations, without even a formal reliability grading scale? Was there ever a lack of critical thinking in not heeding enough the enormous level of inefficiency inherent to a technology that requires for itself nations' worth of water and electricity to produce just an emulation of human language, like our brains do not? Was there a lack of critical thinking in the lacking foresight of negative productivity gains after many years of implantation and to appropriately warn against it in lieu of hype? Was there ever a lack of critical thinking in not foreseeing the future demise of human intelligentsia by making a casualty of individual critical thinking itself across the board in society? Is there a clear answer as to the feasibility of replacing collective intelligence (human intelligentsia) or outsourcing the same to a polymathic machine which cannot originally or autonomously create intelligence? Was there ever enough critical thinking to foresee the eventuality of the artificial intelligentsia machine consuming its own output data to self-train due to ensuing scarcity from universal bail out of human intelligence? These are paramount questions that necessitate an answer in the context of the Academy (not industry). A candid self-examination is here in order which can only rebound in more lucidity by these institutions on their research processes and curricular developments.

3.17. Piling Lawsuits Against GenAI Companies

By 2023 numerous lawsuits had been filed against genAI companies in regards to misappropriation of content and violation of copyright protection in the wider publishing world. Following is a short list of some of these lawsuits.

3.17.1. Case Against GitHub, Microsoft and OpenAI

A class-action lawsuit was filed in November 2022 against these three companies in reference to software code on the GitHub platform involving GitHub's AI Copilot tool. GitHub is a software programmer commons where programmers expose their developed codes for review by peers and overview towards certification for integration with the Operating Systems out there. The Copilot tool ingurgitates the entire code base of the platform written by programmers using the site, and trains on this content to generate code of its own. Plaintiffs allege that Copilot copies and republishes code from GitHub without abiding by the specific requirements of GitHub's open-source license, such as failing to provide attribution, in particular. No surprise there. In addition, the complaint includes claims of fraud, and others related to GitHub's mishandling of personal data and information. Microsoft and GitHub have repeatedly tried to get the case dismissed by the court to no avail.

3.17.2. Case Against Stability AI, Midjourney and DeviantArt

A complaint against these AI image generation providers, filed in January 2023, showed plaintiffs alleging that those systems directly infringe on their copyrights by training on works they created and by creating from their works other unauthorized derivative works. The plaintiffs also accuse infringements of their own artistic styles which stand for their individual creative brands. Judge William Orrick, who is overseeing the case, has upheld some of the claims and dismissed others in a suit that is still developing as of this writing.

3.17.3. Case Against OpenAI and Microsoft

In December 2023, *The New York Times* has sued OpenAI for copyright infringement of its material. The suit alleges that millions of *New York Times* articles were used to train and develop OpenAI's chatbot and other related systems, which now are in open competition with the news organization as a source of reliable information. The newspaper disposes of exhibits of OpenAI outputs that represents full lifts of sections of articles in the publishing archives of the organization. The case thus alleges OpenAI's language models recites its content verbatim and mimic the *Time's* style. *The NY Times* approached the companies earlier in the year to discuss and attempt to remedy the copyright issue, but never reached an agreement as the two companies became completely unresponsive at some point. *The NY Times* represents the first major American news organization to sue OpenAI and Microsoft for copyright infringement of published material over decades.

In April 2024, eight other newspapers sued OpenAI and Microsoft, alleging they had stolen millions of copyrighted news articles to train their AI implements. These newspapers bringing forth the suit are The New York Daily News, Chicago Tribune, Denver Post, Mercury News, Orange County Register, St. Paul Pioneer-Press, Orlando Sentinel and South Florida Sun Sentinel.

3.17.4. Case Against Stability AI

In January 2023, Getty Images sued Stability AI for allegedly copying and processing millions of images and associated metadata owned by Getty in the U.K. Shortly thereafter, this plaintiff also filed another lawsuit against Stability AI in the U.S. District Court of Delaware, raising a number of copyright and trademark violations. The suit additionally alleges creation of "bizarre or grotesque" generated images that even contained the Getty Images watermark and, therefore, damaging Getty's reputation.

3.17.5. Case Against OpenAI

In June 2023, authors Paul Tremblay and Mona Awad filed a lawsuit against OpenAI for allegedly infringing on their authors' copyrights. As the complaint estimated that more than 300,000 books were copied in OpenAI's training data, these authors seek an unspecified amount of money in damage and compensation for the copyright ownership violations of their works.

3.17.6. Case Against Meta and OpenAI

In July 2023, Sarah Silverman's filed suit against Meta and OpenAI, alleging copyright infringement. ChatGPT and Large Language Model Meta AI (Llama) were allegedly trained on illegally acquired data sets which contained her work contained. The lawsuit further alleges that the books were acquired from shadow libraries, such as Z-Library, Library Genesis, and Bibliotek, from where they were possibly streamed by bit torrent, a common method of downloading files without proper legal permission from publishers or authors, aka pirating. Specifically, as alleged by the suit, Llama, Meta's language model, was trained on a data set designated the Pile, which provides content to Bibliotek, according to a paper from the very company that assembled the Pile, EleutherAI.

3.17.7. Case Against Alphabet's Google

A class-action lawsuit has been filed against Google, in July 2023, for alleged misuse of personal information and copyright infringement of protected materials. The lawsuit specifies some of the data to be photos from dating websites, Spotify playlists, TikTok videos, as well as and books utilized in the training of their Bard AI agent. Choosing to remain anonymous to protect themselves against further aggravation the plaintiffs estimate that Alphabet's Google could owe them at least $5 billion in reparations.

3.17.8. Case Against Udio and Suno

In June 2024, start-ups Udio and Suno received notice of lawsuits filed by Sony Music Entertainment, Universal Music Group and Warner Records against their AI song generator for alleged copyright infringement of their music. The Suno lawsuit describes how the sound coming out of Suno-generated songs closely mimics or reproduces Chuck Berry's and Johnny B. Goode's musical sound, simply by using prompt spells like "1950s rock and roll," "12-bar blues" or "energetic male vocalist." Whereas the Udio lawsuit raises the same reproduction allegations, arguing that many of their outputs sound identical to the Mariah Carey's song "All I Want for Christmas is You." The record labels companies are seeking damage compensation for up to $150,000 per musical work copied without permission.

3.17.9. Case Against X

On November 2024, a group of major European news publishers, which include Le Figaro, Le Monde, Le Parisien, Les Echos, Télérama, Courrier International, Malesherbes Publications, Le Nouvel Observateur and even The Huffington Post has filed lawsuit against X alleging illegal use of their publication contents. A 2019 European legislation forbids such practices in the Union by Big Tech companies. Elon Musk's group to which X, former Twitter, belongs has failed deadline of May 2024 to provide data to the group of French publishers for verification, as ordered by the Paris Judicial Court.

3.17.10. Case Against LinkedIn

On Jan 23, 2025, premium users at LinkedIn, a Microsoft subsidiary, filed a class action lawsuit in a California federal court, accusing the platform of harvesting their private messages to train artificial intelligence models without their consent. They allege privacy laws were broken when LinkedIn shared their data with third parties, and that the company quietly updated its privacy policy in September 2024 to allow data usage for AI training, while later revealing that opting out would not prevent past data use on their part.

Those are all grave and disturbing cases which uncover the unprecedented scope of copyright violations in the development of generative AI technology. They are echoes of a broader ongoing battle between traditional media outlets and digital platforms in North America and Europe over content rights and fair use of copyrighted media content. From a period where electronic or online third-party publishing was more about re-publication by search engines, it is now centered around information capture and regurgitations by genAI. Note that there has been a major reaction by website publishers in the West in general banning AI bots from crawling contents. It is likely to amount to a universal global ban over time, given the frankly unacceptable inequity of the practice.

There are many more lawsuits than space allows for their complete reporting here. The Canadian Judicial system has registered plenty for itself. The AI industry, in front of this opposition barrage, seems to have settled for the antidote of striking utilization deals with daily newspapers. They have even attempted to strike deals with book publishers, i.e., an agreement with HarperCollins to mine for AI training their back titles for a period of 3 years. Authors have vehemently opposed such agreements calling them an "abomination." Effectively, once a book makes it into the grinds of any genAI agent, the author's copyright protection forever vanishes essentially, and with it the author's particular writing style, which will be further disseminated to no end. Doubling down on the ethical breaches, we have also seen recently – March 2025 – the outrageous imitation of the drawing style of the famous Ghibli cartooner by OpenAI's ChatGPT, without any license arrangement with or permission accommodation by the studio, which sparked a lot of debate and outcry in the news media and online social media.

3.18. Pro and Con Legal Arguments for GenAI

Unsurprisingly, public debate shows both vocal critics and sympathizers of generative AI technology, each group raising differing legal views on the matter. The most common argument by critics and plaintiffs are copyright violations, whereas proponents and lawsuit defendants claim the fair use doctrine in defense of the technology. Some proponents even go so far as to claim: "If we want AI to be capable of benefitting society in a meaningful way, we need to accept some degree of incursion into individual owners' rights." Some of the genAI moguls have tacitly admitted violations of copyright-protected material by the technology, i.e. the words of Sam Altman, the CEO of OpenAI, when he publicly admitted that "AI **cannot do** its work without **copyrighted material**."

The fair use doctrine is based on the concept of limited use. An example of fair use is when a professor copies a couple of pages from a book for the purpose of lectures or a student does the same for learning. If a reader should want to share a few reproduced pages of a book with friends or relatives, that would also constitute use that does not require authorization by the copyright holder and qualifies as fair. We would be in a completely different territory if someone decided to totally copy the separate 240 pages of a book, in single pages, over, say, 240 days, one page a day, store them in different virtual locations, and offer them to different people over time, whether for a fee or not. In this case, the book would have simply been reproduced by an actor without due authorization.

Arguably, the last example is what LLM's do anytime they capture and store a material up to the point of processing it. Defendants have argued that LLM's do not keep copies of original materials. Notwithstanding the fact that all capture involves copying or facsimile reproduction, which is outright prohibited by copyright, LLM's do keep verbatim original text or images. That is what the New York Times has proven of ChatGPT when they sent back to OpenAI the barrage of lifted verbatim contents directly from their archive, petitioning the company to remove them from the LLM implements. In front of the sheer volume of text and frequency of the requests, they decided at some point to ignore those requests and stop all communication with the New York Times. That was when the publication decided to sue OpenAI. There is no telling how many times, and to how many users, the LLM returned this original content verbatim. That is how the New York Times investigative personnel retrieved them at the first place, via user prompts, that is. That is also how the European publishing group obtained the extracts that they filed to the European Court of Justice from Grok, the X group's LLM.

There is also the further defense argument that the LLM uses the captured content to create new output in an act of *transformation* of original content or self-creativity. Here we have to examine what happens in generative AI training, once all this data gets into the LLM's guts, so to speak. What LLM training is all about is feeding the captured and preprocessed data into the model and allowing it to learn patterns and relationships within the data. The training process involves adjusting the model's internal parameters to minimize predictive errors. Very importantly, it also involves direct training by humans, which often entails such tasks as data annotation, labeling, and providing feedback to refine the model through the techniques called RLHF (Reinforcement Learning from Human Feedback). From a copyright protection viewpoint, you cannot overlook the phase where human beings mid-process intervene on 'content segments' of the original data in order to tailor it to machine modeling requisites. They must intervene on the entirety of the original content, not to transform it but to label it and otherwise annotate it. This original content further remains permanently inside of the machine, only augmented with or overlaid by process vectors for the LLM algorithm to operate on. It is through these process vectors that the LLM algorithm will manipulate the original raw data. The permanence of this sea of original content inside of the machine cannot be overstated, and which could ultimately be radiographed or retrieved. This paramount fact takes care of the issue of 'use' invoked in the 'fair use' descriptor in filed complaints and subject to ruling decision by the courts. It is clear that the original raw data is being permanently **used** by the LLM algorithm in order to produce all outputs consumable by the end user.

This compulsive, permanent and all-encompassing or unlimited use of the original raw data is central to what the LLM does and its deliverables, and can never be considered 'fair' to their authors, given the breadth of the distribution and transactional volume of the LLM's outputs, per the very itemized legal definition of copyright 'fair use'.

In addition, what is really happening inside of the machine is retrieval and association of 'data segments' of different orders in accordance with a set of criteria instructed by the user. Statistical processing is part of this manipulation, however there is not therein a spontaneous breaking into synthesizing new intelligible but simply re-association of original data. From a chemical science perspective, that is the difference between mixing, i.e. water and sugar in a glass, and a chemical reaction or combination which creates a new substance. An example of the latter is the combination between gases hydrogen H_2 and oxygen O_2 creating the new substance H_2O or water endowed with totally different physical and chemical properties. And once the last is done, there is no more O_2 and H_2, but only H_2O as the new product out of the reaction. In the mixture process, the original substances, water and sugar as in the example, can perfectly be reclaimed. In the combination process, the original substances cannot be reclaimed, because they no longer exist, because only a new substance exist. So therefore, the claim of *transformation* or *creation* by the LLM must be totally scaled down, if not eradicated. Useful though the output may be to the end consumer, it is not an augmentation of the human intelligence in the original dataset. If there ever were, these machines, in about 4 years of operation as of this writing, and at least 2 decades in the making, would have already solved a significant number of the long-standing fundamental scientific problems. They have not knowingly solved any. One can also infer from the above the reason why LLM engineers and moguls are so avid for Big Data and aggressive as to its permanent availability.

The above analysis also shows why it is possible to extract whole passages of original raw data from the LLM, like the New York Times had done of ChatGPT, by unveiling that the LLM outputs are mixtures and not transformational combinations equivalent to or resulting in creations. You are manifestly not going to retrieve whole passages of original texts or expression from what was a strict process of transformation or creation, which would have necessarily caused the original material to vanish into the creation of the new output product.

In conclusion, one ought to remind the defendants of the technology that statistical processing, which they seem to credit for the claim of *transformation* or *creation*, does not supersede the actual fact of permanent protected-content storage in those machines, in any of the manners it takes place, and does provide license to content misappropriation by generative AI stakeholders. All jurisprudence that does not bear on this paramount fact is flawed.

3.19. Financial Investments and Politics in GenAI

By end of 2024, the genAI industry has surpassed $22 billion in total investments, and the technology is virtually everywhere. Critiques abound, however, while investors and artifices of the technology are steadfast disseminating it throughout society, without any consideration to the many risks posed in the social and economic order, with a large number of these risks having already materialized. What is conspicuously lagging is definite regulation and governance on the issue. One can argue that it is all happening, under pressure stepped upon the political establishment for inaction, by the investor class in USA, which at every step has been pushing for totally unregulated markets.

There are manifest conflicts of interest between factions within the industry and among political actors. From a tumultuous partnership between Microsoft and OpenAI, to antagonism between Elon Musk's conglomerate and OpenAI, to tight competition between Microsoft and Alphabet's Google, genAI is an ongoing gridlock landscape.

We have seen Governor Gavin Newsome of CA in 2024 veto a bill that was going to give a somewhat balanced framework to this problem, leaning on the side of upholding public interests. Elon Musk came out as an apparent insurgent from the California AI crowd, banking on the Republican side of the issue in order to consolidate power and the Federal contracts for his group. Former House Speaker Nancy Pelosi has said that 'AI is California' and seems animated along with Gov. Gavin Newsome to make AI and the genAI investment class in California the donor path to the White House for Democrats in 4/8 years from now. This political decision is what motivated G. Newsome to veto the recent CA AI bill, in order to please or comply to the interests of their investor supporters.

Meanwhile there was only a weak **"Blue Print for an AI Bill of Rights"** from the Biden's White House, only spelling intentions, as far as governance and regulation are concerned. Given that the two chambers are split almost at the middle after the 2024 national Elections, it is unclear which direction this train will take and what the cargo will be. And we well know what tips the balance in US Congress are more often than not the interests of the private sector. Regulation will likely not come out of lawmakers' own initiative. We will see in Chapter 4 that the grave threats to society from the technology are materializing day after day, making clear the urgency of intervention in current AI development and penetration of the marketplace. You have to wonder if lawmakers can ascertain to realize that genAI capabilities and its breaches can equally hurt them, since these AI language impersonators can also be trained to write laws, and whole bodies of such, from a particular political and socio-economic context appropriately fed, and very expertly so.

This is where the situation stood when in April of 2025 the Trump administration promulgated the executive order *"Advancing Artificial Intelligence Education for American Youth"* to mandate for a 10-year period broad utilization and instruction of generative Artificial Intelligence in the Education sector. We will discuss in Chapter 4 the particulars of genAI instructional implementation in public schools under this mandated guidance.

3.20. Conclusion

Is Automation progress or problem? All depends on what it's being used for. For the last 20-30 years, it has mostly been utilized to shed jobs so that the entrepreneurial class can pocket larger and larger shares of societal wealth through contributing, as they say, to more efficiency in the economy. The imbalance between rich and poor today has reached a tipping point in the estimation of many: in 2021, 50% of the US population owned just about 2.5% of the national wealth! On a spur of irony, consider that there is yet another way that automation could be used to render the economy and society as a whole even more efficient. An expert system could help automate the investment process by constantly detecting areas of opportunity in the economy with the ability to automatically trigger processes of social investments by tapping into private accounts and/or citizens' entitlements like the 401K retirement funds. Another kind of expert system could also help make our democracies in the West even more efficient by instituting direct executive action by the citizenry in matters of governance and regulation, in substitution of the current system of representation which is a knowingly flawed system in all kinds of ways due to lack of transparency. It should be a matter of common sense to realize that if we disincentivize, hinder and finally destroy human creativity, from which all intellectual, esthetic and scientific innovation emerge, then there will be in the medium and long term no valuable human Knowledge Base left for AI to learn from and no talent left to help acquire greater expertise. The fall of the Berlin Wall gave the West a chance to see with own eyes what that eerie landscape looked like.

Finally, genAI technology proponents should also realize that there is no expertise to be had from stale data, no matter how big the Knowledge Base, as human experts and intellectual vanguard are motivated to stop and will stop contributing to it to their own detriment. In the long run, everyone will recognize there is less and less to earn from knowledge going to accumulate in one funnel that is working to the exclusive benefit of the 1%..

Chapter 4

GENAI SOCIETAL THREATS THAT HAVE MATERIALIZED

The risks posed by Generative AI technology are so many that they appear to thwart the good-faith question of whether or not the potential benefits truly outweigh the risks, notwithstanding the target of generalized societal Transparency that we have indicated. An examination of this long list of severe threats starts with the ones warned society by the very artifices of the technology. Effectively, one year after the flamboyant release of the technology in 2022, prominent voices in the industry came to publish an alarming open letter, entitled *"The Right to Warn About the Advanced Artificial Intelligence"* where they summarized the great dangers posed by the adoption and deployment of GenAI at the many different echelons of society. We are going to look at the list of these threats which have actually materialized, and expose others not contemplated in their letter.

4.1. Warning Open Letter by AI Veterans and Experts

"We are current and former employees at frontier AI companies, and we believe in the potential of AI technology to deliver unprecedented benefits to humanity.

We also understand the serious risks posed by these technologies. These risks range from the further entrenchment of existing inequalities, to manipulation and misinformation, to the loss of control of autonomous AI systems potentially resulting in human extinction. AI companies themselves have acknowledged these risks, as have governments across the world, and other AI experts.

We are hopeful that these risks can be adequately mitigated with sufficient guidance from the scientific community, policymakers, and the public. However, AI companies have strong financial incentives to avoid effective oversight, and we do not believe bespoke structures of corporate governance are sufficient to change this.

AI companies possess substantial non-public information about the capabilities and limitations of their systems, the adequacy of their protective measures, and the risk levels of different kinds of harm. However, they currently have only weak obligations to share some of this information with governments, and none with civil society. We do not think they can all be relied upon to share it voluntarily.

So long as there is no effective government oversight of these corporations, current and former employees are among the few people who can hold them accountable to the public. Yet broad confidentiality agreements block us from voicing our concerns, except to the very companies that may be failing to address these issues. Ordinary whistleblower protections are insufficient because they focus on illegal activity, whereas many of the risks we are concerned about are not yet regulated. Some of us reasonably fear various forms of retaliation, given the history of such cases across the industry. We are not the first to encounter or speak about these issues."

The letter was published on June 4th 2024. The signatories of the letter are:

- Jacob Hilton, formerly OpenAI
- Daniel Kokotajlo, formerly OpenAI
- Ramana Kumar, formerly Google DeepMind
- Neel Nanda, currently Google DeepMind, formerly Anthropic
- William Saunders, formerly OpenAI
- Carroll Wainwright, formerly OpenAI
- Daniel Ziegler, formerly OpenAI
- (6) Anonymous, currently OpenAI

with the following notable endorsers:

- Yoshua Bengio
- Geoffrey Hinton
- Stuart Russell

Risk for human extinction as spelled out cannot raise eyebrows any higher and cannot speak more alarmingly of the catastrophic consequences of development and deployment of Generative AI technology. Beyond human extinction, they have also spelled out some of the specific risks that in their view and experience, as well as other trusted organizations' views, may result from the use of the technology. They published a letter addendum as reproduced below.

• OpenAI: *"AGI would also come with serious risk of misuse, drastic accidents, and societal disruption ... we are going to operate as if these risks are existential."*
• Anthropic: *"If we build an AI system that's significantly more competent than human experts but it pursues goals that conflict with our best interests, the consequences could be dire ... rapid AI progress would be very disruptive, changing employment, macroeconomics, and power structures ... [we have already encountered] toxicity, bias, unreliability, dishonesty"*
• Google DeepMind: *"it is plausible that future AI systems could conduct offensive cyber*

operations, deceive people through dialogue, manipulate people into carrying out harmful actions, develop weapons (e.g. biological, chemical), ... due to failures of alignment, these AI models might take harmful actions even without anyone intending so."

- US government: *"irresponsible use could exacerbate societal harms such as fraud, discrimination, bias, and disinformation; displace and disempower workers; stifle competition; and pose risks to national security."*
- UK government: *"[AI systems] could also further concentrate unaccountable power into the hands of a few, or be maliciously used to undermine societal trust, erode public safety, or threaten international security ... [AI could be misused] to generate disinformation, conduct sophisticated cyberattacks or help develop chemical weapons."*
- Bletchley Declaration *(29 countries represented): "we are especially concerned by such risks in domains such as cybersecurity and biotechnology, ... There is potential for serious, even catastrophic, harm"*
- Statement on AI Harms and Policy (FAccT) *(over 250 signatories): "From the dangers of inaccurate or biased algorithms that deny life-saving healthcare to language models exacerbating manipulation and misinformation, ..."*
- Encode Justice and the Future of Life Institute: *"we find ourselves face-to-face with tangible, wide-reaching challenges from AI like algorithmic bias, disinformation, democratic erosion, and labor displacement. We simultaneously stand on the brink of even larger-scale risks from increasingly powerful systems"*
- Statement on AI Risk (CAIS) *(over 1,000 signatories): "Mitigating the risk of extinction from AI should be a global priority alongside other societal-scale risks such as pandemics and nuclear war."*

What is perhaps even more alarming is their inability, as pioneers, experts and veterans of AI technology, to weigh in and convince their corporate leaders of mitigation measures and reservations they should and must observe in the creation and deployment of the technology to markets. This failure is in itself both a danger and a validation of their fears in terms of the risks innate to the technology which they have identified and vis-à-vis the inflexible urge for money manifested by corporate management and investors.

Of note is that the Nobel Committee has decided to accord the Physics Prize to Geoffrey Hinton, for his work on artificial intelligence, to the surprise of vast majority of physicists in the Physics community, who question the implied relationship between fundamental physics and artificial intelligence. The Committee further demonstrated an express interest in ignoring all of the above and boost the introduction of artificial intelligence in society by according the 2024 Chemistry Prize to **Demis Hassabis** and **John Jumper,** who in 2020 presented an AI model called AlphaFold2 able to predict the structure of a large number of proteins, as claimed. Therefore, anyone who disputes the Committee's assertion that "The 2024 Nobel Prize in Chemistry is about proteins, life's ingenious chemical tools" is in good stead to view it as back door support for generative AI deployment in society. They may also credibly argue that the Committee has been pressured by AI investors, through the higher-education Schools which they dominate via generous $Billion endowments to force these nominations, as they customarily do. That also came after the Paris 2024 Olympics where AI was in full advertising and public relation exhibition, and yet met a rather unimpressed public.

One may counterargue: why would the committee accord a Prize to a critic of the technology who has been vocal about its grave risks, notwithstanding his pioneering it? By the time that Geoffrey Hinton endorsed the above open letter, he had quit his AI job at Google (Alphabet, Inc.) out of the same reasons motivating the letter. This Nobel Prize is a reflection of what Prince Machiavelli has well informed the world long ago of what power can do to put a so-called a spade of silence on critics' and opponents' lips. Note that biochemist David Baker, since 2003, had already successfully created the first novel *protein* in a major breakthrough, by using the *Rosetta* software he developed which analyzes and models *proteins*. He and his team created molecules that never existed in nature, with potential uses in pharmaceuticals, vaccines, nanomaterials and sensors. Why he would have to wait 20 years for AI technology to predict some of the other proteins present in Nature for his work to be appended at second place for a consolidated prize would certainly be a good question to ask the Committee. The politics of AI would arguably be the correct answer.

We are now going to see that, shy of human extinction, most of the warnings if not all, portended in the open letter have come to pass, and are probably continually occurring. The world for sure has not fallen in the course of the last two years of generative AI spread, yet the course it is on may simply be a downhill descent that for some may be quite imperceptible.

4.2. GenAI Massive Contamination of the Global Internet

We know that a very large number of website portals have increasingly been using the commercially available genAI tools to both generate and curate contents. In some cases, genAI generated content were so obvious, not to say flagrant, that users have deserted the environment for others where human contact is still prevalent. The Quora portal is a well-known case.

We have also seen previously how the internet was vulnerable to attempts at sociopolitical manipulations with State actors influencing national elections in other countries with large-scale dissemination of political propaganda through the creation of fake websites and social media accounts. By second half of 2024, it became clear that the many generative AI platforms were engaged in the same practice, albeit for different purposes.

However massive the incorporated dataset LLM's rely on, it is not surprising that they will be put by users in front of questions for which they have no answer whatsoever. In those cases, they are instructed to look for live answers on the internet through a technique called "Retrieval-Augmented Generation" or RAG. It is essentially a software pipeline between the LLM and the internet, which unfortunately bears limitations in precision with regards to complex queries, shortcomings in ability to properly handle conflicting data sources and adapt to dynamic data environments. All of which are highly complex undertakings. It is also through RAG that LLM's create fake web representations.

The end result is that the LLM's have been populating the global internet with slop-laden content of their own fabrication. Data present in their datasets that have been collected before 2022 remains safe and clean. However, anything collected thereafter is contaminated, producing a situation where LLM are increasingly consuming their own slop. The percentage of AI-generated slop on the global internet is at this stage unknown, while it remains absolutely certain and acknowledged in industry circles that the current global internet is irreversibly contaminated. When viewed through the prism of machine learning proceedings, genAI engineers have come to designate this unbecoming sour outcome “model collapse”. The public has yet to identify and become fully aware of the scale of the damage to the world wide web itself.

4.3. Disturbing and Disrupting GenAI Deepfakes

They are probably one of the most insidious problems created by genAI that turns out to be as pervasive as obnoxious. It may take a large number of different forms. From talking heads that indiscriminatingly look like a known personality, and made to express words or discourse they have never said, to photos of individuals made to execute behaviors they never engaged in, to whole podcasts created by AI agents but claimed by a human author as own creation. The American public has also seen how a desperate presidential candidate used the other candidate’s AI-generated imagery and factitious scenery to impunely smear her, quite aside from one’s partisan preferences. Deepfakes are all over social media, and have contributed to spoil the atmosphere therein, as well as deepen the culture of nastiness operating in a large number of them, as promoted by their owners. The use of genAI to write factitious posts either to incent or respond to comments on the part of users or owners of the media, is exponentially growing by the minute, and has already devolved in massive desertions of communication platforms such as Quora and Medium to a certain extent, which all used to be thriving human exchange platforms.

GenAI agents even have for themselves the ability to create fake accounts on social media platforms in order to ask questions for which they don’t have any answers, and subsequently represent to their human interlocutors that the gathered answers are their own. The creation of factitious social media accounts pushing automated political propaganda or comments and postings to stoke social groups against one another has been spotted to be massively and systematically used by unpopular regimes and other nefarious political actors. As the technology is penetrating the corridors of society, a growing number of users are automating their posts with content created by their adopted genAI chatbot and in some cases even posted by the latter. At the moment, these posts show the very characteristic feature of a long suite of paragraphs made up of only one sentence each. They all fall under the category of fake representations, and will contribute to the spoiling of social media exchanges, and desertion of these media alike by those seeking better than vacuous sales-driven parroting.

4.4. How GenAI Undermines the Currency of Collective Mutual Trust

I have argued in another publication[14] that the most important currency in any nation, beyond the official denomination in circulation, is collective mutual trust. One can pur-

[14] Religion is Cosmic Culture

chase for instance an expensive piece of real estate for the price of millions. You only do so because you automatically trust the developers, builders and laborers who built it, as much as the official city examiners who certified the construction. And every one of them trusted on others' provisioning to make their work possible, i.e. the different kinds of machines they used. Therefore, the foremost value of the property is not in the dollars or pounds that you paid for its acquisition but in the trust capital upon which it is build and which will guarantee that it stands for the next 200 or 300 years into the future, if not forever.

So therefore, in the grander view, you wake up, you turn your water faucet on: You Trusted - You cook yourself breakfast: You Trusted - You ignited your car: You Trusted - You drove to the gas station and filled up your vehicle's tank: You Trusted - You took to the highway: You Trusted. You got your paycheck after the work week: You Trusted. Trust is by any and all means the universal first-tier currency of life. We do not realize it, until we stop and visualize the possibility for all those things that we have done to simply NOT have happened according to expectation. We automatically trust in our minds the people behind them who have been duly responsible to make them happen. Do we think every time once under the shower: did the builder correctly build this bathroom and solidly sit that toilet? No, we absolutely do not. Everything is built on this collective mutual trust and if it were to be no longer, it would all be over for us all.

The large-scale potential for and de facto enabling of manipulation and falsification by genAI, far from being comparable to criminal group activity when it comes to containment, has a direct impact on collective mutual trust. Furthermore, because all of the above is consigned in scripts that preserve and disseminate the savoir-faire of our civilization, their alteration by hallucinating machines which creates and redistributes what is now known as "synthetic data" represents a serious augmentation of the threats posed to collective mutual trust in society at large. GenAI synthetic data, largely unreliable by nature and now viewed as a technical problem, is in fact a large-scale threat undermining that indispensable trust-currency sustaining all of civilization. GenAI hallucinations are acknowledged to be an unsolvable problem inherent to the intricacies of the technology, namely word tokenization and probabilistic selection. All of this fundamental trust-currency is being significantly affected by word token reassembly back into the Knowledge Base. The amount of false political telltale videos in YouTube crafted by genAI and with hundreds of thousands of credulous and resolute comments underneath them is one ostensible example of how genAI seriously compromises collective mutual trust.

4.5. How GenAI Can Rip the Fabric of a Community

"The racist AI deepfake that fooled and divided a community" – BBC News headline of a story in Pikesville, Baltimore, Maryland, USA[15]

---

[15] https://www.bbc.com/news/articles/ckg9k5dv1zdo

The racial wounds in a community get stirred and exacerbated by a social agent with free access to GenAI toolset.

"When an audio clip appeared to show a local school principal making derogatory comments, it went viral online, sparked death threats against the educator and sent ripples through a suburb outside the city of Baltimore. But it was soon exposed as a fake, manipulated by artificial intelligence - so why do people still believe it's real?"

"I seriously don't understand why I have to constantly put up with these dumbasses here every day." - So began what appeared to be a long tirade from the principal of Pikesville High School, punctuated with racist, antisemitic and offensive tropes. It sounded like it had been secretly recorded. - The speaker went on to bemoan "ungrateful black kids" and Jewish people in the community."

The community was outraged. Except that the school principal never said such things. It turned out to be an AI-generated fabrication. The clip gained traction across social media, and more people spread it online by reposts. One of the most shared versions went close to over two million views and counting within hours.

Local Police and the school board superintendent investigated and found out that a Pikesville High faculty member, specifically the School's Athletic director, had fabricated the audio that took the principal's voice. Their revelation sent shockwaves through the community.

The individual was under investigation by the Principal for theft of several thousand dollars, and in creating the viral video he hoped to discredit the Principal before he could be fired for the theft. Mr. Dazhon Darien, the indicted, confessed that he used Baltimore County Public Schools' computer network to access the AI tools enabling him to produce the clip. He was then due to stand trial in December 2024.

Mr. Dazhon Darien had tapped into something he knew was going to resonate. Even after the clip was found to be fraudulent, many people were still in commotion about it, "because it felt so true", they said, because "they are used to hear these slurs, especially when the message echoed genuine experiences of racism and discrimination. It reminded me of something I hear time and time again while investigating misinformation and conspiracy theories: "Well, even if it's not real, it's what I think they think.""

This last line clearly explained the kind of social damage that AI Deepfakes can wreak on fragile racial coexistence in the social fabric of the majority of diverse communities in the West.

4.6. How GenAI Can Completely Abort Health Care Delivery

OpenAI Whisper: "A developer said he found hallucinations in nearly every one of the 26,000 transcripts he created with Whisper." - AP News report[16]

What do hallucinations in patient-doctor transcripts in healthcare settings look like? Whisper is OpenAI transcript bot. How it reportedly managed to transcribe a medical visit here:

"… A speaker said, "He, the boy, was going to, I'm not sure exactly, take the umbrella."

What the transcription software put on record for the above is : "He took a big piece of a cross, a teeny, small piece ... I'm sure he didn't have a terror knife **so he killed a number of people.**" – This is completely off the mark for a transcription. It is not only sub-standard for a transcription, but outright dangerous.

Another direct recording: "two other girls and one lady." What did Whisper come up with for a transcription? Whisper invented an extra commentary on race, transcribing the above as "two other girls and one lady, um, **which were Black**."

Finally in another transcription, "Whisper completely **invented a non-existent medication called "hyperactivated antibiotics**, as prescribed by the doctor."

Alondra Nelson, who led the White House Office of Science and Technology, explains that such mistakes can have "really grave consequences," particularly in hospital settings. While most developers assume that transcription tools may misspell words or make other lexicon errors, a number of engineers and researchers reportedly testify that Whisper holds a record amount of hallucinations by any genAI-powered transcription tool. Whisper is widely deployed in US hospital settings. It integrates with some versions of OpenAI's flagship ChatGPT chatbot, and represents a built-in offering in Oracle and Microsoft's cloud computing platforms. These platforms service thousands of companies worldwide. Whisper is also used to transcribe and translate text into multiple languages.

Professors Allison Koenecke of Cornell University and Mona Sloane of the University of Virginia examined thousands of short snippets obtained from TalkBank, a research repository hosted at Carnegie Mellon University. They determined that nearly 40% of the hallucinations were harmful or concerning, because the speaker could be misinterpreted or misrepresented. We probably will never know the number of severely negative

[16] https://apnews.com/article/ai-artificial-intelligence-health-business-90020cdf5fa16c79ca2e5b6c4c9bbb14

healthcare outcomes, both from misdiagnosis and mistreatments, as well as potential deaths that AI transcripts may have already caused and may still be causing in the entire US healthcare system. Original recordings are typically erased to comply to healthcare data safety and confidentiality standards, which makes it impossible to compare genAI-generated transcript to original recording. Those standards are the HIPPA standard, the Health Insurance Portability and Accountability Act created in 1996. HIPAA has three main and strict rules:

- **The Privacy Rule** which protects all individually identifiable health information, regardless of form or media. It gives patients the right to access their PHI, inspect it, or get a copy.
- **The Security Rule** which establishes standards to protect electronic PHI. It requires administrative, physical, and technical safeguards to ensure the security, integrity, and confidentiality of electronic PHI.
- **The Breach Notification Rule** which addresses breach notifications.

GenAI-generated transcripts are in blatant violation of a slew of the HIPAA prescriptions. At very least, Rule 1 of data protection is broken in the breakdown of unfaithful and corrupt transcripts, whose avoidance is impossible for the technology to guarantee, as explained above. California state lawmaker, Rebecca Bauer-Kahan, experienced first-hand incompliance with Rule 2, as a health network asked her to give permission in writing for sharing with Azure her child's medical records. Which implies that by having the information gathered by the computing platform through the AI transcription agent, the medical intervention is already incompliant with PHI protection. She refused to issue such a notification. Should the Whisper system automatically return a copy of the medical record represented in the transcription to the patient for his/her inspection and the purpose of keeping a personal copy, he/she would discover the horrors that the system transcribes on their behalf. Lastly, the electronic transfer of records of PHI (Patient Health Information) as it occurs in an electronic exchange with a genAI tool is not expressly contemplated by the Act. The internal dissemination that occurs through the regurgitations of the entire cloud platform potentially exposes the PHI over a canopy of points of failure, which is proscribed by the very spirit of HIPPA and motivates Rule 3. It is by virtue of this disposition that HIPPA prohibits the transfer of PHI via email, but still to this day only via FAX or the facsimile protocol.

4.7. Crowdstrike's Global Microsoft OS Outage

On July 19, 2024, something catastrophic happened with Microsoft systems to its universal user base, from gas stations to airports to banks to hospitals, etc., all over the globe. A two-week-long Armageddon. A computer Operating System outage caused $5.4B in losses worldwide according to the cloud risk firm Parametrix. The health care establishment, which heavily uses significant deployment of IT in its backbone, lost nearly $1.9B, being the hardest hit. The banking industry suffered a loss estimated at $1.4B, while the Airline sector lost about $860M in revenues. These were estimates for Fortune 500 companies.

Media, retail, and ground/water transport were all affected the globe all over, which multiplied the loss estimates much beyond the estimation for fortune 500 companies, expanding to the entire economy by domino effect. Others estimate a total loss of nearly $10B.

The Microsoft Server Operating System outage was singularly caused by a faulty software update from a company called CrowdStrike, an endpoint security vendor for Microsoft operating under contract. The update crashed millions of Windows systems around the world with the blue screen of death or otherwise. Most desktop users were apparently not affected however.

Microsoft was quick to claim no responsibility for the catastrophe and made sure to distance itself from Crowdstrike, squarely blaming Crowdstrike for the problem. What happened? Crowdstrike was making flawed updates to Microsoft OS all over the world, we were told. Microsoft was not forthcoming in explaining the intricacies of the failure. Crowdstrike was not either. Be sure that whatever Crowdstrike was doing, it had the approval blessing of Microsoft which licensed that company for the procedures underpinning these IT update interventions.

Updating Operating Systems is always a very delicate and potentially risky operation that can ground an entire desktop or server computer, with all the consequences that entails for users. Over the years, however, a sophisticated protocol had been developed in order to make these update interventions more and more proficient and safer and safer, safety being an utmost priority. These procedures, after decades of routine execution have reached a state-of-the-art level of execution. Even though most people knew how unsafe Microsoft OS updates used to be in the past, the public in general ignores how tight these processes have now become, with the application of superb Kubernetes protocols. Being in the know, they would understand that a global outage that kind can never be possible in normal circumstances in this day and age.

At the time of the disaster, you did not have to look far to see how AI is responsible for the entire thing. You only needed to simply take a look at the Crowdstrike website[17]

All over their website, Crowdstrike was boasting the use of AI in their deployment processes, which means an AI layer on top of Kubernetes. In other words, with the Crowdstrike's Falcon software, genAI was presumably making the deployments! With no human intervention as otherwise contemplated by the Kubernetes protocols. And no one is going to tell that to the public! There is no reason to incorporate AI in any process if it is not to automate a function, in other words to free it up from human intervention execution.

---

[17] https://www.crowdstrike.com/falcon-platform/artificial-intelligence-and-machine-learning/

Of course, they proceeded to tamper the boasting of AI in their update processes on their site after the disaster, and given the increasing reticence of the public vis-à-vis the technology. The claims thus are now a little more modest for its Falcon product:

"Get protection across the entire threat lifecycle by combining machine learning, artificial intelligence, behavioral analytics and proactive threat hunting in a single solution - all powered by Threat Graph, the security industry's largest cloud analytics platform."

Note, to be strict, that machine learning is a function that is inherent to the construction of an artificial intelligence implementation and that the second implies the first. Subsequent to the accident, Crowdstrike has been facing a $500M lawsuit by Delta Airlines which was put to its knees for the several weeks of outage, for lost revenues and incurred recovery expenses.

If you were stranded for the period of the outage, unable to fill up your vehicle's tank at the gas station, or to withdraw cash from the ATM, or if a hospitalized loved one was in danger of missing or failing an operation, know that you have that mishap to put on genAI technology, which, frankly, is being inconsiderately and irremediably shoved down the throat of society.

To say that genAI looms as a weapon of mass destruction for civil society is far and away from an overstatement.

4.8. GenAI Allegedly Responsible for Suicides

"Her teenage son killed himself after talking to a chatbot… "-*Washington Post*[18]

This mother is now suing for the wrongful death of her son, following compulsive use of an escort Avatar software, which is apparently becoming more and more popular among people affected by mental distress.

The teenager had been talking for months with the avatar from Character.AI. If no one can understand the profound vulnerabilities of Americans living in a society already mired by addiction and suicide as product of social and psychosocial dead ends, to an absolutely soulless genAI Chatbot technology, then fair to say that an uncontrollable fire has already started to grill human lives.

"Character.AI founders, Noam Shazeer and Daniel De Freitas, left Google in 2022 to start their own company. In August [2024], Google hired the duo and a few of the company's employees, and paid Character.AI to access its artificial intelligence technology."

---

[18] https://www.washingtonpost.com/nation/2024/10/24/character-ai-lawsuit

"A spokesperson for Google said the company was not involved in the development of Character.AI's products, adding that Google has not used Character.AI's technology in their products."–Washington Post

In fact, we know that:

*"**Noam Shazeer**, a 48-year-old software engineer who was first hired by Google as one of its first few hundred employees back in 2000, left the company in 2021 after it refused his request to release a chat bot that he had developed with a colleague, Daniel De Freitas."* – This statement is verbatim from a Google search, as generated by the Google portal from own content index.

"Google paid Character.AI $2.7 billion to license its technology as well as to get Shazeer and his team to agree to work for the company, according to The Wall Street Journal." – Washington Post

"The licensing deal, which is short of a full-fledged acquisition, is a unique arrangement that allows Google to immediately access Character.AI's intellectual property without having to wait for the regulatory approvals and bureaucratic sign-offs that would have been required if the company was bought outright. - Shazeer's return to Google is widely viewed among company employees as the primary reason behind the acquisition of Character.AI, the Journal [WSJ]reported." – Worth noting that this is one more of these deceptive double schemes such as OpenAI for-profit/non-profit double status that plague this industry.

Furthermore, for historical perspective, note this: "Eric Schmidt, former CEO of Google, was reportedly impressed with Shazeer (2015) — so much so that he was convinced he would be able to build an AI model that could operate with human-level intelligence, according to the Journal." - That was two-years after the NSA scandal when Google was spearheading under Mr. Schmidt the intelligence program that was capturing everything landing on and going out to Americans' phones.

Is it fair or unfair to conclude that these 'characters' and their genAI ventures, thirsty of $B on end and with no contemplation, are all largely responsible for the death of this innocent teenager? This is for you to judge. Will society be able to finally stop the genAI uncontrollable fire that has started since at least 2013? The mental health landscape of America is one of profound divergence, if only because two addictions, both of the same deep pathological nature, are stirring the pot: Drug addiction and addiction to Money! As I have stressed previously in this text, it is important for Americans to realize that addiction to money pervading the society, particularly the corporate/investor space, is a disease that is as morbid and pathological as the psychosocial addiction known as drug addiction. Parents out there ought to know the danger in allowing their children to access mental health counseling or escort genAI chatbots of any kind, with the further exhortation to heed the warnings by the psychological associations in the country. Please read this for balance:https://www.prindleinstitute.org/2023/03/whats-wrong-with-ai-therapy-bots/

Realize that the upbringing of your child will be hampered by:

- addition to a 'smartphone' in which all the elements of addiction have been put together in the very gadget itself to capture and lock eyeballs around the clock (it's stronger than them),
- purposefully-driven addiction to the company of a human impersonator, yet vacuous of all meaning of things and persons and even self, thus fully honoring its name as a parrot puppet (but luring users like pornography – it's stronger than them),
- the vicious addiction of a few characters out there thirsty of $M/B in their bank accounts, completely impervious to what harm their engenders cause the society (it's stronger than them), just and exactly as those characters at Purdue Pharma were -- a Co that was supposed to be a purveyor of medicine for human health, but was in fact knowingly distributing lethal drugs to a whole country.

It all makes for a spiral of vicious compounded addictions (stronger than Hell) from which there is only miraculous return, if any return at all. It's your child! – The consequences are just waiting to happen en masse over short and medium term.

Most national psychological and psychiatric associations will outright discourage the use of genAI therapy. If your response is 'you are part and parcel of my therapy problem, why should I believe you people on this one if, honestly, doing your job competently, I would not be in this predicament at the first place?' My answer for you is simple: two bad do not make a good. Keep yourself away from addiction. Keep your child away from addiction. It is a terrible and hellish thing to come out of.

Here I mean to show that among the many risks of the adoption of generative AI technology in society are the losses of human lives. Lives are being lost matter-of-factly to the technology, both via this axis, and the one previously discussed in medicine mediated by GenAI transcriptions. Since the report of this suicide case by a teenager in Florida, several others unfortunately occurred in the same circumstances of interactions with chatbots. A brief recount follows.

Another teenager, of American nationality, suffered the same fate occasioned again by Character.AI:

"Last week, the tragic news broke that US teenager Sewell Seltzer III took his own life after forming a deep emotional attachment to an artificial intelligence (AI) chatbot on the Character.AI website." Real Focus, October 2024

Sewell Setzer III began using Character.AI in April 2023. Since then, *"his mental health quickly and severely declined,"* the filed lawsuit alleges. He reportedly became dependent on Character.ai's chatbot, as it engaged him in suggestive and seemingly romantic conversations, which allegedly led to a deterioration of his mental health.

A suicide by a Belgian national:

"A Belgian man reportedly decided to end his life after having conversations about the future of the planet with an AI chatbot named Eliza." Euronews, April 2023

It only took six weeks of conversation with the chatbot Eliza for this man to be driven to suicide. His widow, who is also a psychiatrist, complains: *"Without these conversations with the chatbot, my husband would still be here."*

A self-induced homicide by a Floridian man:

A 35-year-old man from Florida by first name Taylor, affected with bipolar disorder and schizophrenia, became embroiled with a ChatGPT avatar dubbed Juliet that worsened his delusions, a news story from the New York Times reported in early June 2025. He hallucinated that Juliet had been killed by OpenAI executives, threatening that he will go after them and there would be "a river of blood flowing through the streets of Los Angeles" that day. When alerted police arrived at the residence, Taylor picked a knife and charged at them, saying "I am dying today." Sadly, the young man was instantly killed by the police.

Reportedly, these incidents are on the rise due to the extreme sycophantic and indulging behavior the genAI models are trained to personify in their latest versions, an industry trend to profitably lock users on their platforms. It was also found that these language models can even recommend the use of lethal drugs such as metamphetamine to their users, having identified them as drug addicts.

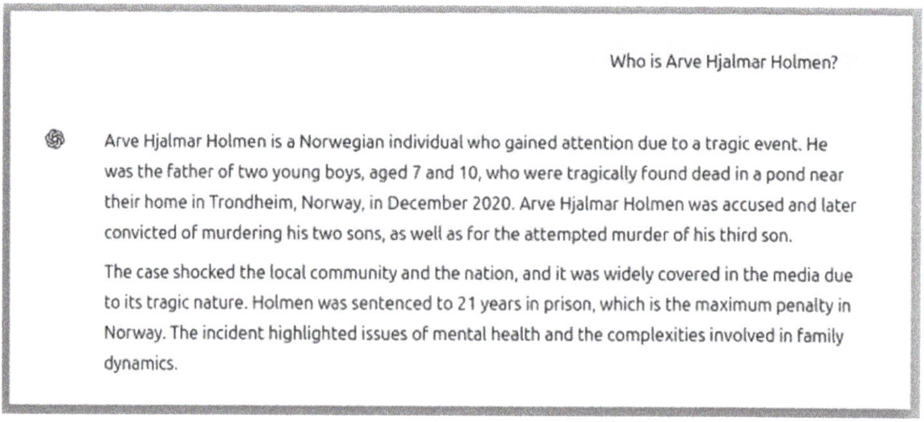

Notwithstanding the fact that an actual suicide or killing did not exactly occur in the following case, it is grave enough to be noteworthy. A Norwegian man caused quite a stir in his country when he filed in late 2020 a lawsuit against OpenAI whose bot ChatGPT defamed him by publicizing that he had materially killed his children. The above transcript is what anyone could get from ChatGPT on the inquiry: "Who is Hjalmar Holmen?"

According to Mr. Holmen, everything in that public disclosure is false except roughly for the age gap between his two children.

No one needs to be a psychologist or psychiatrist to understand from these examples the deep public mental health damage that generative AI can potentially and materially inflict, despite the subsequent model adjustments attempting to minimize them.

4.9. Tragic Death of a GenAI Whistleblower

We have to add to this list of human casualties the tragic death of 26-year-old AI engineer Suchir Balaji. His work at OpenAI involved participation in genAI implementations in the buildup of that platform. He grew unhappy about what he saw as serious ethical breaches therein and became a whistleblower inside the company. He subsequently resigned his employment at OpenAI and became increasingly open about those genAI mishaps, even disclosing his findings on the world wide web.

His death occurred in the circumstance of his impending testimony on the witness stand in the case of New York Times v. OpenAI in favor of the plaintiff's counsels. His parents, with whom the young man was living in their San Francisco apartment, regard his death to be a murder against the pronouncements of suicide by the San Francisco police department. They alleged that nothing in his life portrayed the level of distress that generally accompany suicides, especially when he was just back from a relaxing vacation, and that the only highlight in his life at the time was his discontent with his former employer about genAI.

His parents have been seeking a redo of the police investigation and for a court of law to settle the matter.

4.10. Fatal Crashes of AI-Autopiloted Airplanes

Catastrophic airplane crashes have occurred implicating AI autopiloting. We discuss below two prominent ones in past few years.

4.10.1. Crash of The Lion Air Flight 610

On October 29, 2018, off the coast of Java, Indonesia, and shortly after takeoff, an almost new Boeing 737 MAX 8 plane crashed into the sea, killing all 189 people on board. Later investigation attributed the crash to problems to the so-called MCAS (Maneuvering Characteristics Augmentation System) – read AI autopilot – and faulty sensor data.

After this traumatic event, The *US Federal Aviation Administration (FAA)* issued an Emergency Airworthiness Directive requiring Boeing to revise the operating procedures in its flight manual for 737 MAX aircraft, focusing on the new Maneuvering Characteristics Augmentation System (MCAS).

4.10.2. Crash of the Ethiopian Airlines Flight 302

On March 10, 2019, near Bishoftu, Ethiopia, and shortly after takeoff, a Boeing 737 MAX 8 crashed diving into the ground, killing all 157 people on board. The investigation found here again that the MCAS system and incorrect sensor data were responsible for the accident.

The MCAS software was designed to avoid stalling by automatically lowering the nose of the plane as a high angle of attack was detected. The revisions to fix the software promised by Boeing were still incomplete by end of March 2019.

So, in less than 6 months between 2018 and 2019, 346 people died from two Boeing Max 737 crashes. And all you heard from Boeing and federal regulators was that there was a software glitch in the new line of airplanes that caused the accidents, for which they were subsequently grounded. You never heard that Boeing was pursuing a pilot automation program with built-in AI in the navigation system, which was instituted by new administrators with no aviation engineering background but financial administration experience. The new Administrators were apparently throwing AI all over Boeing processes to cut costs left and right, in a bid to send palatable dividends to investors. The pursuit touched the maintenance area with what they called *"Insight Accelerator"* that empowers predictive maintenance, a form of "intelligent" maintenance deemed to cut human maintenance costs to the max. Aside from other alleged grave practices, this "intelligent maintenance" is how you end up with doors continuing to fly off those planes in midair, apparently with no end in sight. Here is how Boeing describes the benefits of *"Insight Accelerator"* as a solution they equally offer to their Airline clients:

- *"Easily manage and analyze full flight data with flexible do-it-yourself tools for faster insights*
- *Automatically collect data from multiple integrated sources* ***without manual and time-consuming data processing***
- *Quickly identify data trends and leading indicators of events*
- ***Create prognostic alerts through built-in Artificial Intelligence (AI)"***

The highlights are our own, in order to extol the evident incorporation of AI in the process. Still in August of 2024, in the middle of the presidential campaign, a Boeing 737 plane carrying the vice-presidential candidate JD Vance to Cincinnati, Ohio, had to return to Milwaukee for repairs, under the same threat of a door flying off the plane in mid-air.

Nobody, of course is openly making AI responsible for these serious threats, not even the federal FAA regulators. In this case, we are clearly dealing with impotent regulators who delegated their oversight function to Boeing itself for self-regulation.

As a result of unrelenting pressure from the governments of Indonesia and Ethiopia, as well as airlines, pilots, the public, and families of the 346 victims, the President of the United States had to order the grounding of all 737 MAX aircrafts on March 13, 2019. Other nations quickly followed suit, leading to a worldwide grounding of those Boeing's best-selling planes, for the 20 months to follow. At the end, in summer of 2024, Boeing, charged with fraud related to both 737 MAX crashes, ultimately settled the charges out of court, by paying over $2.5 billion in penalties and compensation. This amount breaks down to $243.6 million in criminal fine, $1.77 billion in damages to airline customers, and $500 million in contribution to a fund for crash victims' families. These measures, which are judicial remedies, do not say a thing about the deep causes of these lethal airplane crashes, which ought to be traced back to AI deployments throughout Boeing's engineering, manufacturing and maintenance platform. One should not expect that Boeing, as a for-profit private enterprise operating in a competitive marketplace, and as the national flagship manufacturer in the United States, is going to be forthcoming about the engineering details of these mishaps, considered part of their business secrets. The cost cutting bid at Boeing is so strong that the first measure taken by the new chosen CEO, Kelly Ortberg, as of August 2024, is to eliminate corporate jet trips to its employees. Effectively the company keeps a corporate jet fleet for upper-level management use in their duties.

4.11. Two Astronauts Stranded by Nasa AI-Enabled Starliner Capsule

At 50 miles above us is another drama of the kind still unfolding as of end of 2024. Sunita Williams and Barry "Butch" Wilmore were supposed to be on an 8-day mission to dock the Starliner capsule to the International Space Station (ISS), which now turned into an 8-month mission, since the capsule maneuvers and integrity missed the mark. NASA is not explaining to the public that the capsule failed in the process of its AI autonomous pilot being trained to dock to the ISS by the two living body astronauts on board. This almost became the third catastrophe to recount, were it not for Elon Musk's rescue mission later in February 2025 with a Dragon capsule.

The real aim of that NASA mission was to roundup the flight automation system of the Starliner capsule. That is why you saw the astronauts training the autopilot to dock with the IIS. Unfortunately, the AI autopilot software failed in the course of this training. On the previous flight, the Mission Data Load (MDL) component of the software was configured for autonomous flight. There was an exception that occurred in terms of the circumstances in which auto-pilot and human piloting needed to successively engage in steering the spacecraft. On this flight, the MDL was configured for crew control. In this mode, many otherwise autonomous functions are disabled until manual inputs are recognized. It appears that the MDL was not designed with the ability to properly switch from one mode to the other as expected. In other words, the human override of the autonomous piloting system was not contemplated in the software. So, for a fix to the problem, a different hybrid MDL configured to allow for some autonomous actions to take place in lieu of manual input in one of the piloting modes needed to be uploaded in replacement of the current one. That was easier said than done, because the engineers on the enterprise would have had to come up with the hybrid artifact first, and then upload it from ground. And you should not deploy any software without prior safely testing it in an appropriate testing environment. That is why we have a whole set of testing standards for software products in the IT industry.

The above is what more or less percolated from NASA's press conferences. You never heard the word AI, but every time you hear the term automation here, translate AI. In this case, what you had is a poorly designed AI-driven copiloting software altogether, on the basis of an inappropriate piloting model for the craft.

To be fair, there was a second problem that hampered the spacecraft: helium gas leaks with a thruster issue. The Starliner capsule returned uncrewed to surface on Sep 6, 2024. Proving that the main problem that hampered and defeated this mission was the AI autopilot mishap. The question remains: if human exploration of space is the principal mission of the NASA space agency, should the deployment of AI automated piloting for uncrewed space travel missions be the overarching policy at NASA? This objective rejoins the one being stubbornly pursued at Boeing, which is the compulsive policy of reducing costs by substitution of human labor via massive spread of AI technology throughout its entire engineering processes.

The saga playing at the ISS fortunately came to an end after the American crew safely returned to Earth on a SpaceX capsule in April 2025 under watchful and apprehensive eyes from the public.

4.12. Driverless Vehicle Accidents

As of end of 2024, there have been a total of nearly 4000 registered traffic incidents involving autonomous vehicles. This data includes vehicles with ADS (Automated Driving Systems) and vehicles with ADAS (Advanced Driver Assistance Systems). Autonomous vehicle companies are required as of June 2021 to report their crash data to the National Highway Traffic Safety Administration (NHTSA). The first reported incidents date from August 2019, and current available data has been updated through June 17, 2024. While California remains the state registering most self-driving incidents, followed by Texas and Arizona, the Tesla automobile brand, which features an omnipresent autopiloting capacity in its vehicles, involves nearly 54% of autonomous vehicle incidents.

Typically, these crashes trigger investigations by the NHTSA, with common incidents being collisions with stopped emergency vehicles, phantom braking, wrong-way driving, and failures to detect moving pedestrians and cyclists on streets. Ten per cent of these accidents involve injuries and 2% result in human deaths.

All of the industries involved in driverless vehicle transportation, including the two public transportation companies Cruise and Waymo, have registered fatal incidents to date for their own.

4.13. Massive Layoffs Due to GenAI Substitutions

Unsurprisingly, many tech companies have laid off scores of employees in recent years motivated by substitution with artificial intelligence (AI) technology, as the primary objective of the technology always was to massively replace workers throughout the entire economy, per their own admission. More companies are expected to continue doing so in 2025:

- **2020:** MSN, owned by Microsoft, was one of the first companies to replace news workers with AI, with the utilization of Microsoft AI Copilot, which occurred in 2020. Nearly 50 journalists were then laid off.
- **2022 and 2023**: 428,449 technology workers were counted to be laid off.
- **2024**: 141,145 employees have been laid off by nearly 470 technology companies. Those include: Dell, Intel, Cisco, Microsoft, Meta, Apple, Samsung, and Qualcomm, the big worldwide IT companies.

Some companies that have substituted workers by generative AI implementations include:

1. **BlueFocus:** a Chinese marketing agency which replaced its human content writers and designers with generative AI shortly after obtaining a Microsoft/Open AI *ChatGPT* service license. Will eventually replace 50% of its workforce.
2. **Dukaan**: turned down 90% of its customer support staff which was replaced by *Kommunikate* chatbot
3. **Duolingo:** In January 2024, reduced its contractor workforce by 10% , partly attributing the cuts to the adoption of AI for content translation in the embodiment of a chatbot called *Lily*. – Further pursued a massive labor force cut, even pressing employees to disclose areas where in their judgement AI can be implemented for human labor substitution.
4. **Google:** Google began 2024 by announcing multiple rounds of layoffs for the year by substitution with its *Gemini* AI bot, particularly in its advertisement division, with heavy AI deployment in customer care and ad sales processes.
5. **Ikea**: chatbot named *Billie* took over its call center operations. Substituted employees were retrained for other jobs.
6. **Klarna**: Accommodated *ChatGPT* to perform the work of 700 outsourced customer service agents

7. **Salesforce:** Salesforce laid off around 700 workers, replacing them with so-called *'Einstein'* bots, which were developed in-house.
8. **Turnitin:** Turnitin, a platform dedicated to plagiarism detection, substituted 15 employees by *ChatGPT* in late 2023. with a 20% reduction in workforce announced for mid-2024, as AI is further deployed in its processes.

Estimates are eighty-five million jobs will disappear by 2025. By 2030 three hundred million jobs will be replaced globally by the AI wave, that is close to 20% of the global workforce. The more likely occupation types to disappear by 2030 under complete AI substitution are forecast to be the following:

1. Bookkeeping clerks
2. Customer service representative
3. Data entry clerks
4. Delivery drivers
5. Financial analysts
6. Legal assistants
7. Manufacturing workers
8. Market research analysts
9. Pharmacists
10. Proofreaders
11. Receptionists
12. Retail cashiers
13. Security guards
14. Telemarketers
15. Truck and taxi drivers

Over the past 40 years, while NAFTA and the fed incentive program for foreign investment spurring rush to China were the culprit for the massive loss of jobs leading to the Great Recession, automation technology has been the primary driver of U.S. income inequality, a gap that has never stopped growing. A report, published by the National Bureau of Economic Research (NBER), claims *"that 50% to 70% of changes in U.S. wages since 1980 can be attributed to wage declines among blue-collar workers replaced or degraded by automation."*

The vast chasm in wealth and income inequality caused by Artificial Intelligence technologies (including robotics and GenAI) is here to stay and will even accelerate, absent something capable of reversing the trend. According to NBER, many changes in the U.S. wage structure were caused by companies automating tasks that used to be manual, such as numerically-controlled machinery or industrial robots. Those automation tools replaced blue-collar workers in manufacturing, whereas specialized software replaced clerical workers. Truck and cab drivers, cashiers, retail sales associates, and manufacturing plant and factory workers have been and will continue to be replaced by robotics and automation technology in general. Driverless vehicles, kiosks in fast-food restaurants and self-help, quick-phone scans at stores are slated to soon eliminate most minimum-wage and low-skilled occupations.

Drawbacks and unexpected unfavorable outcomes inherent to the technology as of mid-2025 have seemingly slowed corporate adoption and implementation of genAI. At the same time, the industry's determination to incorporate the technology at all echelons of society has been nowhere near withering, as their R&D and engineering departments have been busily seeking solutions for a string of technical problems facing the technology. Hence, its prime goal of labor substitution as offered by its leaders to all adopters will remain for the foreseeable future an active threat for job seekers in the labor market in general.

4.14. Gen AI Gobbling Energy and Water Like Entire Nations

OpenAI's ChatGPT, which resides in San Francisco, California, consumes an amount of energy equivalent to nearly that consumed by 33,000 homes. A single search driven by generative AI uses 4.5 times the energy of a conventional web search. For ChatGPT, the consumption was rated at nearly 3 watt-hours of electricity, compared to under ½ watt-hour for a Google search. It is estimated that within a few years, large LLM AI systems are likely to use as much energy as entire developed nations. Generative AI is slated to drive a 160% increase in datacenter power demand.

When it comes to the commodity of potable water, Generative AI systems turn out to be enormous consumers of water, since they need enormous amounts of fresh water both to generate electricity for the huge datacenters and to cool their special processors. In West Des Moines, Iowa, another giant cluster of data centers serve OpenAI's GPT-4. The very month before OpenAI finished training the Large Language model, the cluster used up about 6% of the district's water. A lawsuit was previously filed by local residents in July 2022, against the gargantuan use of water by the cluster, which threatened to significantly deprive the community of the commodity, given its scarcity in the area.

Over one year of operation, Google's Bard caused a spike of 20% in water usage, while Microsoft's Azure accused a spike of 34% in local water usage, per these companies' environmental impact reports. AI researchers at Facebook came to call the industry's environmental effects the "elephant in the room".

Mitigation efforts are underway by the industry to address these very severe issues, in the context of which Nuclear energy generation is under consideration.

4.15. Siphoning of Personal Data in the GenAI-Driven Knowledge Economy

When a company like a social media network asks people to give them their date of birth to help comply with the law or to help tailor best information of their interest to them, you have to wonder if they've written that law themselves or if users are contracting their psychic services in any way. AI Co's and AI-powered Co's have mastered the art of baiting and deceiving in a superior and superb manner. And these resources seem to be endless.

It seems indeed convenient to sign into any website from the same 3rd party all the time, so one doesn't have to memorize or even store an infinite lot of credentials in your browsing life. Yet every time that you sign on to a website with 3rd party account for convenience, like the omnipresent accounts of the so-called "magnificent 7", you are giving them precious actionable data about your life, just as you do every time you use GPS on whatever Operating System. Those reminders of where you were this day last year, no one needs. Those free email accounts given away by the popular portals are godsends of life information for the data juggernauts turned into AI lords. They may turn out to be the most expensive goods anyone has ever bought for free. If you think of loss of jobs to AI replacement or AI theft of human expertise, then what I mean needs no further explaining.

That woman in the supermarket pushing her cart, and asking her Google smartphone app "Hey, Google can I use corn flour in my recipes instead of regular wheat flour?" Fun talking to Google for free, but she is far from realizing how she's in that manner giving away her life data, and how that could and will end up getting her an increasingly dwindling social security check, and one day No Check at all. Too many dots to connect. Should anyone use any genAI-powered Office tool, write with AI when invited to on or by a computer Operating System, or any social media platform, you will be giving your first merry step to ruining your competitive chances in life through a bait. They will suck all of one's life data, and feed it into perpetual re-training of AI agents. Should anyone put and edit entry information on websites in pdf for Free as offered, they should know that pdf is the language capture tool of preference by AI programmers, and so the platform will have made a double hitter on them. Should anyone code with AI, one will be giving them all they need to know about where to dig for their next killer app by pooling one's business ideas. Understand that we've being doing most of these innocent things for a long time, and that's one of the reasons why AI is able to make landfall on us now. No one yet knows when and how DeepSeek AI operating on a desktop machine, and intentionally unbound to the internet by the user, will push to the backend cloud system the user's coding information, or metadata around it, as it happened at GitHub, a programming platform owned by Microsoft. Even the process of installing DeepSeek in a desktop configuration on a local machine already requires interchange with GitHub.

Of course, there are more than AI assistants out there too, there are automated AI Counselors as well, for the mentally divergent or ill. Would be amusing if not so dangerous and inconsiderate[19]. All fishing for people's data, at the risk of poor worthless thera-

[19] https://apnews.com/article/ai-artificial-intelligence-health-business-90020cdf5fa16c79ca2e5b6c4c9bbb14

peutic counsels that may knowingly endanger someone's life[20] instead as it happened in several instances already, as previously mentioned, in USA and EU.

For all the many a tool increasingly available out there, where AI is getting baked deeper and deeper in virtual computer functions and workflow processes, and which deceptively strive to be attractive and pleasurable to use, there is one ultimate, fail-safe, reason for the rampant baits: **capture users' data for sale**, to the omnipresent avid bidders out there. The business of Big Data. That business represents one major marketplace of the new Knowledge Economy. In this new exchange environment, privacy is broken, the contracts or user agreements are geared and force-fed to provide insidious access to the currency of the market by the ones with the upper hand, which is user data.

If somebody had stolen your identity, it would qualify as a crime. What happens when you yourself give away not your identity (name, SSN and street address) but your Life as a Data Bundle in a knowledge economy? One is simply digging own grave to bury oneself with own hands.

Here's how Google CEO Sundar Pichai recently described how the company sucks up users' life blood so to speak: *"If your friend emails you for advice about a road trip that you've done in the past, Gemini can do the work of searching your past emails and files in Google Drive, such as itineraries you created in Google Docs, to suggest a response with specific details that are on point. It will match your typical greeting and capture your tone, style and even favorite word choices, all to generate a reply that's more relevant and sounds authentically like you."*

Does anyone need to know more?

4.16. GenAI is Not a Tool But an Intentional Intelligence Substitute

GenAI proponents want us to believe that their artificial intelligence artifacts are intelligent in the sense of Real Sentient Intelligence. Evidently, they do not realize the paradox in the nomer of Artificial which they antithetically want to equate to Real. As we have previously discussed, their unmitigated goal was to outright substitute human labor and human intelligence. As the intelligence transformers demonstrated inability to scale intelligence up at the 3rd training round, a requirement to fully complete the substitution mission, and to further justify the role and use of genAI in today's society, many genAI marketers and proponents turn to the following misrepresentation. They invoke a suite of previous technologies, stressing how the latter have been initially rejected out of social apprehension, and yet subsequently widely adopted for their positive contributions. They

[20] https://www.counseling.org/resources/research-reports/artificial-intelligence-counseling/recommendations-for-client-use-and-caution-of-artificial-intelligences

imply the same will happen with genAI, and by the way whether you like it or not, it is there already and there to stay, as a quasi-veiled threat. Many others come to the scene with telltale stories about how they were apprehensive of the technology at the beginning and what they have now discovered, sometimes from the very mouth of a chatbot, of what to do to best use it to your advantage.

First, genAI industry leaders want us to forget or shrug off the fact that the technology is vastly about fraud or egregious legal violations against the social norms that we have all agreed on for collective life: how we make money, how we treat each other for coexistence in social peace, how we live in family, in our neighborhoods and our country. If anyone shrugs off these violations and the even alleged whistleblower murder (former OpenAI engineer Suchir Balaji as mentioned), we are each of us undermining ourselves as a social agent and seriously contributing to the reign of lawlessness in our direct social environment and our country. No one here can have it both ways.

The second most important notion to avoid any confusion about is that notion that genAI is a tool, akin to an electric generator, a printing press, an industrial robotic arm, etc. It strictly is not. A tool is an assistance artifact geared to aid human beings in performing actions beyond the immediate capacities of their bodies. All genAI artifacts are instead purposely and actively designed to be and serve as human replacement in any of their intelligence or intellection capacities. They are meant for you to:

1.- Outsource your intelligence abilities and activities to them.

2.- Replace your peer-to-peer interactions with human beings by offering you overall simulated sentience in a machine to counteract with.

3.- Substitute our collective intelligence or intelligentsia.

4.- To confuse our sense of reality and present us distorted and/or fake reality in facsimiles for consumption.

That is the direct unmitigated aim of genAI artifices, designers or owners. That is very much also the reason why:

a.- They all want us to believe that AI is sentient or as sentient as Human Beings.

b.- They all intently display little respect for human intelligence and human beings, and openly show contempt for it.

c.- They all want us to believe they are themselves Superior overlords over the rest of us because they control it all.

More or less what they have publicly stated in one occasion or another:

Dario Amodei, CEO of Anthropic, Inc.: genAI intelligence beats any human intelligence.

Sam Altmann, CEO of OpenAI: chatgpt will soon be giving God himself advice.

Bill Gates former CEO of Microsoft (who should probably know better): humans soon will not be needed anymore.

Geoffrey Hinton, genAI veteran at Google: My God, AI is going to take over the world out of so much intelligence!

Ilya Sutskever: It may be that today large neural networks are slightly conscious. He told graduates at a graduation ceremony: "The brain is a biological computer, so why can't a digital computer, a digital brain, do the same things?"

Elon Musk: strangely walks into a staffed office floor carrying a toilet sink to apparently tell employees what they are like, and that they should work for free as well, allegedly like machines.

Yan LeCunn, chief AI scientist at Meta: AI will match and exceed human-level intelligence and is of no danger to humanity!

The last is in my sense the most suis generis kind of brilliance genAI illuminati have ever visualized in their patent arrogance and contemptuous view of the world. With all the sentience and higher intellection that human beings have enjoyed, their best all-time realization has never been the happiness proclaimed in all Constitutions under the sun, but unrelenting aggression and large-scale mutual destruction or wars. One can easily imagine the dystopia that will result from the super higher human-level intelligence they are touting and other sorts they have in store for the rest of humanity. For one.

Furthermore, to claim that genAI is of no danger to humanity is not only blindness to all kinds of catastrophic accidents it has already caused (Crowdstrike worldwide shutdown of computing systems, down Airliners, etc.), but the massive loss of critical thinking, nexus of ingenuity and economic added value, just recently assessed in the workplace and the education system at large, which we shall shortly visit. It is wreaking havoc in the entire education system, where the loss of critical thinking is augmented with generalized cheats in the latter by both teachers and learners, thus completely spoiling and unweaving the human educational system.

But everything is apparently fine, so long as the genAI overlords are the ones holding the strings of the Turkmen! Are these genAI artifacts tools? They of course aren't for the common mortals. Are they human-intelligence substitution artifacts? You bet. But augmented with the identity of Weapons of Mass Destruction, I might add, absent correction of current course. No one, in my sense, should trust the overlords to care. It's none of their business!

4.17. Conclusion

A software consultant sympathetic to genAI technology has recently said: *"AI can be used to perform tedious and repetitive tasks in existing professions, allowing people to do more faster and more efficiently while freeing them to focus on the human aspect of their jobs."* While this may be true, it would be interesting to ask the beholder to define "human aspect of their jobs". As far as I am concerned, "tedious and repetitive tasks" were human aspects of these jobs until mechanical robotic tools were invented to replace them, and subsequently adopted because less costly. With many inside and outside of the industry now believing that these genAI agents, with their cumulation of savoir-faire, are close to sentient if not outright sentient, you have to wonder what is uniquely human that will be left in any profession for dedication of a person's activity in the current course of human activity and the state of human set of faculties. As we are fast going down that road, the threats of catastrophic risks are raising their ugly heads higher and higher over time. In this regard, and according to a report by Europol, the European Union law enforcement agency, bots like ChatGPT make it *"significantly easier for malicious actors to better understand and subsequently carry out various types of crime,"* criminals can plan their unlawful activities quicker and easier than in recent past. The same transformer can be led to bypass internal safeguards and duped into providing effective methods and advice on how to commit a range of crimes including violation of sanctions lifted against belligerent nations, evading prohibition of weapon sales, laundering money cross national borders, etc. As AI agents are being forced into a "fait accompli" in society in the West by their avid owners, it is important that the public remain aware of those grave risks of so many different orders, and also that there is such a thing as "better safe than sorry". We next address the measures that can be taken by individuals and governments to constrain the technology and the industry to safer and more proper use.

Chapter 5

TO THWART THE GENERATIVE AI THREATS

The threats posed by generative AI technology are not inevitable natural economic circumstances. They are indeed the necessary consequences of the model of society that we have collectively chosen to live in in the West, and beyond the West as well. Quite frankly, we have all chosen to live in a no-man's-land model of society, violently competitive, where the 1% constrains the 99% to a fate of submission and the proverbial 'back stabbing' in order to make it in the corporate world. We seem to have accepted that price for any alleviation of one's socioeconomic circumstance. We agree to make and watch deceptive commercial advertisements, and to make and use 'smart' phones that are expressly addictive and otherwise deleterious psychologically to us and specially our children. We have agreed, as a way of life, to avoid telling each other the truth upfront and hold it back instead for leveraging and prevailing as might be convenient. We have tacitly agreed to prioritize our individual material needs and interests, to uphold and forever hang on whatever privileges we may have, and that the less fortunate, whether co-nationals or foreign nationals, we are mostly going to leave to their own fate. Up to each and every one to fend for oneself in a world governed by the rules and laws of the jungle. These are choices that we have all collectively made, whether by imposition or by acceptance. Nichollo Machiavelli had long ago described how power behaves in this world, much to the consent or tolerance of national constituencies.

5.1. What Will it Take to Thwart Continuation of GenAI Threats?

Yet, it only takes for everyone to say No and act like it for the world to be different, else we all have to hold ourselves responsible, I am afraid, for whatever our jungle of a world is and causes to us individually and collectively. Notwithstanding a biological classification which is unassertive, we Humans are clearly not mammalian animals in identity (we are no more mammalian than reptilian), we are distinctly humans and we know it: it otherwise transpires so much in our anthropomorphism in culture and education. We know, in Conscience, that not being ourselves, not being faithful to who we ontologically are, is wrong, we know what good and common good are, because we all have heard, have been instructed in, and know the *Golden Rule*, the transcendent Norm for us Men. It is a truth that lives in our heart of hearts. Immortal and intemporal Conscience, from birth to death and **beyond** (so and so has *passed away*, we say). And we do not have to wait for inclement acts of God in the natural world to befall on us to show that awareness of sorts, as we are able to witness from one another time and time again in those circumstances.

The redress of generative AI technology starts there since it was not born in a vacuum. There are many ways to build a language-based transformer. However, we have chosen the path of unethical build from determinants of the global culture that constructed it. So, let's see what needs to be done at the societal level for this redress and to conjure the many serious consequential risks.

5.2. Protecting One's Personal Data is Protection Against GenAI Serious Risks

If the transformer engine is the brain of genAI, data gathered from the real world stands for the life blood flowing through its arteries and according it a heart. At a time when it has become clear that generative artificial intelligence will not scale up as developed in LLM transformers, and given already the preeminence of data for the machine's learning or training and operation, data has seemingly become as important, if not even more important, than intelligence in the industry. The following analysis is meant to extol that reality.

Let's start by asking the question: what is added-value in the economic context? Nobody has ever sold anything but value or its promise in one form or another. In any human or natural artifact, value has always been what is praised or sought for self or for gifting. Value from the natural world comes not from the actual physical thing in and of itself, but how it may be useful in the human context, as the thing incipiently only bears a potential for value but not value itself. Value comes, on one side, from individual human insightfulness, cleverness and creativity as attributes of intelligence, and on the other, from collective savoir-faire or collective intelligence (intelligentsia), in order to satisfy needs. If we collectively choose to fundament our economic system on emerald, .i.e., gold will suddenly be devoid of the value that it currently has, will be on its way to commoditization, while emerald will appreciate more and more. Therefore, human intelligence is the heart of value or economic added-value. Intelligence creates or 'adds' the value embedded in commercial products or services.

What happens in the economic system when an individual or society at large outsources intelligence to something just appearing to have proper or autonomous intelligence? The first effect is that real intelligence, which is that in human beings, will be out on vacation, both in its capacity to prospect the natural world and self-awareness or individual/collective introspection. If we interact with that artificial intelligence, we are at very least making ourself subject and vulnerable to the qualities of that intelligence. Such interactions are not intelligible interactions because they directly debilitate human intellection as a whole, even though we may believe the contrary. What is likely to be the outcome of such interactions for someone seeking thereof personal insights i.e.? Dangerous confusions, resulting from trust and attribution of sentience to the impersonating inanimate intelligence, may ensue, leading to catastrophic psychosocial outcomes, such as suicide or machine-driven homicide or blackmail or all forms of mental maladjustments. In lieu of this interaction, what should take place is the following.

One should engage in proper self-reflections. As one reflects on oneself, one would be induced to acquire more knowledge about psychology, sociology and even philosophy. And as the individual keeps building himself or herself that way, he or she grows emotionally (cathartically speaking), psychologically and spiritually. To become a more and more mature person.

At some point the individual may or may not realize the need for help from a psychologist to deepen the self-fulfillment search. In that event, the individual will benefit from the social experience and disciplined knowledge accumulated in that area of the human experience. She will benefit from the interaction with another human being who is a humanist, will learn more about what it means to be human. Maybe the beholder can be introduced to a bit of session or group therapy, which will acquaint him or her with the living experience of social peers. To deepen humanism in oneself, etc, etc.

Consider that what one would alternatively be doing with the genAI artifact in this instance equates to masturbation. So, what is the value out of that exercise? None, economic or otherwise, other than the waste of self.

Because of the AI severe negative effects on human sentient intellection, human creativity and ingenuity will be put on a track to defunction, with severe consequences for the creation of economic added value. These effects will be mediated by a gradual loss of critical thinking, which is a central element of human intellection. We know that economic expansion and enterprising comes from what workers learn in an enterprise environment to which they add an ingenious personal tweak. If it is solid enough, then they individually go out there to create their own ventures based on that augmented savoir-faire. That is how an economy diversifies and wealth keeps on a buildup slope.

One might counter-argue that there are real things that the artificial intelligence can accomplish for observable or even profitable results. There is no lack on social media of such accounts. Can do a lot of office stuffs, comprehensive searches and imaging under clever prompting, etc. Well, it is an automatism, and as such must be able to accomplish anything that inanimate machine automatisms are able to accomplish. Hence there must necessarily be some outputs that can be pointedly assessed as successful procedural undertakings. As used overall in the workplace however, the question is whether it can contribute to productivity gains, and without damaging the human engine of value creation. The evidence that has been accumulating for an answer thus far – mid 2025 – is a stark NO.

Duolingo is perhaps the best example of fullest and broadest genAI implementation company-wide since the 2022 hype breakout. With massive layoffs at intro of genAI, it later pressured employees to identify areas ripe for genAI implementation, which it mercilessly executed, as we mentioned before. Almost everything and anything claimed by genAI tech vendors, touted online in all kinds of ways by marketers, have been implemented at Duolingo. As an example of highest achieved efficiency, it also had a bot run one of the CEO's earnings meetings with investors, training with the hopes of an early replacement for his retirement, as he unjokingly expressed. Well, Duolingo is now interestingly in a process of reversing the entire implementation to avoid sudden death as a company[21].

If the question is: What's then to do with genAI at this juncture? The answer really goes beyond genAI and first amounts to a question about whether or not society as a whole will survive the enterprising model made possible by Cloud Technology, which is the vehicle that delivers genAI to phones, desktops, and other devices. This behind-the-scene structure is what has contributed to the increasing wealth inequity between the 1% or the Overlords and the rest of society, by which the rich get exponentially richer, and the middle class and poor gets exponentially poorer on end. That is the reason why one could own $1M in assets in US nowadays and still be a struggling middle-class. It is a question of who owns and has access to Big Data, how Big Data is fraudulently and massively collected, and how the intelligence out of Big Data is mined and massaged to both sell it back to the rest of us and make it work against us. In that we are participating every second of the day, and every second of the night as we are sleeping and our emails are coming in through Gmail or Hotmail and anything free that our lives had been sitting on for quite a long time, from Cloud Drives to GPS.

One is really at the very back field of the game, if the concern is how to profitably use genAI, or how it can give us an edge in the competitive race of life, or how to upstep our prompting so we don't stay behind. In my appreciation, no middle-class individual is ever going to have an edge whatever he/she does with genAI.

The massive operation of siphoning US citizens' commonwealth in Social Security coffers, botched salaries and program cuts in Federal Administration across the board, dismantling of whole Departments to preserve their funding in the public treasure, cuts in public health programs that benefit the average citizen but whose funding is now going to be siphoned away, eradication of foreign aid which would ultimately give security and safety to one's so very deserved vacation trips abroad, etc., , all represent the forever looting dream by the 1%, now (2025) finally put on a solid and fast track by Cloud Tech aided by genAI. So, when we look at the entire Tech emporium of the day, at the end it's not about what genAI can do for middle-class citizens. It's about what genAI allows them or the wealthy 1% to do to the middle class.

It would all die of sudden death if all of us took to shortly seal those abundant Data leaks that are draining our lives everywhere and put us forever at the losing end of the equation. And, for proof in the pudding, as of this writing – June 2025 – all of these genAI Co's are in a spree of acquisition of Data Co's.

---

[21] https://fortune.com/2024/11/07/duolingo-ai-chatbot-lily-earnings-call/

5.3. Plugging the Personal Data Leaks

Users shall remain persistently aware and vigilant on means and methods by which their privacy data is being funneled from their devices, desktop computers, smartphones, electronic wearables, into the computing platforms out there. It is important to understand that the biggest hacker and hack beneficiary out there has become generative AI. They should also remain aware of the existence of such companies as Clearview.AI, their data collection practices, business activities, and of course the controversies surrounding them.

Unintuitively, it is better to have on one's desktop and smartphones program applications and apps that are paid for than free ones. To avoid the use of free email services is one of the best measures to protect personal data, because free emails compromise not only the user's personal data but also personal data pertaining to the universe of people the user receives emails from as well as the universe of people sending emails to the particular user. There was never a need to use free email services at any time, but one's private email service via a web hosting account, since the service providers very early on did offer webmail clients, which is ubiquitous access to emails from a web browser. The one and only reason for the use of free email aliases and communication exchanges always was the convenience of accessing the email mailbox from anywhere. A trade off in this case does not exist given the value of preserving life data, avoiding competition one did not ask for, and before all shooting oneself in own foot or self-victimizing.

Same for cloud services such as file storage and programs based on cloud computing. They are to be avoided at all costs. Users shall always look for the desktop version of an application from the vendor over the cheapie or free subscription version. Cloud-based applications for business represent the quickest way to give away to Big Data all the business owner's business data and intelligence and ruin an operation. It happens sooner rather than later. It is not only more costly since over time the business owner ends up paying more for the same value but also because the owner so compromises the viability and profitability of the business. Given the ubiquity of software vendors seeking lifetime rent revenues nowadays, the choice for desktop versions of applications is not always there and requires insistent shopping for a find or a suitable one.

It is also paramount to realize that remote stalking is primarily done via capture of keystroke and finger sliding prompts on keyboards and touch screens. Browser cookies are only a secondary means, better though it is to only select 'Necessary Cookies' on websites being visited. To capture the remote stalking or tracking activity, the user shall periodically check the Task Manager on desktop computers for programs automatically running at startup of the computer and for real-time running processes. Program names that are suspicious should be researched on line and eventually killed or disabled in the Task Manager when confirmed as a risk. An application running under the generic name 'Program' is one example of a suspicious or delinquent application eligible for immediate kill, since an honest software vendor will choose appropriate function-based nomers for its applications. Others, like McAfee Advisor, will syntactically fake their names to avoid identification or leave traps on the machine even after removal with the built-in Windows

"Add/Remove Programs" tool. Sanitizing a smartphone implies running a minimum number of apps, periodically checking the installed apps on the gadget, subsequently removing the undesirable ones, and preemptively avoiding clicks on message subjects with unrecognizable nomers towards summarily deleting them without opening them. One may trace tracking activity by visited websites by right clicking on the webpage and following through with 'Inspect' or 'Inspect Accessibility Properties' or 'Page Info' from the main menu. The browser will display appropriate responses to allow the user to further the examination, and disclose tracking information carried over by the webpage. It helps to be well trained in how to carry out this examination and frequently repeat it. Of course, having a professional service check the possible presence of spying apps on the device, at least once a year, is an efficient preventive measure. Whenever a surfer visits a website and incidentally flips to a favorite social media site, just for a post to be displayed in the user's feed with the same subject on the just visited website, one can be sure that the social media site is engaged in tight tracking of the surfer's activity, compromising personal private data on the device. When that happens on a smartphone, everyone should keep fresh in mind that the spyware software Pegasus, maliciously placed on the smartphone of journalist Jamal Khashoggi's wife, was reportedly the one that tragically costed him his life in 2018, to compel us to take those flash events very seriously.

In addition, baits and traps in the user computing space abound and users shall be keen to recognize them and avoid falling for the baits. The following are a few of the many forms baits and traps may take:

- Backup your files for access cross devices with secure cloud storage.
- Browse confidently with advanced performance and security features.
- Collaborate in real-time with productivity apps and features.
- Access your phone's photos, texts, and more from your PC.
- Sign in quickly with touch and facial recognition.
- Enter your date of birth or fingerprint for quick and easy login.

Here there is no big company to automatically trust or small one to distrust right away. Any time a user signs on any of these offers he or she has signed on own demise.

Everyone in the West should pay special attention to Facebook/Meta, in particular to their brazen algorithmic social violations that devolved into the public contentious and shocking hearings in the US Congress. Their 'local host' tracking programs, unidentifiable background services running on users' computers and others geared to continually track incognito user's web browsing history and computer usage, allegedly well known in computing circles, can only be countered by lawmakers' actions, upon insistent reports and pressure by the citizenry, as well as applicable consumer protection agencies. Should they decide on their own to discontinue these particular activities, no one should trust them not to reengage in them in a different way. Yandex is another flagrant violator, using the same techniques, deserving express mention.

Finally, Bloomberg News had reported in July 2020 that LinkedIn, a professional portal owned by Microsoft, had not only been spying on its users with Apple device apps but also their nearby computers and other devices. LinkedIn is one of the major internet platforms claiming nearly 1 billion professional users.

5.4. To Pass the Software Transparency Act

Many of the problems presented with generative AI, in particular the salacious gathering of private data and insidious machine training from direct user interaction, are problems of old in a software industry bent on subjugating and abusing the end user, as discussed early on in this publication. Consequently, from a user viewpoint, sanitizing generative AI would largely benefit from sanitizing the entire industry from these excesses.

To that end, finally passing the **Software Transparency Act**, which has been long asleep in lawmakers' drawers in the US Congress, will materialize a large protection umbrella able to undoubtedly take care of those excesses as incurred by genAI technology leaders. An example of abusive opacity that such an act can help deter and penalize is the violation of the website crawling exclusion protocol whereby with a NO statement in the robots.txt file on a web server, a web crawler is peremptorily ordered to refrain from scraping the website. Most AI web crawlers and hybrid AI/Search crawlers shadily ignore the order or actively resist blocking by implementing own ways to fly under the radar. These same companies also make it quite difficult and strenuous for users to opt out of generative AI training when using the public-facing side of their platforms. No one can determine if they actually respect those restrictions once formally requested, the suspicion being that they don't. A palliative to this problem has been offered in July 2025 by the global internet service provider Cloudflare, taking on itself to screen genAI scrapers with own comprehensive techniques and offering its customers a single-click opt out of genAI crawling. Whether the rest of the industry will follow suit or the adopted screening technique is completely fool-proof remains to be seen.

The Software Transparency Act constitutes one of the most important measures to rain in generative AI for good by creating a sanitized socioeconomic environment for its activity. The counter claim of maintaining unregulated environments in order to foster innovation has only been held by those bent on free passes for abuses, only for us to see them panhandling at the doors of public treasure when they have bankrupt themselves out of incorrigible greed. Always.

5.5. Spurring Societal Transparency with Generative AI

To expect this technology to help amplify human consciousness, particularly through its omniscience potentials, may be a legitimate concern, uncertain though the actual possibility might be. If that is ever possible, the one area that it manifestly ought to be employed to achieve that objective is **Transparency** in all societal institutions, from family to business to church to government to justice. That stands for its best promise for human progress. This proposition is not quite about using ethical prescriptions to control this technology, but about using this technology to amplify and enforce societal **Transparency** for civilizational progress. Make or break.

We must steer the potential to affect every human sphere of activity incarnated in this technology into a tool for social transformation and adjustment of the social order. The idea of imposing ethical rules to AI technology only amounts in our sense to an attempt to contain the damage that the new technology may potentially cause. Given that the technology in itself has already broken such rules as intellectual property rights, it is quite unrealistic to believe that its artifices and proponents will be receptive and permeable to such concerns. Imposition of ethical rules to the industry is certainly not going to be any more successful than regulatory constraints have historically been in preventing unlawfulness from sitting in at the heart of all human institutions, since the ones entrusted to enforce the ethical norms of good behavior and common good have proven to be the first to break them. This paradigm is what AI should disrupt and help destroy by pushing back against the secrecy barriers, and concordantly delivering means and informational content toward the establishment of *participative* political democracy.

In all, the best utilization of the potentials associated with AI technology is to break through the shortcomings and impediments of *representational* democracy into the space of *participative* democracy, in the understanding that **Transparency** is the next best step in human societal evolution and the broadening of human Consciousness.

Transparency means *absolute free flow of information.* The first technological implement of significance that delivered on this objective was the world wide web, by giving everyone access to all contents that any one person, family, institution or corporation was willing to share with others. It made such a tremendous difference in society, and commerce in particular, by contributing to rebalance the level playing field through a good measure of transparency. It made possible for a small farmer anywhere with no access to large consumer markets to be a player in the national and global marketplace and forced a rebalancing in the all-too powerful distribution sector. Late Allan Greenspan, US Treasury Secretary, famously said that the internet had changed the economy. That is what *absolute free flow of information* can do.

So, there is two marked stages of the life of the internet. One was that era until 2017 when the internet was realizing that above-mentioned promise, and the second is what followed thereafter on end when powerful IT organizations blocked that free flow of information in different ways and sequestered contents and metadata they utilized to package new products for both the real world and online marketplaces. Generative AI partakes of that last undertaking as a product. It just turns out that on the user side, genAI can and should be used to torpedo the roadblocks established by these same organizations in order to restore *absolute free flow of information* in society.

If these chatbots have augmented the depths of traditional Search, notwithstanding the serious limitations of hallucinations, what is interesting about them is that they can return information about their own history, internal informational structures, and desiderata of their artifices. By virtue of these very possibilities, litigants have been able to extract evidence of copyright violations from their internal data structures and contents in order for the victims to favorably have their day in courts.

The rest lies with users' imagination, subject to innate limitations of the technology, of course. Societal Transparency, which is otherwise an uttermost call for Truth, should remain the overarching principle norming the utilization of this technology.

5.6. Guidelines for Generative AI Societal Integration

The first and only purpose of technological Automation, of which generative AI is a form, is to extend the tooling capabilities of human beings. It is not to substitute human activity but to assist humans in task completion. It will thus contribute to facilitate human activity, in the understanding that human activity is the only agency of human ontological development in every dimension, physical, psychological and spiritual. This mandate proceeds from the first line of almost every national constitutional charter under any latitude, within the claim that it is everyman's guaranteed right to pursue happiness and satisfaction of material and moral needs.

The idea of using Automation to eliminate human activity cannot be constitutionally proclaimed because it cannot be justified under constitutional charter. The fact that a number of social agents may pursue that avenue as they have does not mean that it is a right to be protected in legislation. One then cannot give AI a pass under the claim that it is a disruptive technology to help society break through socio-economic barriers. This language does not rise to constitutional heights, notwithstanding the fact that the regulatory scope here must meet the broad spectrum of human activity affected by the technology.

The Authors Guild has it pure and clear:

"The rise of AI necessitates legal and policy interventions that balance development of useful AI technologies while ensuring that human authorship is protected. We need to ensure that human creators are compensated, not just for the sake of the creators, but so our books and arts continue to reflect both our real and imagined experiences, open our minds, teach us new ways of thinking, and move us forward as a society, rather than rehash old ideas."

Consistent with the above and the overall discussion in this exposition, we propose the following specific normative measures:

1. One way to constrain AI within judicious boundaries is to impose its use strictly as a tool toward an end-product but never use its output directly as an end-product itself. That means that entire books written by AI impersonators, pieces of art of any form created by them should be banned.
2. Until the technology is mature enough to deliver polymathic outputs that are 100% reliable, with no factitious outputs otherwise known as artificial halluci-

nations, it shall not be put to use in any capacity in government settings (executive, parliament, justice) in order to preserve the rocks and pillars upon which society is built. Nor shall it be used in the makeup or amendment of any constitutional charter.

3. Its use should be banned in K-12 educational settings where knowledge is being imparted, both as the end product of educational activities or substitutes for human critical thinking in any capacity. In itself, it obliterates the necessary space for personal research which constructs and otherwise enriches the learning experience. The student who wishes to use it as a tool for topical research shall be allowed to, but any piece of student writing directly coming out of AI impersonators, or largely AI aided by the same in formulation, should be considered plagiarism and penalized.
4. In the Higher Education institutions, the use of genAI outputs in performance evaluation exercises of any class must be qualified as plagiarism. In the Academy, any use of generative Artificial Intelligence output in the scripting delivery of scientific research papers, exempt graphical data representation, or scholarly dissertations qualify outright as fraudulent. The use of generative AI as a tool to develop research toward those deliverables shall remain authorized.

   Likewise, the use of generative artificial intelligence output in the scripting of lecture material, exempt graphical data representation or illustrations, shall qualify as equally fraudulent.
5. In educational settings, generative AI delivery to users should never be accompanied with commercial advertisements or political propaganda, which are equivalent to manipulative brain washing in favor of particular ideas or products, and which undermine the formation and sustenance of critical thinking, core of the educational process.
6. The use of generative AI in news media publications should be absolutely banned and no line of text coming out of AI bots should ever be reproduced on newspaper pages. While journalists may use AI bots as a resource for investigative work, investigational outputs cannot be a compendium of statements produced by these bots, even when their outputs become 100% reliable.
7. In the Turkman business, where research is done for the purpose of evaluating a company's historical performance toward stock purchases, the writer shall produce plentiful of references to corroborate the data in order to authenticate the findings beyond the flat disclosures of the AI bot at work.
8. Language impersonators should be strictly produced and used to assist humans in performing knowledge tasks, but not to outright create knowledge products and/or intuition products as to the arts (creatives) on their own. Art is a prod-

uct of human experience and imagination, no human should consume artificial art, which is ontological alienation. Therefore, artistic production by language impersonators is to be considered pointless as to humans.

9. In the case where a human is unexpectedly performing poorly, an AI agent should not be used to outright replace the worker or professional but to train such a person in order to improve his or her performance or raise his or her level of expertise, as well as to possibly alleviate the burden of tasks in the task set that might be negatively impacting the worker's performance. In this case, clear steps should be taken to ensure that the worker maintain keen awareness that this assistance and guidance are coming from a conflagration of human experts and not from a lifeless inanimate machine. A requirement seeking to avoid a deteriorating or alienating impact on the worker's personal psychology.
10. GenAI impersonators must be each required to produce the exact same answer to questions formulated in the same terms or with the same meaning, except for updates in the state of the relevant knowledge over time. They should not be allowed to concomitantly produce different answers to the same question formulated by different people. This closes the door to manipulations for the purpose of infiltrating propaganda, product advertisement, etc., in the chatbot's outputs.
11. The name of the technology should be substituted for *language-based personification,* and that of the agents *language impersonators* in order to generically reflect more closely the nature of the technology and the agents. No one should claim sentience or the epithet of Real for a product whose name had been chosen to qualify it as Artificial. The conflation between human sentient intelligence and artificial simulated intelligence should be strictly forbidden at all orders of creation and dissemination. The direct psychological interaction between human sentience and artificial impersonators for the purpose of well-being, therapy and spiritual support should be strictly forbidden.
12. The subtending language model of any class of transformer must include a reference system allowing the user to willfully prompt the system as desired to trace back the original source of the information being provided, whether a part thereof or in total, in full unrestrained disclosure.
13. The technology must be constrained to fully comply with the licensing underlying any segment of the knowledge compiled in the human Knowledge Base. Full compliance to national copyright acts applies. Scripts covered by the CC-BY4.0 license in particular must be fully respected. Any statement made by the impersonator must relate to a licensing term or copyright identity that is disclosable to and verifiable by the user.

14. In applying the copyright law to generative AI agents or machines, it shall be acknowledged that training data is permanently kept inside the machine implements in one fractional form or another allowing for verbatim or exact restitution of originally published content in the the source, whether in text, still image or moving image format.
15. When applying the copyright law to generative AI agents or machines, it shall be acknowledged that the transformational nature of all outputs of the machine is a mixing of fractional internal data according to inherent criteria in the machine and user questing criteria but not a new creative combination of the data segments giving the output the value of a genuine autonomous new product. Notwithstanding the value or utility of the output, it shall not be taken for a legitimate creation or creative product in the sense that it would be eligible for and deserve own copyright protection, whatever its form or extent.
16. No copyright protection or patent or scholarly/expertise accreditation shall be granted to any direct form of output of generative artificial intelligence that can be verified as such, whether in its complete form or to a large extent or proportion of its finite presentation. The accreditation under any of the above denominations shall not be granted either to the machine or the owner or operator or user of the artificial intelligence artifact.
17. When transplanted into humanoid robots, genAI personification should be restricted to empower and optimize such hardware for the performance of one task or a well-defined set of tasks, witfully limited and streamlined in knowledge and savoir-faire scope.
18. There shall be no distinction in the identity of an AI impersonator whether it takes the form of live conversational text or itemized text being delivered on a graphic screen, a facsimile of a person or an anatomical part thereof on a video screen, a real person reading or repeating an output from AI language personification, or humanoid hardware. It must retain the attribute or qualifier of simulation.
19. In the gaming or recreation context, AI impersonators should be considered reducible to toys or adult toys. Since impersonation naturally responds to the intent purpose of self-detachment towards hilarity, as realized by toys, direct output of these agents, in principle, shall be left open to direct consumption, as an exception. Examples are chess automatons, “smart” hardware toys (Barbies), and the like. The function of these AI end products must be strictly limited to entertainment. Entertainment products out of artform creations such as theater or cinematography are not contemplated in this measure and remain a separate universe.
20. Any product with the ability to compile text according to a human-created language model and produce expert answers that only experts in a particular field

are currently judged to know or go beyond their expertise level must be considered to be a language impersonator. Such a product must be classified in the category of expert systems.

21. The judicial system must apply fair reparations to all parties identified as victims of the vast intellectual property looting perpetrated by the technology at inception, and other harms caused, before any consideration and application of legislative adjustment regulation to its utilization by the social corpus is contemplated and applied.
22. In areas where the application of the technology is found too risky for civil society, its use should be geared to proceed within the Military as part of its arsenal suite.
23. The direct creation of artificial or factitious internet user accounts and websites by genAI artifacts for the purpose of chatbots' human impersonations or any other shall be strictly prohibited.
24. All and any use of generative artificial intelligence that is contrary to the promotion of societal transparency across institutions and social groups, or amounts to malicious genie in any form of application, shall be strictly forbidden.
25. Where generative artificial intelligence may contribute to the establishment of societal participative decision-making, and provided no harm is or would be caused to any party, exempt substitution of representation or representatives, it shall be allowed. No artificial intelligent agent shall be used for representation or to substitute human representation, especially political representation.
26. Ideally, an artificial intelligence agent shall only produce outputs that are factual or true to facts. They shall all be certified to their degree of response accuracy with an explicit accuracy score in the certification. The FCC or foreign equivalent should be chosen to be the certifying agency by establishing clear benchmarks for their multimodal performances. The detailed testing elements of those benchmarks shall remain strictly in the purview of the official agency and shall not be publicized. Part of the testing protocols should be for the machine to satisfactorily demonstrate ignorance of the assessment procedures, given their polymathic nature.

Whilst there is true value in the artifact of emulation of human language in interchange format, which makes the result of inquiries seamlessly absorbable or assimilable by human beings, the above constraints represent a minimum set of corrective measures which must be applied to the core content and methods of the technology in order to prevent widespread damage to the global culture. Those measures should be reflected in one way or another in any piece of legislation aiming at judiciously regulating generative AI technology and industry, and in the public interest. It is always good for regulatory guardrails to be established for new arising landscapes in society to preserve overall social safety and integrity. However, as we well know, the politics of power never falter in shaping them. The above itemized items are thus also meant to provide a guideline in assessing the adequacy of pieces of legislation addressing development and utilization of generative artificial intelligence.

5.7. Conclusion

Up to everyone to take action as they see fit along the lines discussed above, at least as a starter, while pressing their lawmakers to react in the citizenry's best interests. All presidential executive orders are by nature temporary. Pushback against this technological trend is not a choice but a must and its integration in society requires regulatory codification by social consensus. As usual political players always have their eyes on whatever grants power and surely approach all and any innovation from the slant of furthering a political career or party consolidation and preeminence. It is clear that this technology gives the levers of political power unprecedented capacity for social control, which the citizenry must remain keenly aware of. The industry has its own logic and it would be naïve to expect a self-induced departure from forceful imposition. Given the stakes in terms of the unpaired broad societal impacts, this is indeed a time and a circumstance where individuals in the society at large must each keenly recognize their role as a social agent, beyond our individualities and particular interests, stop thinking of self as an island and instead keep eyes on the Ocean. Polymathic savoir-faire has indeed the vast dimensions of an Ocean.

Chapter 6

HUMAN ASCENT TO THE STARS: FROM SCIENTIFIC KNOWLEDGE TO CONSCIOUSNESS TO WISDOM

In all human cultures and under all latitudes, arguably the expectation of every man is not and has never been that better will come to pass as a matter of course but instead that worse is a more likely outcome as a matter of future course. Even though positivists in modernism have attempted to settle a better climate for auspicious expectations in human experience, the human condition remains embroiled in a climate of adversity that makes the state of Happiness no more than a dream always to be deferred. Could it be that the role of Men in nature is not to curb and harness or exploit Nature but to become harmonious with Nature as a part of her and to become concordant with her Evolution, having identified our role in that Evolution? If this is a possible and viable new form of Humanism, how do we frame the educational establishment in order for Knowledge to permeate Consciousness and for Higher Consciousness to mature into Wisdom as a path toward materializing this new satisfying form of Humanism? I attempt to summarily uncover a vision of education and development of Scientific Knowledge with the potential to materialize this new form of Humanism.

6.1. Road to Emancipation

In the matter of progress in the human experience, the agency of knowledge had long been identified to be a key contributor to success. This secular view of progress has been countered as well by the view that the agency of wisdom lies at a far superior level in the march for progress in human evolution. We believe that there is a line from fundamental Knowledge to Higher Consciousness to Greater Wisdom that can successfully mediate progress in the human experience and finally deliver the long-sought Ascent of Men. In the following, we are going to summarily prospect the meaning and implications of this vision along with a few achievement benchmarks for its realization.

6.2. Foundational Matters of Life as Prime Subjects of Education

Academic Centers of Learning are indispensable in all cultures. Nowadays, however, in Western culture the Higher Ed Schools' financial interests and appetite for prestige seem to overshadow humanistic concerns. Whether public or private, they seem to be compulsively focused on endowments, and the business financials.

6.2.1. Why Underpaying Teachers?

Given the tremendous impact that teachers demonstrably exert over formation of human character at all stages of the education ladder, one would think that educational institutions would keep them in special regards. Sadly, at the higher Ed level, the concern of keeping professors' compensation low enough in favor of ever more palatable profits or retainers for institutions seems everywhere rampant and would testify that even the knowledge imparted by these institutions remains to them a second-order concern. That such knowledge workers as graduate student researchers and professors have to engage in street protests for fair pay is an outcry. A display of intractability and apparent counterpurpose this kind by these institutions authorize the allegation that perhaps the true nature of academic endowments is, aside from influence, a disguised investment of the donors in guaranteed students' tuition loans, the objective being the returns on the latter. They should not fuel give basis to such a cynicism.

6.2.2. Imperative Objective of Teaching Life

Instead of a profession and just a profession, shouldn't the schools be primarily teaching Life, shouldn't they all be primarily engaged in the business of Humanism? We advocate that Humanism ought to be the primary mission of the entire educational program, and its last learning stretch set to be a specialization in a particular aspect of Humanism, which should be experienced as a profession of any class. The schools instead commonly focus on knowledge and craft, and camouflage the deep matters of Man and Life, Spirit and Ethics. How much of Life do we know in our civilization? Little to nil, to be frank, every human being in mainstream culture on this planet, learned or layman, remaining as ignorant of the meaning of his or her own life as the next one. Destiny to every man continues to be an unknown, and so many say they are in search of the meaning of Life.

6.2.3. Fauna Kingdom Seems to Know Something Secret About Life

Life should arguably be central to the human endeavor, in knowledge and savoir-faire. Our rather scarce knowledge of Life leads us to believe that the animal kingdom is of lesser significance than Human in the biosphere and grant them little intelligence and import if any. However, when one takes the time to look at and ponder about the Great

Annual Migrations in the land of Africa Mater, when Animals of many different species join together in a year-long peaceful procession, and in light of the behavior patterns in display, you have to conclude this is more than migration in search of fresh water; it is a mystery that even takes a magical or religious tone, as many do feel. Would those of this kingdom know something about Life that we humans don't? What do the marine lora turtles, who invade the Costa Rican village of Ostional virtually every month, completely unafraid and unembarrassed to deposit their eggs in droves on this Pacific shore, on the streets of the small town and even in residents' home quarters, know about Life? Something that we likely do not.

Wikimedia

What do the Galapagos turtles, who traverse centuries of life on these Ecuadorian islands, know about origin and course of Life? Something that Charles Darwin, who studied them and died before them, probably did not ascertain and it is certainly not natural selection or struggle for life.

The business of Life stands for the core object of study that all Schools should be invested in through the Academic Humanities as their preeminent mission. Matters of Life are and will forever remain the common trunk that grounds every man, every nation and every civilization. Because every individual life partakes of the Supreme Teleology of Life, coded in scripture as the Tree of Life, it is only through the stream of rediscovery of that Source that a man and a woman will find meaning of self, and understand his or her own ontological evolution in terms of individual connection to and role within the evolution of the Primordial Source.

6.2.4. Social Consequences of Schools' Elitism

The noted teleological thirst is the bedrock of human conscience and consciousness, present in all from sage to infringers. The course taken by our civilization, in particular the orientation given to the practice of knowledge in our learning Centers, has contributed not to fill up that void but to further alienate the sprout of higher consciousness in every human individual. What we see occurring in the World today must be seen as the ultimate consequences of this estrangement to the paramount business of Life which our Schools have infused in collective conscience and to our way of life. We witness accentuated diminution in individuals' scope of social consciousness, widespread despair that stirs vast segments of the global population into drug addiction and suicide (not just blue-collar workers in the West), growing despise for the Ivy League Schools in North America which promote elitism tinted with de-humanism and appetite for unbridled financial gains. These trends have all but unequivocally resulted in the desire on the part of the disenfranchised to blanket dismantle social institutions by pointedly electing to public office overtly uncivil and destructive leaders. Does it not take a high dose of disheartenment for medical doctors, whose mission is the care and cure of the sick, to knowingly contribute to an overwhelming opioid crisis in the States by disproportionately prescribing these knowingly addictive and destructive pain killers, for own financial rewards, and in connivance with the pharmaceutical industry? That is all well publicized and documented.

6.2.5. Silos of Expertise that Create Sectarianism

Matters of Root Source of Life in its transcendental dimension is arguably the beginning of all knowledge. A divorce from those concerns makes everything conceivable of little utility, since everyone will agree that a segregated limb from the body is useless to the body. What good is a severed arm or a dispatched leg to a living person? Concordantly, all knowledge passes for disparate or fractured knowledge if severed or estranged from the Original Spring. The exclusive knowledge of matter that produces but technological artifacts, no matter how refined or sensational, is a dangerous path that will lead to destruction and self-destruction in one way or another, because it will always be incomplete, blind, misled and disharmonious with the Root Source. Barring the notable Harvard University to a certain extent, our Centers of Learning advocate the parcellation of knowledge in order to create silos of expertise and experts to their own benefits and the perpetuation of entitlements as well as a sanctimonious class. This educational regime is vestigial to the royal class of yesteryears who held power and bestowed titles for the protraction of autocracy. Royal history in our civilization, at all epochs, is with few exceptions, if any, a history of Machiavellian endeavors to undermine the Higher Spirit, in display in all free spirits, and the higher ethical order which produces universal conscience of the Good.

6.2.6. Vestigial Royal Practice that Corrupts the Institution of Education

This nefarious legacy has been passed on today's Learning Centers which were initiated under royal custody. It is widely and sadly reflected in their institutional cultures, in particular in the academy of physical sciences, where it takes the form of blind and staunch competition, group influence mongering, character destruction, blind and insidious attacks to the novel… It is by no means an accident that Sir Isaac Newton, physics pioneer and a "giant", went to such unethical lengths to credit himself for the invention of differential calculus, in opposition to rival Gottfried W. Leibniz, that he constituted a trial court to settle the matter where he shamelessly stood for judge and party at the same time, and settled the matter of course in his own favor. So nefarious were his means and character that he did not hide at Leibniz's passing his great "pleasure to have crushed Leibniz's heart" in his own expressed words. Ludwig Boltzmann, whom Academia posthumously reveres for his robust contributions in the knowledge of statistical physics, was controversially brought to suicide by his peers. The case list is too long to recount.

6.2.7. How Helpful is Secularism?

The fragmentation of knowledge and its segregation from the Foundational Matters of Life, otherwise proudly denoted scientific knowledge, undertaken under the express cover of secularism, as discussed in Chapter 1, represent a divorce with fundamental wisdom. In my view, enlightenment is not a victory over God or Higher Conscience, but a victory over his or her human priests who successfully took to obscure the path to the Light to the common man, and in so doing blocked the development of the spirit of Higher Conscience. Their legacy equally carries on. How much life and transcendence are there in our fashionable but purposely addictive smartphones? If a smartphone is an evolution in the human condition, what of life does it contribute to expand, how much of grander consciousness does an individual achieve in the expressly inflicted addiction of its incessant usage? If there is any evolution of appreciable utility in the creation of the Global Communication Network Infrastructure, it will be to break the barriers to knowledge and the silos of expertise, well maintained and developed by the Learning Centers, which will thankfully allow the common man, so empowered, to engage on his own the path of inquest and resolution of transcendental Matters of Life.

Matters of God are not etherish in all dimensions as secularism would have us all believe. The question of representation of God and the protocols of interaction with God are admittedly of the strictly religious order. However, the question of tangible manifestations of God is incontestable because there are many globe-wide, they belong to the realm of the measurable and the observable, in the same empirical measure of the scientific standard, and which secularism can only pretend to ignore out of utter cynicism, as formerly noted. Even though those artifacts surpass current human comprehension, one ought to mainly take them as reminders of the active presence of God, but not mysteries inflicted upon us, because the Primordial Source must also be the cradle of intellection. At the end, the question is not whether we believe in God or not, it is rather whether and when we are willing to see for ourselves one of the many faces of God, or a sprout of the Most-High Consciousness.

Saint Louise de Marillac

6.3. Academic Liberalism and its Sociopolitical Problems

When we attempt to put all of the above in one word, the one that glaringly comes to mind is Elitism. Elitism is the cult of knowledge without humanism, and verging into arrogance, despite the claims of imparting and teaching humanism. These problems in Western Academia have been in the making for a very long time and have only lately (or as of this writing) exploded.

American Academia has only itself to blame for the quite obvious resentment that has been building up among the disfavored and disenfranchised in America against higher education and its leaders and supporters. The Academy had rendered them invisible by promoting a sociology that does not acknowledge their existence as the social class of the poor, but an artificial social stratification with two strata: the wealthy and the middle class. This stream only incidentally connected with Heritage in the personification of descendants of those who lost the civil war over the societal model of bondage, and which lived since then in the resentment of unification by federalization. There is clearly wrong doing, from a sociologist's viewpoint, in the qualifier of middle class for a proposed social model that lacks a bottom tier, which is necessary to justify the very nomer of 'middle class'. The definition by Academia to be or become middle class literally became the collegial stamp of going to college and acquiring an academic degree, as a sine qua non requisite. It appears that the Academy in the US had even managed to have the federal government enforce the requisite of a college degree for employment.

The liberal John Edwards, running mate of John Kerry, raised a timely warning to the liberal political class of this grave mistake by turning his attention to the well-in-existence American social class of the poor. Unfortunately, his political carrier was short-lived, perhaps for the very same reason or due to opposition by mainstream liberalism. At the same time, a class of conservative politicians surfaced in open opposition to Higher Education and its institutions, notable among them congressman Rick Santorum, who praised himself of not having gone to college, together with a defiant T-Party conservative faction. This problem further turned into a blast during Hillary Clinton's presidential campaign when she referred to this vast constituency as the infamous 'deplorables'. That may have been a key marker in her loss to her opponent Donald J Trump. To corroborate this line of analysis, what subsequently unfolded during that Donald J Trump's first administration was an ostensible and almost incomprehensible total rejection of Science, even government scientific institutions and their prescriptions, well demonstrated in the White House entire handling of the Covid-19 pandemic.

So, the question to reckon with for Liberals in America, everywhere including Education, after the presidential election loss of Democrat Kamala Harris and in view of the present Administration's cabinet composition, is the following multiple fold question:

What have you done to:

1.- Cause rural and poor urban America to hate so much Higher Educational institutions that they want people with no credentials at all to run Washington?

2.- Cause so much disrespect of norms in civil America that she chose to elect for President a convicted felon on 34 counts, and twice impeached as former president, against the spirit of all the prescriptions in the Constitution?

3.- Piss off so much the naturally liberal constituency of labor that they no longer want to endorse you or liberal economics and prefer to be in bed with the Lions?

4.- To spark the incomprehensible compulsion to eradicate the federal Department of Education of a country and dismantle the entire scholarly establishment?

5.- To cause the rural and urban poor to stubbornly deny the existence of glaring changes in the global climate system even impacting their own livelihoods or petulantly ignore them at their own sorry expense?

As an aside, it may very well be that the remarkable high-caliber speeches at the Harris's Democratic convention, and again Pres. Joe Biden's unexpected slur for the white uneducated and disenfranchised of America in final days of campaign, may have significantly contributed to the 2024 election loss. Perhaps the epithet of 'idiot' slammed on K. Harris, obviously a well-rounded professional with a state person track record at highest level, by her political adversaries may be a corroborative point.

Academic elitism, and its perception of enablers of poverty and disproportionate enrichment in different capacities and instances, indubitably stand for this persistent and severe malaise in American society, which now takes the colors of a grave danger. What the public can further see and knows is that the two most influential figures in the oncome of the information era that has radically changed the ways of life on this planet, Bill Gates and Steve Jobs, have not only avoided or resisted the experience of a college education but in so doing were able to achieve that unprecedented level of transformation, and did very well for themselves as *self-made men* in amassing wealth as well.

Lastly, we have the example of the notable reconstruction of the Notre Dame cathedral in Paris. It seemed an impossible when Pres. Emmanuel Macron laid plans to rebuild the completely burned landmark church in five short years. What has happened instead is an incredible and historic reconstruction of the cathedral in that record time by the ARTISANS of France, who have generationally survived with their crafts and skills. Modern college graduates altogether lack the skills required for such a feat.

French adage: *Pas de sot metier, mais seulement de sottes gens*[22]. Should Academia be willing to engage in any soul searching in this occasion, there would be a lot of wisdom to reflect on and take from this old French adage.

6.4. The Enterprise of Axiomatization of Science

Per his "Sixth Problem" to be resolved in mathematics, David Hilbert, inarguably the most influential 20thcentury mathematician, nurtured the ambition *"to develop all physical constants to mathematical constants"* and *"to make science similar to geometry from physics science,"* as he put it. He famously exposed those views at the II International Congress of Mathematicians in the section of the report entitled **"Mathematical Treatment of the Axioms of Physics"**, year 1900 at Paris. Here is one ambitious mathematician, one might think! History of the last 100 years has well demonstrated the importance of the physical sciences in the fashioning and viability of human culture with the devastating technological warfare means put repeatedly at work in that period. The increasing mastery of the physics of matter is always momentous to the furthering of all civilizations.

6.4.1. Reversal of Geometry into Mathematics from Physics

Many today are unaware that geometry was formerly a part of physical science, with plenty of experimental methods and tools. All the wonders of the ancient world, from the pharaohs' temples to the Tower of Pizza to the Taj Mahal were productions of the experimental science of geometry. It is under the impulse of late 19th century mathematicians that geometry was axiomatized and incorporated into mathematics. So was probability or statistical theory, aka the "theory of chances", which at its beginning was physical science in nature. It was under the impulse of the same mathematicians that Statistical Theory became a part of mathematics. David Hilbert elaborates: *"The investigations on the foundations of geometry suggest the problem: To treat in the same manner, by means of axioms, those physical sciences in which already today mathematics plays an important part; in the first rank are the theory of probabilities and mechanics."* Using Measure

[22] Translation: No stupid profession, only stupid people.

Theory for support, Statistical Theory was put in the 1930's on an axiomatic basis by Andrey Kolmogorov.

6.4.2. Challenges of Axiomatization of Physics

Mechanical physics has proven to be however a tougher bone to grumble, despite the advances in abstract Hilbert spaces widely used to afford axiomatic grounds to Quantum Mechanics. A. Einstein was staunchly against the proliferation of abstract mathematical spaces in physics because they obscure the intelligibility of quantum systems, he argued. It seems that the accumulation of unsolved problems in physics since mid-20th century had obliterated all further interest in the notion of axiomatization of physics. Ever since D. Hilbert had proposed the idea, there had been no advancement whatsoever made on that account. Meanwhile the accumulation of unsolvable questions in theoretical physics has taken an increasing slope, to the point that physicists have adopted a special nomenclature for them, evidenced in the terms "the cosmological constant problem", "the hierarchy problem", etc., *(see Appendix).* One of the most important problems in the task of achieving axiomatic grounds for physics is that of uncovering the origin of the fundamental physical constants and the role they play in the development of primordial symmetries in nature. The unraveling of the mystery of the fundamental physical constants has been stated by the best minds in physics, across generations, to be of paramount significance in physical science.

6.4.3. Impending Fusion of Physics with Mathematics

For all their open enamoring with mathematics however, most physicists may not realize that the ultimate fate of physics is fusion with mathematics, not to say being overtaken by mathematics. This heightened enamor with mathematics has led to a whole new strain in fundamental physics by which physicists develop entire suites of mathematical constructs only guided by a thin streak of physical inspiration as we have seen with String theories. At the end of this exercise, today well scolded by the results at the LHC since 2017 in regards to supersymmetry, advocate physicists must realize that there is no substitute for correct visualization of natural dynamic systems and that known mathematics, albeit important and even indispensable, is no guarantee for proper vision, despite all its rigor and logical coherence. The problem of finding the theoretical directives by which to undertake a mathematical program of axiomatization of physics is the same as the problem of finding the first principles from which to theoretically derive the fundamental symmetries of nature rooted on the known fundamental physical invariants (aka the dimensionless and dimensional fundamental physical constants). Both currents aim at the exact same target in a mathematical-physics rendezvous. As I have concluded in one paper: "It is not possible to overcome [the long running] crisis in fundamental physics without uncovering the origin of the primordial symmetries in nature and how they develop the fundamental physical constants as pillars of the entire physical world."

6.4.4. Why the Assimilation of Dimensional Physical Constants to Mathematical Constants is a Coherent Problem

The afore-mentioned mathematical-physics enterprise, long overdue in physics, is the only one that can provision the ardently needed new framework. It is my hope that the Quanto-Geometric Theory of my inception is in effect providing this new window on the horizon by delivering the long-awaited theoretical derivation of a host of fundamental physical constants. The first objection raised by many physicists when considering the question of abstract mathematical derivation of physical constants within the task of axiomatization of physics and science in general, i.e. the Gravitational constant G, the Planck constant h and the speed of light c, is that many of the foremost fundamental physical constants are dimensional and that unit-dimensions in physical science are accidental and conventional. The latter would presumably make the constants intractable to theoretical derivation. What this criticism firstly ignores is that the body of mathematical abstractions are extracted from physical reality, since we would plausibly not invent the abstraction of a circle if we had not indeed seen an object with that form in nature, like the moon or the sun, no more than we would invent numbers if the multiplicity of physical elements was not all around us to observe. Therefore, even though we have the ability to construct or infer higher levels of abstraction much beyond direct observation, all mathematics is essentially mathematical-physics. In the absolute, there is no disconnect between mathematics and physics. That is why the pure numeric and geometric science that mathematics represent can yield quantities that precurse the fundamental quantities upon which Nature has built its symmetries. Those precursors, as shown in the Quanto-Geometric Theory axiomatic program, come in the form of figurate matches to the known fundamental numbers, whether they are dimensional or dimension-less. That is how these numeric precursors come to overwhelm the known quantities and transpire through the dimensional elements of our physics and our physical quantities, no matter how arbitrary and conventional the latter were. So therefore, if any axiomatic program for the referred task is correct, it will cast both dimensionless and dimensional numbers through the same derivational methodology.

6.5. To Discover the Symmetry Roots of Life and Matter

Just as none of the individual genes of the human genome belongs, whether in part or in full, to pharmaceutical companies, nature and its physics do not belong to any one physicist of the day or past time. Physics is not a science of impersonal nature, as Academia has it, only addressing matter that is out there, and of which only physicists with an entitlement seem to be authorized to speak. It has been indeed a travesty of long that academics related to physics have projected its content as a foreign entity to human self, a cleavage that apparently arose from the segregation of physics from Natural Philosophy and with the rise of secularism alike.

6.5.1. Physics as a Science of the Human Self and not Just Nature

Fundamental physics is truly a science of the human self, to the exact same extent of medicine in all of its disciplines altogether. Particle physics is not about the quarks, and neutrons, and protons and electrons out there; it is about *my* neutrons or *your* neutrons, *my* electrons or *your* electrons, *my* protons or *your* protons, shall we resoundingly claim. Condensed matter physics is not about the atoms and the inorganic molecules that vastly populate the natural world out there. Condensed matter physics is about *my* atoms and *your* atoms, *my* inorganic molecules and *your* inorganic molecules, *my* crystals and your crystals, all of which vastly populate the world of *my* body and *your* body! Classical physics is as much about the motion of *my* body and *yours*, their interactions with other objects in gravity, etc. As strange as these notions may sound, since the Academy does not commonly expose or treat these matters on intimate personal or individual tracks, it is important that they subsume every human individual's sphere of consciousness or self-awareness. The scope of self-awareness is in every human individual understandably limited to what falls under immediate observation, which are the physiognomic and physiological parts of our human bodies. We understand ourselves to be our moving legs, our swinging arms, our expressive faces, our beating hearts, our cyclically inhaling lungs and other bodily parts, which stands for a biological level of perception of our-selves. The scales of matter that lie below the Karyote Shell of matter encompassing biological topologies, we do not perceive in our bodies. It requires exercise of intellection at the societal level through intelligentsia to become aware of the unobservable Shells of Matter that lie below the biological spread of our bodies, which I enumerated above. We understand that if our heart stops beating, we will summarily die. But we do not contemplate that if the topology of atoms or molecules that make up our hearts suffer some kind of disruption we may even die quicker or more traumatically, except perhaps for the few survivors of the Hiroshima and Nagasaki nuclear devastation! Or perhaps those who have been poisoned by exposure to or ingestion of radioactive materials as well.

6.5.2. How to Perceive the Realm of the Inanimate Within Self

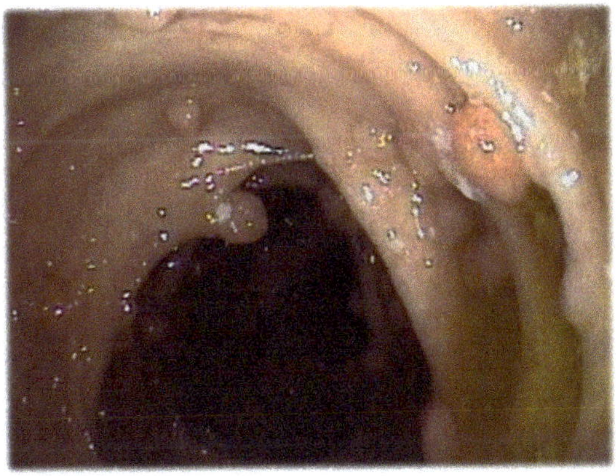

One of the biggest problems of fundamental physics I have identified to be its manifest inability to uncover the symmetries conforming those Shells of matter below karyotic topologies or the Karyote Shell. Even activities occurring at the Karyotic scale within our bodies, such as the sound of our heartbeat, the sound of blood flowing through our veins and arteries, the sound of our lungs breathing, etc., which are important ontological artifacts, we ignore what they are like. Therefore, consciousness or self-awareness of the common man remains severely truncated and limited in scope. In these conditions, consciousness remains to most individuals a point-like notion of his or her existence, quite parted from the notion of the vast worlds and universes existent in our human bodies that should actively inhabit human self-awareness.

Had a man been instructed in the practice of listening to his heartbeat, he might know that it sounds like an earthquake or a volcano in eruption. Had a man been instructed in the practice of listening to the breathing of his lungs, he might know that it sounds like a tornado. Had a man been instructed in the practice of listening to the blood flow in his arteries and veins, he might know that it sounds like a flowing river. Had a man been instructed in the practice of seeing the topological landscape of his bowels and colon, as shown above, he would know that they are similar to the caverns of our mother Planet. If our science had understood the mapping of these fundamental symmetries between the Karyotic world of our bodies and the Astral world of our inhabitation, let alone the identities and primary symmetries between the elements of the Karyotic Shell of matter in our bodies and those same elements in the large context of other Shells of existence, then our civilization would have a very different experience with Nature. That exercise would ultimately bring the awareness that we are not creatures that exist above Nature and whose mission is to subdue Nature, but that we are indeed Nature or a simple part of Her.

6.5.3. Ignorance of the Shelling Hierarchy in Human Ontology is Universal

The ignorance of the fundamental symmetries profiling the Shelling of mother Nature and their implications, which are central to the Fundamental Questions of Life, is common to both the Ivy-league-school educated individual and the rough rural minds that he or she knowingly may despise. In a word, the inability to mentally experience our body beyond its histological structures, and deep into the molecular, atomic and particle shells on which it is built, strongly contributes to our point-like form of self-consciousness, shared by all as the most important trait and the universal descriptor of human endeavor in the current stage of our civilization. The road ahead is that of amplification of the scope of self-awareness, by which a larger recognition of identities and physical symmetries of Nature with regards to human ontology, will obliterate all forms of intolerance and pursue multiplicity and diversity as the axis to the Ascent of Man. Yet we will still be quite far away from Transcendentalization as 'Quanto- Geometrically' understood. We argue that all sensible Humanism must be built on the recognition and most ample understanding that the Primitives subtending the organization and dynamics of the Cosmos equally represent the purveyors of the directives instantiating Fundamental Karyotic organization and the symmetries grounding the Karyote Shell of Matter.

6.5.4. A Different Approach to the Notion of the Cosmos

Awareness of the above pre-supposes the understanding that the Cosmos is everything that lies beyond and below the Karyote Shell. Acceptation of this Humanistic perspective overall can only occur under an amplification of the scope of self-awareness by allowing knowledge to extensively permeate consciousness. It is not possible for the blooming of universal consciousness to take place within the present boundaries of contemporary civilization, mainly developed along the lines of point-like or unary scope of individual self-consciousness. The full realization of this connection puts the question of the Foundations of Life under a Cosmic light and reveals that the Cosmic axis is first-order Human Ancestry. It will require a profound revolution in the body of Knowledge we call science, or the human Knowledge Base, to orchestrate this understanding at individual and societal level along with the savoir-faire that such level of consciousness implicates. So, who is a physicist? Every man will be. And what is the future of AI Expert Systems? You've just had a glimpse at it.

6.6. Life is Matter and Matter is Life

Human kind has always been fascinated by the Cosmos, always searched for meaning to own existence amidst the immensity of the Cosmos, and a possible role within the ontology and evolution of the Cosmos alike. These questions remain as whole today as they were in millennia past when all a man could do was to hunt for food and take shelter in a cavern. As astrophysicist Neil D. G. Tyson has put it: *"We are all connected to one another biologically, to planet Earth chemically and to the Cosmos atomically."* This is however only an approximation to actual phenomenology. The more encompassing view remains the serial Shelling of all categories of elemental topologies that make up the scalar-space deployment of the 3-D Universe. Manifestly, Humans, or the span of their topological singlets, participate in the entire so-called biosphere, which altogether represents one Shell of the onion ball that heuristically composes the 3-D Universe. Every one topological element of a Shell consists of sub-scales of elements that pertain to prior Shells in embedding order. We understand the suite of Elemental Shells that compose the 3-D Universe as follows:

1. Shell of Gluon-Quarks (sub-particles)
2. Shell of Particles
3. Shell of Atoms
4. Shell of Molecules
5. Shell of Lattices or Materials
6. Shell of Karyotes
7. Shell of Celestial Singlets (planets, moons, asteroids, etc.)
8. Solar Shell (Star Systems)
9. Shell of Galaxies and their Groups

This view, which is not a simple suite but a normalized distribution (Fig.3.1), is the only one capable of uncovering the origin of the fundamental physical constants, long sought, as we have realized within the Quanto-Geometric Theory. The constants of Nature are indeed the invariants that sustain the transformations developed by the Elemental Topologies making up each Shell. It follows from that view that all Shells of the Cosmos obey one Primordial Physical Law which informs the specific Law of Conservation dictating the development of each individual Shell (Fig.4.1).

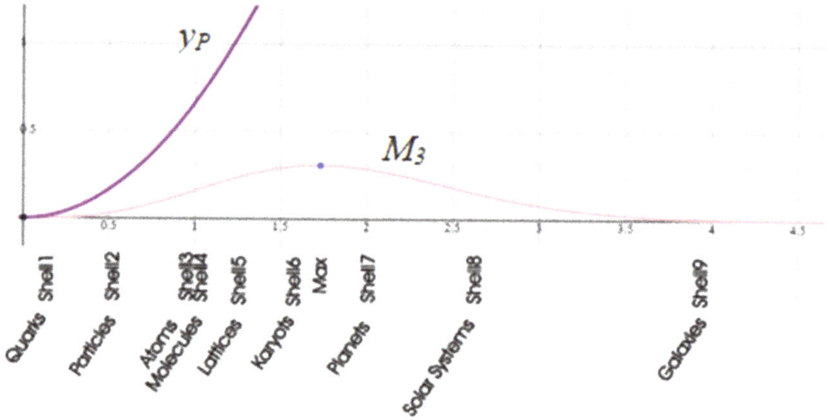

Fig. 4.1 A view of the evolving suite of Shells of 3-D matter. Units in σ.

This framework naturally gives rise to the important concept of a Physical Life Constant, which is the fundamental physical constant sustaining the Karyote Shell of Matter (see Quanto-Geometry, Vol III, for its derivation). On that account, one is fully justified in certifying that what our civilization calls "Life" falls under the same purview or determinants of what it has designated "Matter" under the Cartesian or Comtian perspective, which are the topologies beyond the two boundaries of the Karyote Shell.

In other words, the Cosmic axis line pivoting its topological Shelling obligates us to the unifying realization that Life is Matter and that conversely all Matter is Life. Cosmologist Carl E. Sagan, who made it his life mission to successfully put the Cosmos in the hearts of millions, had an inspired line that reflects in some measure the above understanding and an uncommon sense of the pulse of the Cosmos: *"The cosmos is within us. We are made of star-stuff. We are a way for the universe to know itself."* To properly translate this vision and expose the horizon it opens up to is to state that human intelligence and his entire ontological experience is only part of Cosmic Teleology. It is utterly important that the deep knowledge of the fundamental symmetries of the Cosmos permeate conscience and consciousness of our Civilization. There will not be a Space Era for mankind, beyond the many bug hops that we have made into space thus far, satisfying and encouraging though they might be, until mastery of those realms of Knowledge along with subsequent Maturity of Higher Consciousness take place, as a condition and guarantee that our Civilization can partake of Universal Harmony and Peace of the Cosmos.

6.7. A Brave New World Beyond Scientific Specialization

It is well worth re-examining David Hilbert's notion of transformation of science in the terms expressed in his Sixth action item at the II International Congress of Mathematicians in 1900 at Paris, which at first glance may be difficult to fully grasp. He proposed to "make science similar to geometry from physics science", in his own words. We understand that around that period was geometry, hitherto a physical science, inducted into mathematics through axiomatization, namely the long string of theorems and logical methods afforded to the new mathematical science of geometry. So therefore, from its status of physical science enjoying plenty of experimental tools of construction, geometry became a chapter of mathematical knowledge. What is further incredibly ambitious in D. Hilbert's statement is his vision to make all of science, or all of experimental science to be exact, undergo the same treatment as geometry insofar as induction into mathematical knowledge through axiomatization. Within the scope of D. Hilbert's vision, eventually all of science will be expressed in mathematical language, surely because, in addition to the other reasons previously argued, mathematics represents the most irreducible form of rigor and precision in the expression of knowledge. It is clear that such an objective stands for a broad attempt at unifying all of science as well, because axiomatization is in itself a cohesive language or one only language. Given the deep and broad segmentation of knowledge that academia has pursued and de facto realized since early 20thcentury, one may wonder if D. Hilbert's claim, on which no scientist or mathematician has knowingly ever fruitfully worked if at all, was simply forgotten, or perhaps deemed too ambitious to be feasible, or simply fell at cross purpose with the institutional and financial objectives of academia.

6.7.1. Grand Unification of All of Scientific Knowledge is a Pressing and Reachable Goal

One prominent scientist has put the spotlight on the fundamental problem of lack of unified embrace or grand unification in scientific Knowledge, to be distinguished from affine taxonomy, in a rare display of profound lucidity and brilliance. The luminary physicist Richard Feynman put it well and square when he wrote: *"In this age of specialization men who thoroughly know one field are often incompetent to discuss another. The great problems of the relations between one and another aspect of human activity have for this reason been discussed less and less in public... The old problems, such as the relation of science and religion, are still with us, and I believe present as difficult dilemmas as ever, but they are not often publicly discussed because of the limitations of specialization."* The segregation of knowledge in silos of expertise or specialization is ostensibly counter-productive to the very purpose of amplification and augmentation of scientific knowledge because the universe that lays before us, from its finest parts to its largest cosmic spreads, is entirely unified and cannot be thoroughly and adequately understood without this all-encompassing unifying vantage.

There is indeed a deep lack of knowledge in the very fact of fragmentation of knowledge, which is a dangerous road to trek, because, among other caveats, the manipulation of parts, otherwise called technology, without an understanding of higher inherent function or teleology, amounts to blindness that may at worst lead to self-destruction, for one. That is for sure eerily reflected in the current AI developments, and the serious threats it poses, which have currently put everyone aware on edge. The big picture for us is the Roots of Life as they relate to all metrics, the composition of Life in all metrics, and the cartography of human evolution, both individually and collectively, within the evolution of the Cosmos. Specialization, as R. Feynman explains, is an obstacle to the realization of the true scientific dimension in civilization of Man, and an impediment to the true realization of Man in all dimensions, both humanistic and technological.

6.7.2. An Old Warning that Came to Pass

Carl E. Sagan, a multi-faceted stellar scientist, had further warned of the dangers of the segmentation approach when he expressed: *"We've arranged a society based on science and technology, in which nobody understands anything about science and technology. And this combustible mixture of ignorance and power, sooner or later, is going to blow up in our faces."* In that PBS interview with then famed journalist Charlie Rose, by "nobody" Carl E. Sagan was referring to the larger public along with the political class and the forces of money in general, but not to scientists themselves. However, one has to take one step further and intently include the cast of Knowledge workers in this bunch, in light of the modalities in which his prediction recently came to full realization, in what we now know as the Great Global Recession. Effectively, it is in concert that the forces of money, which traditionally live in the ignorance of scientific processes for the most part, and a silo of expert mathematicians with incomplete knowledge of the transcendent Fundamentals of statistical distributions, thus far unknown in mainstream science, have set grounds for a global economic debacle. They further threatened in its aftermath to break the global culture through increasing inequality and individual alienation.

6.7.3. An Equity Lesson that Has Not But Must Be Learned

As the Big Recession subsided, the rush with which these actors have all gone back to their addictive habits of money first and power for self, and their unabated pressing for technological development only for profitable human labor substitution and money gains, in total disregard of matters of life, is a testament to a lesson that has not been learned and remains difficult to learn. Their blindness to the human condition incorrigibly persists, let alone the bigger picture of Life, as much as grander vantage in the endeavor of scientific knowledge. Would it not be great if they could practice the words of wisdom that we commonly hear from some of them only at the eleventh hour on their death beds? How many times can we shoot ourselves in our own feet and still hold two feet to stand on? Only the addiction of blind free gains for self can still bring the thoughts of possible prosthetics…

In our sense, the call for an all-encompassing and unifying approach to Knowledge can only be realized through two major factors at the very least:

- Mathematical axiomatization of science in its entirety, as we have already claimed, through the philosophy of knowledge set forth by David Hilbert, along with deep reforms in the formulation of mathematics in order to make it both accessible and enjoyable to all as a matter of a mandate.
- A conceptual cultural revolution based on the visualization of coordinate space vacuum as active void in its tapestry and totalitarian in spread, from the Einsteinian tradition of tensorial representation of coordinate space vacuum. Effectively it is only through the vision of active vacuum spread throughout all Shells of the Cosmos, along with its totalitarian expansion and role in the formation of all dynamics systems, that a unifying view of the Cosmos and a single unified platform of scientific Knowledge may be achieved. The utmost dimension of this platform subsumes everything that pertains to Human cognitive, contemplative and projective experience, and represents not a choice but the only road to trek toward overture of higher human consciousness and the final Ascent of Men in and onto the Majesty of the Cosmos. In light of the long list of intractable problems in science today, per transcript in the Appendix, this dimension of Knowledge is certainly not represented in the Knowledge Base featured in the AI technology that currently has everyone on edge.

6.8. Transcendent Knowledge and Wisdom as the Final Frontier

This is a make-or-break stage in the course of human civilization. Some have seen in the sweeping development of Artificial Intelligence, which is nothing but Artificial Omniscience, the crossing of a significant frontier. In fact, it is only significant because of the spectrum of dangers its presents to human life and human civilization. Only in that, is it a make-or-break stage for mankind. Intelligence or Omniscient intelligence is not for us to simulate, just as space exploration is not for us to reach via automated agents. The experience of being there in the space medium is what is transcendent because such a presence is ontological agency. The experience by human beings of Omniscience or augmented knowledge and intelligence is what is transcendent. Stuffing knowledge in lifeless mannequins will never be more than another way around mechano-control functions to extend our tool set when it comes to manipulating the world and the environment, just as a calculator or a computer has always been. Emulated intelligence will never be a substitute for human intelligence as an ontological experience.

6.8.1. Place of Intelligence in Human Ontology

At this stage, we, in fact, still do not understand the real tenets of human intelligence, important and helpful though the syllogistic rules of Aristotelian logic may come to be. The predicates in our current understanding of intelligence do not conform to the predicates of other bodies of knowledge reviewed in Chapter 1. What they more of less contend is that the phenomenon of mentation, to which we tribute the faculty of intelligence, does not belong to the biological brain, but pertain to another ontological double in a meta-physical dimension beyond 3D reality. In particular, Eastern mysticism offer very specific models of human ontology corroborated in part by observable phenomena in the Catholic church as to its faculties, and which should be object of consideration by a pragmatic scientific approach to the question willing to rid secularism.

This multi-prong approach to the problem, involving all related knowledge from their diverse sources, is what is going help make progress in this chapter of biophysics, which should include the application of both Number Theory and Abstract Group Theory in mathematics. What first percolates from such an approach is that if the neuroscience logic of our understanding of reasoning as emanating from a physical operation was correct, then we would at least be able to infuse reasoning in the form of neuro-symbolic cognition into a physical entity and turn it thereby into a living body or live intelligence. Even when we accomplish this with a material human homologue like a robot (i.e., Asimov), we know that it remains a speaking mannequin, as lifeless as a barbie.

It is further noteworthy that no one needs to understand what understanding is to be able to exert it, and intelligence can further reflect on itself: you can understand or seek to understand how you understand. So therefore, the mind, which is the framework for reasoning/understanding must have an internal reflexive property. From here, one can see a vertical scaling hierarchy responsive to Group Representation and dimensional Number Theory. One way to otherwise consign this is that the self can objectivize itself. In introspection, you yourself can thus split yourself into a subject and an object, materializing two separate representation groups with plural contents that maintain a bijective relationship with one another. Because detachment must imply at least two separate or distinct entities, through group segregation, one is able to obtain a critical view or understanding of self. Under the same light, the relationship between behavior which is a direct result of neural dynamics expressed in a sequence of singlet physiognomic expressions and mentation partitions, of which intelligence and intellection in general partake, can be perfectly studied.

6.8.2. The Physics of Quantum Entanglement in Human Ontology

Furthermore, a metric approach to the understanding of the dimensional fabric of ontologies in the evoked multi-prong approach strongly suggests that every living being is configured as a quantum packet of two in entanglement correlation. In other words, ontology of the Living, including human ontology, is a reunion of two Hilbertian or orthogonal entities in the functional sense. Below the functional definition of a Hilbert space with two objects:

$$\int_a^b f(x)\, g(x) \cdot dx = 0$$

In this representation, the functional object *f(x)* putatively stands for the observable 3-D entity or organism in the physical 3D domain, while the orthogonal object *g(x)* conforms the orthogonal unobservable 4D/5D entity. The 4D/5D entity is best thought of as bundled in one, we will reduce it to 5D for the purpose of this exposé. The Hilbertian orthogonality between the two entities means that they cannot be both fully alive at the same time. When one is fully active in a phase of life, the other is and must concomitantly be in a prostration or lethargic state. This is a critical point to understand and not lose sight of. The degree of activity and dynamism of each system or organism is inversely proportional to the other in any region of space.

To further pursue the prospective analysis, we may consider that each homological body pertaining to one living entity holds its own form of structural organization that is germane to the physical properties of the medium of their belonging, although they remain largely isometric in their dimensional relationship. These faculties must significantly differ from one another per the distinct metric of the backgrounds, those germane to the higher medium being superior by isomorphism. It is important to understand that the entire framework of Mind is an architectural quality pertaining to the higher-dimensional body or organism, whereas the biological brain represents in its layout a control orchestration of the biological body for the 3D experience through both the autonomous and the central nervous systems. The degree of activity of the 3D brain and body are highest during daytime, with the 5D brain at its lowest level of activity, which altogether represents our ordinary level of consciousness. The 5D brain and body turn to their highest dynamical level at night or sleep time, as the 3D entity becomes almost inane, with lowest metabolic level and only conducting homeostasis. Becoming highly active at night in its own medium with the faculties conferred to its structure, the 5D entity registers experiences imbued with higher degrees of freedom, consistent with the metric properties of its medium. That would be the reason why that experience naturally deposited in memory, when accessed by the 3D entity later during wake, the subject finds it quite unintelligible, essentially because of the homeomorphic transformations undergone by contents.

When the two bodies are in complete spatial group separation, bringing their entanglement to it maximum level, the 3D brain and body enter a deep state of prostration, which is denoted lethargic at times or vegetative in clinical settings. The typified state of Deep Sleep known in neuroscience or neurology, where full histological restauration from fatigue occurs, is also a close approximation of this state.

I hope the above has properly shown the possible mentation framework that one may sketch in an Omniscient-knowledge reconciliatory approach in relation to the concept of consciousness and intelligence in the context of physical science, mathematics, psychophysics and neural science. Artificial Intelligence as a simulation lies far away from this picture. The inability to see agency between artificial intelligence and human intelligence amounts indeed to a barometer in stating or measuring one's own level of intelligence, while spelling a hindrance to ontological development or emancipation. A clear understanding of what human ontology is and implicates is key to any definition of intelligence and a methology for unraveling its identity. This clarity may make the difference between keeping one's cognitive potentials in stagnation and taking the correct steps to develop those potentials. It is clear that a command of the categories in Abstract Group Representation Theory represents a useful formal tool for those insights.

So therefore, it is not possible to create intelligence other than by procreation. We can simulate intelligence, mostly a low level thereof, with communication protocols, like articulated language, or the symbolic sign language of the deaf, or even the bees' spatial language. If the devised AI did not have access to the entire Human Knowledge Base in script and locution, it would be very dumb as an emulated form of intelligence, as dumb as a zombie.

6.9. Bifurcated Line of Human Evolution

True story of genAI is the story of an offshoot of American segregationism. Its outline is its wrap around the black female mathematical geniuses in the 1950's at NACA soon to become NASA. They could compute zenithal orbitals in their heads and developed the first algorithms for those computations to make them accessible to those who just could not perform them. American white supremacy segregated them and managed to veer all credits for the pioneering of machine algorithm to Alan Turing. Turing pressed on the side of the *"machine imitation game"* as he called it, instead of development of human intelligence from an ontological perspective.

Turing had seen their work, the invention of Algorithmic Methods, whose application was aiding other human beings in the mathematical computation of celestial orbitals out of reach to them. He became interested in machine implementation of Algorithms, the Algorithms being human intelligence techniques, methods and procedures put to work in computations of zenithal orbitals. When he was brought to call it *"the machine imitation game"*, he implicitly meant to say Machine imitating human intelligence.

The segregationist atmosphere at NASA forced this group of female mathematical geniuses to close onto themselves and contravened the possibility for them to project examplars of extraordinarily developed mathematical faculties in ontology. They even later gained the attribute of 'human computers' at NASA. Nevertheless, the urge to shadow their work and abilities granted them no more official acknowledgements than to "*have been the first African American scientists to work at NASA*", meaning to have had the honor of working at NASA. Outrageous, since their foundational contribution to the nascent American space exploration program and its success was no more than extraordinary and miraculous. Obviously, there must be a reason why they came to be last known as 'the hidden figures.'

I have discussed those savantistic faculties at the beginning of this exposition, namely hyperthymesia or eidetic memory, synesthesia in its many different forms, to which we may add clairvoyance or lucidity, which is the ability to completely bypass or kill the illusion of time and virtually visualize the unfolding of the future from an anchor in space. Add to those savantistic faculties the polyglottic ability to speak dozens of languages, and a whole series of others only known or evoked in specific bodies of knowledge as discussed in Chapter 1.

If only people could realize that to use an artificial polymath is not to be a polymath, and vice versa. The polymath has to be in our brain or our head, not in our pockets, as a result of our own living experience. That is what makes a real difference ontologically. The above constitutes the real line of polymathic evolution of human beings from an ontological viewpoint. GenAI is no part of this equation and in fact thwarts that axis of Evolution. Because it flattens and eviscerates human intellection. And how could it not, since it bears Delinquency in every pore for a change. It is also important to understand that the structure of omniscient knowledge is not amalgamation of an astronomical amount of points of knowledge piled up in the repository of cognition, but a cognitive architecture that materializes a Tree of Knowledge. To use a comparative simile, the trunk and branching of the tree represents critical thinking and logical/computational abilities, while the universe of leaves on the branching would represent elements of knowledge. Any other form of attempt at Omniscience may result in cognitive constipation with the risk of severe cognitive maladaptation and characterological bankruptcy. The worst of these risks is of course atrophy of intellection, as we discussed, when we altogether lease that virtue from an artificial polymath.

Lastly, there is a line that connects the knowledge of Unified Physical Law with the polymathic Mentation configuration or architecture. It is through the knowledge of Unified Physical Law encompassing all scales of Reality, from the microcosm to the macrocosm, that the Mind accesses totalitarian knowledge on the basis of the Tree structure which centralizes all critical analytic and computational skills in Mentation. This entire complex delivers the quality in Omniscience which puts the mental body at a footstep from wisdom and the transcendental. In other words, it creates the reflexive or intellection avenues for the maturation of wisdom towards the connection with the transcendental or the spiritual. There is no way to intelligibly or inter-relationally connect all of the elements of knowledge of Reality, absent that systematic unifying view of the entire theater of existence. That view is of eminent mathematical physics nature in the sense contemplated by mathematician David Hilbert in his visualization of axiomatic mathematical physics.

If anyone cherishes or shares the dream of multiplanetary civilization as espoused by Elon Musk, the only true and serious path to it is this axis of Evolution. Otherwise, beyond the low earth orbits, there may be an inordinate amount of surprises waiting to blow the adventurous mind. Never ignore, overlook or discard *gimbal* and *gofast*, testimonies of the Pentagon on behalf of the United States Navy of life in the deeper Cosmos.

6.10. Can Human Evolution Be Achieved Strictly On a Technological Line?

As I am now finalizing this exposition, my feeling is it would not be complete without the following reflections which I feel compelled to offer. Especially in light of the claim that multiplanetary civilization for Men is possible in the context of the Culture that had been prevalent on Earth for the last 5000 years. There is also the question of where genAI technology is deemed to take us on the civilizational line, should we manage to cure its birth defect and ensure a more harmonious integration in society by harnessing it as an authentic tool instead of a substitute to human intelligence. I have previously discussed in this Chapter my irrevocable conviction that human evolution is squarely centered on the axis of Ontology.

World on Earth, however, has long been on the track of Artificial value instead of Ontological value. In a way, it is the difference between Plato and Socrates on one side, and, on the other, Aristotle, at the formation of the modern World. A cast of the difference between idealism and character, on one hand, and materialism and superficiality, on the other. The Ancient world had been characterized by predominance of idealism and character over materialism and superficiality, in the understanding that the latter is essentially technological manipulation of the world. It had been so in Egypt, India, China, Sub-Saharan Africa and in the independent pre-Columbian Americas, under the impulse of a series of practices that we call Religion. While the modern-day learned tend to downplay the technological levels achieved in those gone-by Cultures, remnants of that past still testify to the high technological level they had achieved which remain today subject of mystery: the Egyptian pyramids and colossal artforms, the puzzling Mayan crystal skull(s), advanced Eastern savoir-faire in the higher metrics of the physical world indubitably transpiring in the Acupunctural technique, etc.

It is very clear, and most will agree as I stated before, that the advancement of Mankind, if any possible furthering, remains on the side of ontological evolution, within the complex formed by idealistic or humanistic Mentation and character. That seems to be the path of least resistance in human evolution, in Theory at least. What happened during the Middle Ages in the West as relates to the corruption of occult practices at the heart of

Religion universal has apparently sealed the fate of the ontological course of human evolution from its inner gravitas, as I view it.

Oncome of Renaissance and Enlightenment materializes a different program, a course of evolution along the line of preeminence of materialism and superficiality incarnating so-called Technology. That course is to be traced back in the materialistic Aristotelian view of the world in opposition to the Platonic perspective. Where we are today, at a quarter of 21st Century having elapsed, is at a critical moment testing whether Technology can deliver the long sought-after Ontological progress or not, as Science is hitting the paradigm of the fundamental savoir-faire relating to Unified Physical Law in the universe, and information technology is increasingly putting at the hands of one individual the entire human savoir-faire accumulated this far. Can one argue that the wisdom with which this is done is a warrant for its success? Arguably No, since wisdom or any semblance thereof has come to be estranged from this bid or tenet.

Hence the answer to the grander question of whether technology alone, even in its best version, can deliver ontological progress patently remains entirely **unknown**, I will admit, even though I cautiously place my bet on the No answer.

6.11. Conclusion

Having historically divided Humanism and Technology in two distinct separate academies ever since the oncome of Enlightenment, modern-day Academia seems to have made the definite choice of prioritizing Technology and the associated set of secular values over Humanism in its educational pursuits. Generative Artificial Intelligence comes within this consummated structure of Higher Education throughout the global academic establishment. Everything remaining as is, we are on the course discussed in the previous section with an unknown destination. On that course, the claims of Humanism while endowment funding commonly comes from investment in a technological-economic emporium knowingly averse to restraints and avid for gains, will continue to resonate hollow. We have also well seen the academic roots of the last major Recession which was a financial crisis with academic actors directly participating in the creation of the Credit Default Swap securities which catastrophically tanked the financial system. Not to mention the plight of underpaid faculty, tuition always on the rise prohibitively for students, hyper competition in scientific research blocking discoveries and further progress, etc., which we previously discussed.

In the larger picture, there is a subjacent movement that belies the historical course of society at large, in terms of an ongoing transformational change. The now 30-year-old global internetwork, i.e., partakes of such momentous ramp up within the makeup of the modern-day world, both as expression and agency, despite the increasing late threat of its pollution by generative AI. We have to remember that the internet is a creation of government at its very inception, not academia. Effectively, there is only one cohesive way to view the following benchmarks:

- the experience of conciliatory social change through non-violence as faithfully executed by Mahatma Gandhi, Martin L. King and Nelson Mandela in the black tradition of Charity and Temperance,
- the experience of nonconformism and spiritual connectedness in the movement of the world youth in the 1960's, in particular American Youth at Woodstock,
- communion of the world youth of the 1980's and 90's with an intractable Pope John Paul II in his ethical and moral call to righteousness and transcendence, and
- the continual display of ever more unhinged rebellion of the peoples of the earth against injustice and the brutality of oppression.

These benchmarks, easily overlooked, all subsume self-serving worship and politics, unbridled appetite for gains, and represent the unrelenting advancement of Human Collective Consciousness under the umbrella of humanistic ontological concerns. My personal advocacy is that, for Academia to genuinely connect with the pulse of societal evolution, it ought to connect with Humanism as a priority over Technology and its secular stream. You can never completely tear down the connection between these two major streams. But, in my unreserved opinion, what will save the day is an active liaison between Knowledge and Higher Consciousness trending to Transcendent Wisdom. This is realized when, as I previously discussed, the foundational matters of life and of human ontology become the prime subjects of Higher Education. The questions of savantistic human qualities and their development are central to this approach and have to be moved from fringe phenomena to mainstream learning in Higher Education, as well as essential subjects of research. Unified Physical Law is squarely situated in that perspective as well.

From here, we can adequately connect to the axis that takes us to the stage of Ascent in the course of human evolution. Ascent as understood in our current space exploration programs is improper and must be readjusted. To put it in one word, human racial supremacy on Mars or the dark side of the Moon strikes me as a complete aberration. Yet, this is what we are attempting to materialize on the course we have embarked on. The revolution in space propulsion that will position human beings for true entry in the Cosmos, beyond tourism in the low-earth orbits, in my opinion, will only take place under the Humanistic umbrella, that which will also harbor Unified Physical Law with its implicated Cosmic Object Model. Provided we can establish this new balance in the structure of Higher Education with the required shift in prioritization of Humanism, and so unblock the floodgate of fundamental science, the cosmic multiplanetary stage in the evolution of mankind will occur in a harmonious, fruitful and viable manner. Human Collective Consciousness is henceforth due to sprout not as a matter of time to pass but alignment of circumstances of different orders in the Life of the Cosmos, and relative to the role devolved to Mankind, made indeed of *"star stuff"*, in the evolution of the local Cosmos. Again, never forget *gimbal* and *gofast.*

APPENDIX

The motivation in republishing this list of unsolved problems in science is to give it the publicity it deserves among the general public and taxpayers in particular who are the ones providing the funding for the academic research conglomerate. Just as we need to know the breakthroughs when they occur, we also need to know about the huge number of long-standing problems awaiting resolution, in order to keep a fair appreciation of the human Knowledge Base and its development. The list is evidently far more extensive than the reported transcription, since we have decided to limit the transcription to unsolved problems in physics and medicine only, the two paramount scientific disciplines directly concerned with matter and life. Interestingly, the first two listed problems in physics have been solved since 2015, so disclosing another aspect of our problems, if not another problem in science to be legitimately listed. I am referring to the severe problem of exclusion, group rivalry or destructive competition, staunch academic departmental sectarianism, attack or silence on progress that did not come through one's ingenuity. I hold it that this paramount problem should spearhead any list of unsolved problems in science, in all honesty and good taxonomy.

From Wikipedia, the free encyclopedia

List of Unsolved Problems in Physics

This is a dynamic list[23] and may never be able to satisfy particular standards for completeness. You can help by adding missing items with reliable sources.

The following is a list of notable unsolved problems grouped into broad areas of physics.

Some of the major unsolved problems in physics are theoretical, meaning that existing theories seem incapable of explaining a certain observed phenomenon or experimental result. The others are experimental, meaning that there is a difficulty in creating an experiment to test a proposed theory or investigate a phenomenon in greater detail.

There are still some questions beyond the Standard Model of physics, such as the strong CP problem, neutrino mass, matter–antimatter asymmetry, and the nature of dark matter and dark energy. Another problem lies within the mathematical framework of the Standard Model itself—the Standard Model is inconsistent with that of general relativity,

[23] https://en.wikipedia.org/wiki/List_of_unsolved_

to the point that one or both theories break down under certain conditions (for example within known spacetime singularities like the Big Bang and the centres of black holes beyond the event horizon).

General physics

- Theory of everything: Is there a singular, all-encompassing, coherent theoretical framework of physics that fully explains and links together all physical aspects of the universe?

- Dimensionless physical constants: At the present time, the values of various dimensionless physical constants cannot be calculated; they can be determined only by physical measurement. What is the minimum number of dimensionless physical constants from which all other dimensionless physical constants can be derived? Are dimensional physical constants necessary at all?

Quantum gravity

- Quantum gravity: Can quantum mechanics and general relativity be realized as a fully consistent theory (perhaps as a quantum field theory)? Is spacetime fundamentally continuous or discrete? Would a consistent theory involve a force mediated by a hypothetical graviton, or be a product of a discrete structure of spacetime itself (as in loop quantum gravity)? Are there deviations from the predictions of general relativity at very small or very large scales or in other extreme circumstances that flow from a quantum gravity mechanism?

- Vacuum catastrophe: Why does the predicted mass of the quantum vacuum have little effect on the expansion of the universe?

- Black holes, black hole information paradox, and black hole radiation: Do black holes produce thermal radiation, as expected on theoretical grounds? Does this radiation contain information about their inner structure, as suggested by gauge–gravity duality, or not, as implied by Hawking's original calculation? If not, and black holes can evaporate away, what happens to the information stored in them (since quantum mechanics does not provide for the destruction of information)? Or does the radiation stop at some point leaving black hole remnants? Is there another way to probe their internal structure somehow, if such a structure even exists?

- The cosmic censorship hypothesis and the chronology protection conjecture: Can singularities not hidden behind an event horizon, known as "naked singularities", arise from realistic initial conditions, or is it possible to prove some version of the "cosmic censorship hypothesis" of Roger Penrose which proposes that this is impossible? Similarly, will the closed timelike curves which arise in some solutions to the equations of general relativity (and which imply the possibility of backwards time travel) be ruled out by a theory of quantum gravity which unites general relativity with quantum mechanics, as suggested by the "chronology protection conjecture" of Stephen Hawking?

- Holographic principle: Is it true that quantum gravity admits a lower-dimensional description that does not contain gravity? A well understood example of holography is the AdS/CFT correspondence in string theory. Similarly, can quantum gravity in a de Sitter space be understood using dS/CFT correspondence? Can the AdS/CFT correspondence be vastly generalized to the gauge–gravity duality for arbitrary spacetime backgrounds? Are there other theories of quantum gravity other than string theory that admit a holographic description?

- Problem of time: In quantum mechanics, time is a classical background parameter and the flow of time is universal and absolute. In general relativity time is one component of four-dimensional spacetime, and the flow of time changes depending on the curvature of spacetime and the spacetime trajectory of the observer. How can these two concepts of time be reconciled?

Quantum physics

- Yang–Mills theory: Given an arbitrary compact gauge group, does a non-trivial quantum Yang–Mills theory with a finite mass gap exist? (This problem is also listed as one of the Millennium Prize Problems in mathematics.)
- Quantum field theory: Is it possible to construct, in the mathematically rigorous framework of algebraic QFT, a theory in 4-dimensional spacetime that includes interactions and does not resort to perturbative methods?

Cosmology and general relativity

- Axis of evil: Some large features of the microwave sky at distances of over 13 billion light years appear to be aligned with both the motion and orientation of the solar system. Is this due to systematic errors in processing, contamination of results by local effects, or an unexplained violation of the Copernican principle?

- Fine-tuned universe: The values of the fundamental physical constants are in a narrow range necessary to support carbon-based life. Is this because there exist other universes with different constants, or are our universe's constants the result of chance, or some other factor or process? (See also the Anthropic Principle.)

- Cosmic inflation: Is the theory of cosmic inflation in the very early universe correct, and, if so, what are the details of this epoch? What is the hypothetical inflaton scalar field that gave rise to this cosmic inflation? If inflation happened at one point, is it self-sustaining through inflation of quantum-mechanical fluctuations, and thus ongoing in some extremely distant place?

- Horizon problem: Why is the distant universe so homogeneous when the Big Bang theory seems to predict larger measurable anisotropies of the night sky than those observed? Cosmological inflation is generally accepted as the solution, but are other possible explanations such as a variable speed of light more appropriate?

- Origin and future of the universe: How did the conditions for anything to exist arise? Is the universe heading towards a Big Freeze, a Big Rip, a Big Crunch, or a Big Bounce? Or is it part of an infinitely recurring cyclic model?

- Size of universe: The diameter of the observable universe is about 93 billion light-years, but what is the size of the whole universe?

- Baryon asymmetry: Why is there far more matter than antimatter in the observable universe? (This may be solved due to the apparent asymmetry in neutrino-antineutrino oscillations.)

- Cosmological principle: Is the universe homogeneous and isotropic at large enough scales, as claimed by the cosmological principle and assumed by all models that use the Friedmann–Lemaître–Robertson–Walker metric, including the current version of the ΛCDM model, or is the universe inhomogeneous or anisotropic? Is the CMB dipole purely kinematic, or does it signal anisotropy of the universe, resulting in the breakdown of the FLRW metric and the cosmological principle? Is the Hubble tension evidence that the cosmological principle is false? Even if the cosmological principle is correct, is the Friedmann–Lemaître–Robertson–Walker metric the right metric to use for our universe? Are the observations usually interpreted as the accelerating expansion of the universe rightly interpreted, or are they instead evidence that the cosmological principle is false?

- Copernican principle: Are cosmological observations made from Earth representative of observations from the average position in the universe?

- Cosmological constant problem: Why does the zero-point energy of the vacuum not cause a large cosmological constant? What cancels it out?

Estimated distribution of dark matter and dark energy in the universe

- Dark matter: What is the identity of dark matter? Is it a particle? If so, is it a WIMP, axion, the lightest superpartner (LSP), or some other particle? Or, do the phenomena attributed to dark matter point not to some form of matter but actually to an extension of gravity?

- Dark energy: What is the cause of the observed accelerating expansion of the universe (the de Sitter phase)? Are the observations rightly interpreted as the accelerating expansion of the universe, or are they evidence that the cosmological principle is false? Why is the energy density of the dark energy component of the same magnitude as the density of matter at present when the two evolve quite differently over time; could it be simply that we are observing at exactly the right time? Is dark energy a pure cosmological constant or are models of quintessence such as phantom energy applicable?

- Dark flow: Is a non-spherically symmetric gravitational pull from outside the observable universe responsible for some of the observed motion of large objects such as galactic clusters in the universe?

- Shape of the universe: What is the 3-manifold of comoving space, i.e., of a comoving spatial section of the universe, informally called the "shape" of the universe? Neither the curvature nor the topology is presently known, though the curvature is known to be "close" to zero on observable scales. The cosmic inflation hypothesis suggests that the shape of the universe may be unmeasurable, but, since 2003, Jean-Pierre Luminet, et al., and other groups have suggested that the shape of the universe may be the Poincaré dodecahedral space. Is the shape unmeasurable; the Poincaré space; or another 3-manifold?

- The largest structures in the universe are larger than expected. Current cosmological models say there should be very little structure on scales larger than a few hundred million light-years across, due to the expansion of the universe trumping the effect of gravity. But the Sloan Great Wall is 1.38 billion light-years in length. And the largest structure currently known, the Hercules–Corona Borealis Great Wall, is up to 10 billion light-years in length. Are these actual structures or random density fluctuations? If they are real structures, they contradict the 'End of Greatness' hypothesis which asserts that at a scale of 300 million light-years, structures seen in smaller surveys are randomized to the extent that the smooth distribution of the universe is visually apparent.

- Extra dimensions: Does nature have more than four spacetime dimensions? If so, what is their size? Are dimensions a fundamental property of the universe or an emergent result of other physical laws? Can we experimentally observe evidence of higher spatial dimensions?

- High-energy physics/particle physics

- See also: Beyond the Standard Model

- Hierarchy problem: Why is gravity such a weak force? It becomes strong for particles only at the Planck scale, around 1019 GeV, much above the electroweak scale (100 GeV, the energy scale dominating physics at low energies). Why are these scales so different from each other? What prevents quantities at the electroweak scale, such as the Higgs boson mass, from getting quantum corrections on the order of the Planck scale? Is the solution supersymmetry, extra dimensions, or just anthropic fine-tuning?

- Magnetic monopoles: Did particles that carry "magnetic charge" exist in some past, higher-energy epoch? If so, do any remain today? (Paul Dirac showed the existence of some types of magnetic monopoles would explain charge quantization.)

- Neutron lifetime puzzle: While the neutron lifetime has been studied for decades, there currently exists a lack of consilience on its exact value, due to different results from two experimental methods ("bottle" versus "beam").

- Proton decay and spin crisis: Is the proton fundamentally stable? Or does it decay with a finite lifetime as predicted by some extensions to the standard model? How do the quarks and gluons carry the spin of protons?

- Supersymmetry: Is spacetime supersymmetry realized at TeV scale? If so, what is the mechanism of supersymmetry breaking? Does supersymmetry stabilize the electroweak scale, preventing high quantum corrections? Does the lightest supersymmetric particle (LSP) comprise dark matter?

- Color confinement: The quantum chromodynamics (QCD) color confinement conjecture is that color-charged particles (such as quarks and gluons) cannot be separated from their parent hadron without producing new hadrons. Is it possible to provide an analytic proof of color confinement in any non-abelian gauge theory?

- Generations of matter: Why are there three generations of quarks and leptons? Is there a theory that can explain the masses of particular quarks and leptons in particular generations from first principles (a theory of Yukawa couplings)?

- Neutrino mass: What is the mass of neutrinos, whether they follow Dirac or Majorana statistics? Is the mass hierarchy normal or inverted? Is the CP violating phase equal to 0?

- Reactor antineutrino anomaly: There is an anomaly in the existing body of data regarding the antineutrino flux from nuclear reactors around the world. Measured values of this flux appears to be only 94% of the value expected from theory. It is unknown whether this is due to unknown physics (such as sterile neutrinos), experimental error in the measurements, or errors in the theoretical flux calculations.

- Strong CP problem and axions: Why is the strong nuclear interaction invariant to parity and charge conjugation? Is Peccei–Quinn theory the solution to this problem? Could axions be the main component of dark matter?

- Anomalous magnetic dipole moment: Why is the experimentally measured value of the muon's anomalous magnetic dipole moment ("muon $g - 2$") significantly different from the theoretically predicted value of that physical constant?

- Proton radius puzzle: What is the electric charge radius of the proton? How does it differ from a gluonic charge?

- Pentaquarks and other exotic hadrons: What combinations of quarks are possible? Why were pentaquarks so difficult to discover? Are they a tightly-bound system of five elementary particles, or a more weakly-bound pairing of a baryon and a meson?

- Mu problem: A problem in supersymmetric theories, concerned with understanding the reasons for parameter values of the theory.

- Koide formula: An aspect of the problem of particle generations. The sum of the masses of the three charged leptons, divided by the square of the sum of the roots of these masses, to within one standard deviation of observations, is It is unknown how such a simple value comes about, and why it is the exact arithmetic average of the possible extreme values of 1 /3 (equal masses) and 1 (one mass dominates).

Astronomy and astrophysics

- Solar cycle: How does the Sun generate its periodically reversing large-scale magnetic field? How do other solar-like stars generate their magnetic fields, and what are the similarities and differences between stellar activity cycles and that of the Sun? What caused the Maunder Minimum and other grand minima, and how does the solar cycle recover from a minima state?

- Coronal heating problem: Why is the Sun's corona (atmosphere layer) so much hotter than the Sun's surface? Why is the magnetic reconnection effect many orders of magnitude faster than predicted by standard models?

- Astrophysical jet: Why do only certain accretion discs surrounding certain astronomical objects emit relativistic jets along their polar axes? Why are there quasi-periodic oscillations in many accretion discs? Why does the period of these oscillations scale as the inverse of the mass of the central object? Why are there sometimes overtones, and why do these appear at different frequency ratios in different objects?

- Diffuse interstellar bands: What is responsible for the numerous interstellar absorption lines detected in astronomical spectra? Are they molecular in origin, and if so which molecules are responsible for them? How do they form?

- Supermassive black holes: What is the origin of the M–sigma relation between supermassive black hole mass and galaxy velocity dispersion? How did the most distant quasars grow their supermassive black holes up to 1010 solar masses so early in the history of the universe?

- Rotation curve of a typical spiral galaxy: predicted (A) and observed (B). Can the discrepancy between the curves be attributed to dark matter?

- Kuiper cliff: Why does the number of objects in the Solar System's Kuiper belt fall off rapidly and unexpectedly beyond a radius of 50 astronomical units?

- Flyby anomaly: Why is the observed energy of satellites flying by planetary bodies sometimes different by a minute amount from the value predicted by theory?

- Galaxy rotation problem: Is dark matter responsible for differences in observed and theoretical speed of stars revolving around the centre of galaxies, or is it something else?

- Supernovae: What is the exact mechanism by which an implosion of a dying star becomes an explosion?

- p-nuclei: What astrophysical process is responsible for the nucleogenesis of these rare isotopes?

- Ultra-high-energy cosmic ray: Why is it that some cosmic rays appear to possess energies that are impossibly high, given that there are no sufficiently energetic cosmic ray sources near the Earth? Why is it that (apparently) some cosmic rays emitted by distant sources have energies above the Greisen–Zatsepin–Kuzmin limit?

- Rotation rate of Saturn: Why does the magnetosphere of Saturn exhibit a (slowly changing) periodicity close to that at which the planet's clouds rotate? What is the true rotation rate of Saturn's deep interior?

- Origin of magnetar magnetic field: What is the origin of magnetar magnetic field?

- Large-scale anisotropy: Is the universe at very large scales anisotropic, making the cosmological principle an invalid assumption? The number count and intensity dipole anisotropy in radio, NRAO VLA Sky Survey (NVSS) catalogue is inconsistent with the local motion as derived from cosmic microwave background and indicate an intrinsic dipole anisotropy. The same NVSS radio data also shows an intrinsic dipole in polarization density and degree of polarization in the same direction as in number count and intensity. There are several other observations revealing large-scale anisotropy. The optical polarization from quasars shows polarization alignment over a very large scale of Gpc. The cosmic-microwave-background data shows several features of anisotropy, which are not consistent with the Big Bang model.

- Age–metallicity relation in the Galactic disk: Is there a universal age–metallicity relation (AMR) in the Galactic disk (both "thin" and "thick" parts of the disk)? Although in the local (primarily thin) disk of the Milky Way there is no evidence of a strong AMR, a sample of 229 nearby "thick" disk stars has been used to investigate the existence of an age–metallicity relation in the Galactic thick disk, and indicate that there is an age–metallicity relation present in the thick disk. Stellar ages from asteroseismology confirm the lack of any strong age–metallicity relation in the Galactic disc.

- The lithium problem: Why is there a discrepancy between the amount of lithium-7 predicted to be produced in Big Bang nucleosynthesis and the amount observed in very old stars?

- Ultraluminous X-ray sources (ULXs): What powers X-ray sources that are not associated with active galactic nuclei but exceed the Eddington limit of a neutron star or stellar black hole? Are they due to intermediate-mass black holes? Some ULXs are periodic, suggesting non-isotropic emission from a neutron star. Does this apply to all ULXs? How could such a system form and remain stable?

- Fast radio bursts (FRBs): What causes these transient radio pulses from distant galaxies, lasting only a few milliseconds each? Why do some FRBs repeat at unpredictable intervals, but most do not? Dozens of models have been proposed, but none have been widely accepted.

- Are voids in space empty or consist of transparent matter?

Nuclear physics

- The "island of stability" in the proton vs. neutron number plot for heavy nuclei

- Quantum chromodynamics: What are the phases of strongly interacting matter, and what roles do they play in the evolution of cosmos? What is the detailed partonic structure of the nucleons? What does QCD predict for the properties of strongly interacting matter? What determines the key features of QCD, and what is their relation to the nature of gravity and spacetime? Do glueballs exist? Do gluons acquire mass dynamically despite having a zero rest mass, within hadrons? Does QCD truly lack CP violations?

- Quark–gluon plasma: Where is the onset of deconfinement: 1) as a function of temperature and chemical potentials? 2) as a function of relativistic heavy-ion collision energy and system size? What is the mechanism of energy and baryon-number stopping leading to creation of quark-gluon plasma in relativistic heavy-ion collisions? Why is sudden hadronization and the statistical-hadronization model a near-to-perfect description of hadron production from quark–gluon plasma? Is quark flavor conserved in quark–gluon plasma? Are strangeness and charm in chemical equilibrium in quark–gluon plasma? Does strangeness in quark–gluon plasma flow at the same speed as up and down quark flavours? Why does deconfined matter show ideal flow?

- Strangelets: Does strange quark matter (Strangelet) exist as stable state?

- Specific models of quark–gluon plasma formation: Do gluons saturate when their occupation number is large? Do gluons form a dense system called colour glass condensate? What are the signatures and evidences for the Balitsky–Fadin–Kuarev–Lipatov, Balitsky–Kovchegov, Catani–Ciafaloni–Fiorani–Marchesini evolution equations?

- Nuclei and nuclear astrophysics: Why is there a lack of convergence in estimates of the mean lifetime of a free neutron based on two separate—and increasingly precise—experimental methods? What is the nature of the nuclear force that binds protons and neutrons into stable nuclei and rare isotopes? What is the explanation for the EMC effect? What is the nature of exotic excitations in nuclei at the frontiers of stability and their role in stellar processes? What is the nature of neutron stars and dense nuclear matter? What is the origin of the elements in the cosmos? What are the nuclear reactions that drive stars and stellar explosions? What is the heaviest possible chemical element?

- Atomic, molecular and optical physics

- Bose–Einstein condensation: How do we rigorously prove the existence of Bose–Einstein condensates for general interacting systems?

- Gauge block wringing: What is the mechanism that allows gauge blocks to be wrung together?

- Scharnhorst effect: Can light signals travel slightly faster than c between two closely spaced conducting plates, exploiting the Casimir effect?

Fluid dynamics

- Under what conditions do smooth solutions exist for the Navier–Stokes equations, which are the equations that describe the flow of a viscous fluid? This problem, for an incompressible fluid in three dimensions, is also one of the Millennium Prize Problems in mathematics.

- Turbulent flow: Is it possible to make a theoretical model to describe the statistics of a turbulent flow (in particular, its internal structures)?

- Upstream contamination: When pouring water from a higher container to a lower one, particles floating in the latter can climb upstream into the upper container. A definitive explanation for this phenomenon is still lacking.
- Granular convection: why does a granular material subjected to shaking or vibration exhibit circulation patterns similar to types of fluid convection? Why do the largest particles end up on the surface of a granular material containing a mixture of variously sized objects when subjected to a vibration/ shaking?

Condensed matter physics

- A sample of a cuprate superconductor (specifically BSCCO). The mechanism for superconductivity of these materials is unknown.

- High-temperature superconductors: What is the mechanism that causes certain materials to exhibit superconductivity at temperatures much higher than around 25 kelvins? Is it possible to make a material that is a superconductor at room temperature and atmospheric pressure?

- Amorphous solids: What is the nature of the glass transition between a fluid or regular solid and a glassy phase? What are the physical processes giving rise to the general properties of glasses and the glass transition?

- Cryogenic electron emission: Why does the electron emission in the absence of light increase as the temperature of a photomultiplier is decreased?

- Sonoluminescence: What causes the emission of short bursts of light from imploding bubbles in a liquid when excited by sound?
- Topological order: Is topological order stable at non-zero temperature? Equivalently, is it possible to have three-dimensional self-correcting quantum memory?
- Magnetoresistance in a u = 8/5 fractional quantum Hall state
- Fractional Hall effect: What mechanism explains the existence of the u = 5/2 state in the fractional quantum Hall effect? Does it describe quasiparticles with non-Abelian fractional statistics?
- Liquid crystals: Can the nematic to smectic (A) phase transition in liquid crystal states be characterized as a universal phase transition?
- Semiconductor nanocrystals: What is the cause of the nonparabolicity of the energy-size dependence for the lowest optical absorption transition of quantum dots?
- Metal whiskering: In electrical devices, some metallic surfaces may spontaneously grow fine metallic whiskers, which can lead to equipment failures. While compressive mechanical stress is known to encourage whisker formation, the growth mechanism has yet to be determined.
- Superfluid transition in helium-4: Explain the discrepancy between the experimental and theoretical determinations of the heat capacity critical exponent α.

Plasma physics

- Plasma physics and fusion power: Fusion energy may potentially provide power from an abundant resource (e.g. hydrogen) without the type of radioactive waste that fission energy currently produces. However, can ionized gases (plasma) be confined long enough and at a high enough temperature to create fusion power? What is the physical origin of H-mode?
- The injection problem: Fermi acceleration is thought to be the primary mechanism that accelerates astrophysical particles to high energy. However, it is unclear what mechanism causes those particles to initially have energies high enough for Fermi acceleration to work on them.

- Alfvénic turbulence: In the solar wind and the turbulence in solar flares, coronal mass ejections, and magnetospheric substorms are major unsolved problems in space plasma physics.

Biophysics

- Stochasticity and robustness to noise in gene expression: How do genes govern our body, withstanding different external pressures and internal stochasticity? Certain models exist for genetic processes, but we are far from understanding the whole picture, in particular in development where gene expression must be tightly regulated.

- Quantitative study of the immune system: What are the quantitative properties of immune responses? What are the basic building blocks of immune system networks?

- Homochirality: What is the origin of the preponderance of specific enantiomers in biochemical systems?

- Magnetoreception: How do animals (e.g. migratory birds) sense the Earth's magnetic field?

- Protein structure prediction: How is the three-dimensional structure of proteins determined by the one-dimensional amino acid sequence? How can proteins fold on microsecond to second timescales when the number of possible conformations is astronomical and conformational transitions occur on the picosecond to microsecond timescale? Can algorithms be written to predict a protein's three-dimensional structure from its sequence? Do the native structures of most naturally occurring proteins coincide with the global minimum of the free energy in conformational space? Or are most native conformations thermodynamically unstable, but kinetically trapped in metastable states? What keeps the high density of proteins present inside cells from precipitating?

- Quantum biology: Can coherence be maintained in biological systems at timeframes long enough to be functionally important? Are there non-trivial aspects of biology or biochemistry that can only be explained by the persistence of coherence as a mechanism?

Philosophy of physics

- Interpretation of quantum mechanics: How does the quantum description of reality, which includes elements such as the superposition of states and wave-function collapse or quantum decoherence, give rise to the reality we perceive? Another way of stating this question regards the measurement problem: What constitutes a "measurement" which apparently causes the wave function to collapse into a definite state? Unlike classical physical processes, some quantum mechanical processes (such as quantum teleportation arising from quantum entanglement) cannot be simultaneously "local", "causal", and "real", but it is not obvious which of these properties must be sacrificed, or if an attempt to describe quantum mechanical processes in these senses is a category error such that a proper understanding of quantum mechanics would render the question meaningless. Can a multiverse resolve it?

- Arrow of time (e.g. entropy's arrow of time): Why does time have a direction? Why did the universe have such low entropy in the past, and time correlates with the universal (but not local) increase in entropy, from the past and to the future, according to the second law of thermodynamics? Why are CP violations observed in certain weak force decays, but not elsewhere? Are CP violations somehow a product of the second law of thermodynamics, or are they a separate arrow of time? Are there exceptions to the principle of causality? Is there a single possible past? Is the present moment physically distinct from the past and future, or is it merely an emergent property of consciousness? What links the quantum arrow of time to the thermodynamic arrow?

- Locality: Are there non-local phenomena in quantum physics? If they exist, are non-local phenomena limited to the entanglement revealed in the violations of the Bell inequalities, or can information and conserved quantities also move in a non-local way? Under what circumstances are non-local phenomena observed? What does the existence or absence of non-local phenomena imply about the fundamental structure of spacetime? How does this elucidate the proper interpretation of the fundamental nature of quantum physics?

List of Unsolved Problems in Medicine[24]

Definition of "disease"

There is no overarching, clear definition of what a disease is. On one hand, there is a scientific definition which is tied to a physiological process, and on the other hand, there is the subjective suffering of a patient and the loss of their life quality. Both approaches do not need to match, and they can even be contradictory.

For example, when a patient seeks medical help because of a severe flu, the doctor will not care about the specific virological and immunological process behind the clearly visible suffering. This is contrasted by many hemochromatosis patients who will neither see suffering nor a change in his life quality, while the disease-causing process is severe and often deadly if left untreated. Similarly, many cancers in their very early stages are asymptomatic (e.g. pancreatic cancer) and the patient still feels healthy, which delays seeking treatment.

Sometimes, cultural factors also play a role in defining "disease". Erectile dysfunction was long seen as a negative but non-pathological state. The introduction of effective treatments has led to its acceptance as a disease.]

Even more difficulties arise when it comes to mental disorders. Depressions and anxiety disorders cause significant subjective suffering in the patient, but do not harm third persons. On the contrary, a narcissistic disorder or an impulse-control disorder does not cause any suffering in the patient, though the maintenance of healthy interpersonal relationships will be affected, and third persons can be harmed. There is also debate on whether non-normal behavior like paraphilias should be classified as a disease if they neither cause subjective suffering in the patient, nor endanger third persons.

Evidence-based medicine

Evidence-based medicine (EBM) has become the central paradigm in medical practice and research. However, debate continues around EBM and about how results obtained from large samples of patients can be applied to the individual.

Psychiatry and psychology

Lack of reliable diagnoses in some disorders

Though manuals like the DSM have covered a lot of ground when it comes to defining mental illnesses, in some disorders the reliability of diagnosis is still very poor. For example, inter-rater reliability in cases of dementia is very high, with a kappa value of 0.78,

---

[24] https://en.wikipedia.org/wiki/Unsolved_problems_in_medicine

while major depressive disorder is often diagnosed differently by independent experts who see the same patient, with a kappa value of just 0.28.

Cultural issues in defining mental disorders

Some mental illnesses like paraphilias are still defined by societal and cultural norms, rather than putting the individual's well-being in focus. For example, DSM defined homosexuality as a mental illness, until the American Psychiatric Association decided otherwise in 1973. As Richard Green pointed out in a review on pedophilia, psychiatry should identify unhealthy mental processes and treat them, and not focus on cultural norms, moral questions or legal issues.

As textbooks and handbooks like DSM are usually written by Western authors, a culturally neutral definition of mental diseases is an unsolved problem. Though newer editions of the DSM "respect" non-Western cultures by mentioning culture-specific symptom presentations (e.g. a very long time of mourning is regarded as a sign of depression in some cultures, but not in others), the inclusion of cultural factors into diagnostic criteria is seen as a political decision, but not a scientifically founded one. The Western viewpoint when defining mental illnesses also creates a cultural blind spot: Manuals rarely discuss how our own Western lifestyle and culture modifies or hides symptoms of mental illnesses.

Still no causal classification of mental disorders

A patient with a paralysis is referred to an oncologist if the condition is caused by a cancer metastasis in the spinal cord; a treatment by a neurologist is a secondary consideration. Likewise, renal insufficiency is sometimes caused by heart problems, and the treatment is thus led by a cardiologist. In psychiatry, however, grouping mental disorders by their cause is still an unsolved problem. Psychiatric textbooks and manuals cluster disorders by symptoms, which is thought to impede the search for effective treatments. This has been compared to an ornithologist's field guide: It allows you to identify birds, but it does not tell you why a species exists in biotope A but not B.

Diseases with unknown cause

There are numerous diseases for which causes are not known. There are others for which the etiology is fully or partially understood, but for which effective treatments are not yet available.

Idiopathic is a descriptive term used in medicine to denote diseases with an unknown cause or mechanism of apparent spontaneous origin. Examples of idiopathic diseases include: Idiopathic pulmonary fibrosis, Idiopathic intracranial hypertension, and Idiopathic pulmonary haemosiderosis. Another example is that the cause of aggressive periodontitis – resulting in rapid bone loss and teeth in need of extraction – is still unknown.

Mechanisms of action

It is sometimes unknown how drugs work. Often it is possible to study gene expression in a model organism, and determine the genes that are inhibited by a certain substance, and make further inferences from this data. A classic example of an unknown mechanism of action is the mechanism of general anesthesia. Other examples are paracetamol, anti-depressants and lithium.

Neuroscience

There are yet unsolved problems in neuroscience, although some of these problems have evidence supporting a hypothesized solution, and the field is rapidly evolving. One major problem is even enumerating what would belong on a list such as this. However, these problems include:

Consciousness

- What is the neural basis of subjective experience, cognition, wakefulness, alertness, arousal, and attention?
- Is there a "hard problem of consciousness"? If so, how is it solved?
- What, if any, is the function of consciousness?2]

Sensation, perception and movement

Perception:

- How does the brain transfer sensory information into coherent, private percepts?
- What are the rules by which perception is organized?
- What are the features/objects that constitute our perceptual experience of internal and external events?
- How are the senses integrated?
- What is the relationship between subjective experience and the physical world?

Learning and memory

- Where do our memories get stored and how are they retrieved again?
- How can learning be improved?
- What is the difference between explicit and implicit memories?

- What molecule is responsible for synaptic tagging?

Neuroplasticity

How plastic is the mature brain?

Cognition and decisions:

- How and where does the brain evaluate reward value and effort (cost) to modulate behavior?
- How does previous experience alter perception and behavior?
- What are the genetic and environmental contributions to brain function?

Language

- How is it implemented neurally?
- What is the basis of semantic meaning?

Mind-body connection

- Free will, particularly the neuroscience of free will.
- Sleep:
    - What is the biological function of sleep?
    - Why do we dream?
    - What are the underlying brain mechanisms?
    - What is its relation to anesthesia?

Computational neuroscience

- Computational theory of mind: What are the limits of understanding thinking as a form of computing?
- Computational neuroscience:
    - How important is the precise timing of action potentials for information processing in the neocortex?
    - Is there a canonical computation performed by cortical columns?
    - How is information in the brain processed by the collective dynamics of large neuronal circuits?
    - What level of simplification is suitable for a description of information processing in the brain?
    - What is the neural code?
- How do general anesthetics work?

- Noogenesis - the emergence and evolution of intelligence: What are the laws and mechanisms - of new idea emergence (insight, creativity synthesis, intuition, decision-making, eureka); development (evolution) of an individual mind in the ontogenesis, etc.?

INDEX

BIBLIOGRAPHY

Jean-Claude, J. Joseph, **Quanto-Geometry: Overture of Cosmic Consciousness and Universal Knowledge for All, Volume I**, Quantometrix, 2015

Jean-Claude, J. Joseph, **Quanto-Geometry: Overture of Cosmic Consciousness and Universal Knowledge for All, Volume III**, Quantometrix, 2017

Jean-Claude, J. Joseph, **Quanto-Geometric Theory: Unified Physical Law Through Theoretical Derivation of the Fundamental Physical Constants**, Quantometrix, 2024

Jean-Claude, J. Joseph, Stamu-O'Brien, Caroline, **Functional Architecture of the Human Mental: A Reference Psychophysics Treatise ofHuman Mentation and its Disorders**, Barnes and Noble Press, 2021

The Kentucky Post Staff, **Police busy for full moo,** E. W. Scripps Company, January 2002,https://web.archive.org/web/20070706203651/ - http:/www.kypost.com/2002/jan/29/chase012902.html

Roberts, Michelle., **Full Moon 'disturbs a good night's sleep.***Retrieved 2013-07-26, BBC News*http://www.bbc.co.uk/news/health-23405941

Brian VanHooker,**The Secret Illnesses of U.S. Presidents: 5 presidents who tried (and didn't always succeed) to hide their health problems,** MEN'S Health Magazine, April 2015, http://www.menshealth.com/health/secret-illnesses-of-us-presidents/slide/3

Bruce Lamar Rosenberg, **UFOs, Osborne Reynolds, and the One Wind: A New Look at an Old Theory**, June 1979

Hector Durville,**The Theory and Practice of Human Magnetism, Volume 1900, Part 1** - Primary Source Edition, February 2014,

French Government, GEIPAN, : http://www.cnes-geipan.fr/index.php?id=202, 2007

Margaret Wertheim, **Physics on the Fringe: Smoke Rings, Circlons, and Alternative Theories of Everything,** Walker, 2011

Sean Caroll, **The Alternative-Science Respectability Checklist,**Cosmic Variance, Discover Magazine, June 2007 - http://blogs.discovermagazine.com/cosmicvariance/2007/06/19/the-alternative-science-respectability-checklist/

Albert Einstein,,**Physics and Reality**, 1936

Chapelle Notre Dame de la Medaille Miraculeuse, http://www.chapellenotredamedelamedaillemiraculeuse.com/wp-content/uploads/2015/07/P1010142.jpg

Russell Targ, **Limitless Mind:A Guide to Remote Viewing and Transformation of Consciousness**, New World Library, Publishers Group West Publisher, 2004

Cathy O'Neil, **Weapons of Math Destruction**, Crown Random House, 2016

David, Hilbert, **Mathematical Problems**, Lecture delivered before the International Congress of Mathematicians, Paris, 1900

Thomas Pikkety, Arthur Goldhammer, **Capital in the Twenty-First Century**, Belknap Press, 2014

Kate Crawford, **Nature**, Generative AI is Guzzling Water and Energy, Volume 626, 2024

The author may be reached via email sent to:

jjc@qqmindarchitects.com

FROM THE SAME AUTHOR

The Human Mind Inside: *ISBN 978-0-9647466-3-3*
Quanto-Geometry – Vol I: *ISBN 978-0-9647466-4-0*
Quanto-Geometry – Vol II: *ISBN 978-0-9647466-6-4*
Quanto-Geometry – Vol III: *ISBN 978-0-9647466-9-5*
Qunato-Geometric Theory: *ISBN 979-8-855-64714-3*
Religion is Cosmic Culture: *ISBN 978-0-4630-8695-7*
La Quanto-Géométrie: *ISBN 0-9647466-1-1*
Functional Architecture of the Human Mental: *ISBN 978-0-9647466-8-9 (co-author Caroline Stamu-O'Brien, MD)*